ECONOMIC CODE

of

UKRAINE

William E. Butler, a Senior Partner in *Phoenix Law Associates*, is Professor of Comparative Law in the University of London; Academician of the Russian Academy of Natural Sciences and of the National Academy of Sciences of Ukraine; Director, The Vinogradoff Institute, University College London; M. M. Speranskii Professor of International and Comparative Law, Moscow Higher School of Social and Economic Sciences. He read law at Harvard University (J.D.), where he has been Visiting Professor of Law, and holds a Master of Russian Law (LL.M.) from the Academy University of Law, Institute of State and Law, Russian Academy of Sciences. He has advised the Governments of the USSR, Belarus, Russian Federation, Republic Kazakhstan, Kyrgyz Republic, Ukraine, Lithuania, Tadzhikistan, Turkmenistan, and Uzbekistan on aspects of law reform and participated in drafting key legislative acts. He has been a Member of the International Commercial Arbitration Court of the Russian Federation since 1995, and is a member of the District of Columbia Bar.

Maryann E. Gashi-Butler, a Senior Partner of *Phoenix Law Associates*, is an experienced international transactions lawyer who has worked in the United States, England, and Russia. She has been extensively involved in privatization, securities, mergers and acquisitions, and other international transactions for eighteen years, advised the Republic Kyrgyzstan and the Russian Federation on law reform and draft legislation. She read law at Harvard Law School (J.D.) and has an M.A. in Russian Studies from Yale University and a Master of Russian Law (LL.M.) from the Academy University of Law, Institute of State and Law, Russian Academy of Sciences. She is a member of the District of Columbia and Massachusetts Bars.

Phoenix Law Associates is one of the largest firms in Moscow and a leading international firm providing integrated accounting, audit (through our associated JURIS group of companies), business and information services to our clients. We offer turn-key assistance from due diligence and background assessments of potential Russian or foreign investment partners, preparation of legal documentation and legal advice on all aspects of an investment or transaction, legal assistance on questions relating to operations in Russia, accounting, payroll and audit services relating to a transaction or operations, and finally, representation in dispute resolution proceedings (court and international arbitration) in Russia and abroad. We work closely with leading American, European, and other international law firms on transborder transactions and dispute resolution, enabling us to offer an international team of lawyers and advisers best suited to any project.

ECONOMIC CODE

of

UKRAINE

Translated, with an Introduction, by

William E. Butler

Phoenix Law Associates

London
Wildy, Simmonds & Hill
2004

English translation Copyright © 2004 by William Elliott Butler (1939-)

Introduction Copyright © 2004 by William Elliott Butler (1939-)

ISBN 1-898029-68-7

No part of the material protected by this copyright may be reproduced or utilized in any form or by any means, electronic or mechanical, including photocopying, recording, or by any information storage and retrieval system, without written permission from the copyright owner. The moral rights of the author and translator are asserted.

Published by
Wildy, Simmonds & Hill Publishing Ltd.
58 Carey Street
London WC2A 2JB England

Status juris: 1 April 2004

Printed by
Biddles Ltd
King's Lynn, Norfolk

CONTENTS

ECONOMIC CODE OF UKRAINE

***Section I** – Basic Principles of Economic Activity*

Chapter 1   General Provisions 1

Chapter 2   Basic Orientations and Forms of Participation of State and Local Self-Government in Sphere of Economic Management 6

Chapter 3   Limitation of Monopolism and Defense of Subjects of Economic Management and Consumers Against Unfair Competition 24

Chapter 4   Economic Commercial Activity (Entrepreneurship) 38

Chapter 5   Noncommercial Economic Activity 42

***Section II** – Subjects of Economic Management*

Chapter 6   General Provisions 44

Chapter 7   Enterprise 54

Chapter 8   State and Municipal Unitary Enterprises 63

Chapter 9   Economic Societies 71

Chapter 10 Enterprises of Collective Ownership 82

Chapter 11 Private Enterprises. Other Types of Enterprises 96

Chapter 12 Associations of Enterprises 99

Chapter 13 Citizen as Subject of Economic Management. Peculiarities of Status of Other Subjects of Economic Management 108

Section III – Property Basis of Economic Management

Chapter 14 Property of Subjects of Economic Management 113

Chapter 15 Use of Natural Resources in Sphere of Economic Management 124

Chapter 16 Use in Economic Activity of Rights of Intellectual Property 127

Chapter 17 Securities in Economic Activity 133

Chapter 18 Corporative Rights 136

Section IV – Economic Obligations

Chapter 19 General Provisions on Economic Obligations 139

Chapter 20 Economic Contracts 143

Chapter 21 Prices and Price-Formation in Sphere of Economic Management 152

Chapter 22 Fulfillment of Economic Obligations Termination of Obligations 154

Chapter 23 Deeming Subject of Entrepreneurship to be Bankrupt 163

Section V – Responsibility for Violation of Law in Sphere of Economic Management

Chapter 24 General Principles of Responsibility of Participants of Economic Relations 168

Chapter 25 Compensation of Losses in Sphere of Economic Management 173

Chapter 26 Fine and Operational-Economic Sanctions 178

Chapter 27 Administrative-Economic Sanctions 183

Chapter 28 Responsibility of Subjects of Economic Management for Violation of Antimonopoly-Competition Legislation 189

Section VI – Peculiarities of Legal Regulation in Individual Branches of Economic Management

Chapter 29 Branches and Types of Economic Activity 192

Chapter 30 Peculiarities of Legal Regulation of Economic-Trade Activity 195
    §1. Delivery 203
    §2. Contract of Agricultural Procurement of Agricultural Product 203
    §3. Electric Power Supply 205
    §4. Exchange Trade 208
    §5. Lease of Property and Finance Lease 211
    §6. Other Types of Economic-Trade Activity 218

Chapter 31 Commercial Intermediation (Agency Relations) in the Sphere of Economic Management 219

Chapter 32 Legal Regulation of Carriage of Goods 225

Chapter 33 Capital Construction 232

Chapter 34 Legal Regulation of Innovation Activity 239

Chapter 35 Peculiarities of Legal Regulation of Financial
Activity 243
§1. Finances and Banking Activity........................... 243
§2. Insurance 255
§3. Intermediation in Effectuation of Securities
Operation. Stock Exchange 257
§4. Audit 260

Chapter 36 Use in Entrepreneurial Activity of Rights of Other
Subjects of Economic Management (Commercial
Concession) 261

Section VII – Foreign Economic Activity

Chapter 37 General Provisions 267

Chapter 38 Foreign Investments 275

Section VIII – Special Regimes of Economic Management

Chapter 39 Special (Free) Economic Zones 280

Chapter 40 Concessions 282

Chapter 41 Other Types of Special Regimes of Economic
Activity 284

Section IX – Concluding Provisions *289*

ON THE ECONOMIC CODE

W. E. Butler

Of all the codes adopted by member-countries of the Commonwealth of Independent States since the commencement of the transition to a market economy, the Economic Code of Ukraine is the most unusual, most innovative in its own way, piece of legislation to appear. Indeed it is a legislative achievement that defeated even the Soviet authorities.

The family of socialist legal systems was (and is where survivals thereof still operate) perhaps unique in modern civilization for its endeavor to devise *de novo* a system of legal regulation that would combine the vertical relations of administrative-economic and planning law between the State and the subjects of economic law, on one hand, and the horizontal civil-law relations formed between more or less legally equal participants of economic turnover. Within the framework of a socialist planned economy founded upon ideological precepts and canons, the established legal principles included abolition of private ownership of the instruments and means of production by way of nationalization or socialization, a preference for State ownership of the instruments and means of production, and where that was not practicable, various forms of cooperative ownership. The challenge for partisans of economic law was to encourage vertical/horizontal integration of economic legal relations by codifying the fundamental principles of State regulation of a market economy in an economic code.

In Ukraine the legal vestiges of a socialist planned economy have been partially, but not completely, repealed or replaced. The entry into force on 1 January 2004 of the Economic Code of Ukraine and, simultaneously, of the 2003 Civil Code of Ukraine are benchmarks in the transition towards some species of market system.

Although distinctions were drawn in German legal doctrine between "economic" and "civil" law during the early twentieth century, most Anglo-American lawyers are likely to be familiar with the subject through following the debates as traced in western legal writings about the emergence of economic law concepts associated with the "Pashukanis School" during the early 1930s and various revivals of that debate in the Soviet Union during the 1950-60s[1] and again during the 1970-80s, when a Draft Economic Code of the USSR was prepared.[2]

The "economic code school" in Ukraine, most closely associated with Donetsk, adheres closely to the basic structure and subdivisions of the Draft USSR Economic Code dating from the 1970s and elaborated during the 1980s.[3]

Whether justified or not, western jurists will associate "economic law" with a system of central economic planning, an emphasis upon "administration", rather than "management", of the economy. The decision of Ukraine to enact both the "Economic Code" and the "Civil Code" will inevitably be greeted by foreign investors as in some measure the continuation and perpetuation of a legal doctrine that places considerable weight upon a major role for the State in economic relations, even within the context of market economic relations. Perception notwithstanding, however, a command of the Economic Code is absolutely essential for any investor in Ukraine. The reaction of investors to the mere existence of the new Economic and Civil codes will represent an evaluation on their part

---

[1] H. J. Berman, *Justice in the U.S.S.R.* (rev. ed.; 1963).
[2] The Draft was prepared pursuant to an authorization of the Social Sciences Section of the Presidium of the USSR Academy of Sciences adopted 4 April 1969. The Draft Code was to be "a generalized law consolidating the new forms and methods of the economy and leading to a uniform system of normative acts for economic legislation". For the text of the Draft, see W. E. Butler (ed. & transl.), "Economic Code of the USSR (Draft of Basic Provisions)", *Soviet Statutes and Decisions*, XII (1976), 433-483. Also see Butler, *Soviet Law* (1983; 2d ed., 1988).
[3] Compare, for example, V. V. Laptev (ed), Хозяйственное право (Moscow, 1983), with V. K. Mamutov (ed.), Хозяйственное право (Kiev, 2002).

of the "legal risk" associated with their entry into force and the extent to which the two codes genuinely complement one another rather contain elements of overlap, inconsistency, and divergences.

During the 1920s, the Ukrainian SSR was the sole union republic of the Soviet Union to enact an Administrative Code. Now Ukraine has pioneered in a collateral domain of administrative law with the adoption of the Economic Code. Both codes emerged during periods of quasi-market relations; e.g., the New Economic Policy (1921-28) and post-Soviet Ukraine (1991-). There, however, the symmetries disappear, and it remains to be seen whether the Economic Code will serve or obstruct economic relations with its European and CIS neighbors.

ECONOMIC CODE OF UKRAINE

[Signed 16 January 2003, No. 436-IV.
Ведомости Верховной Рады Украины (2003),
Nos. 18-22, item 144]

The Economic Code of Ukraine establishes in accordance with the Constitution of Ukraine the legal foundations of economic activity (or economic management) that shall be based on the diversity of subjects of economic management of various forms of ownership.

The Economic Code of Ukraine shall have the purpose to ensure the growth of business activity of subjects of economic management, development of entrepreneurship, and, on this basis, the increased effectiveness of social production and the social orientation thereof in accordance with the requirements of the Constitution of Ukraine, confirm the social economic order in the economic system of Ukraine, and facilitate the harmonization thereof with other economic systems.

Section I
Basic Principles of Economic Activity

Chapter 1
General Provisions

Article 1. Subject of Regulation

1. The present Code shall determine the basic principles of economic management in Ukraine and regulate economic relations arising in the process of the organization and effectuation of economic activity between subjects of economic management, and also between these subjects and other participants of relations in the sphere of economic management.

Article 2. Participants of Relations in Sphere of Economic Management

1. Subjects of economic management, consumers, agencies of State power and agencies of local self-government endowed with economic competence, and also citizens, social and other organizations which act as founders of subjects of economic management or effectuate relative to them organizational-economic powers on the basis of relations of ownership, shall be participants of relations in the sphere of economic management.

Article 3. Economic Activity and Economic Relations

1. By economic activity in the present Code is understood activity of subjects of economic management in the sphere of social production directed towards the manufacture and realization of products, fulfillment of work, or rendering of services of a value character having a price determination.

2. Economic activity effectuated in order to achieve economic and social results and for the purpose of receiving a profit shall be entrepreneurial, and subjects of entrepreneurship – entrepreneurs. Economic activity may be effectuated also without the purpose of receiving a profit (noncommercial economic activity).

3. Activity of noneconomic subjects directed towards the creation and support of necessary material-technical conditions of the functioning thereof which are effectuated with or without the participation of subjects of economic management shall be the economic provision of activity of noneconomic subjects.

4. The sphere of economic relations shall comprise economic-production, organizational-economic, and intra-economic relations.

5. Economic-production relations are property and other relations arising between subjects of economic management through the direct effectuation of economic activity.

6. By organizational-economic activity in the present Code is understood relations forming between subjects of economic management and subjects of organizational-economic powers in the process of the management of economic activity.

7. Relations forming between structural subdivisions of a subject of economic management and relations of a subject of economic management with its structural subdivisions shall be intra-economic.

Article 4. Delimitation of Relations in Sphere of Economic Management with Other Types of Relations

1. There shall not be the subject of regulation of the present Code:

property and personal nonproperty relations regulated by the Civil Code of Ukraine;

land, mining, forestry, and water relations, relations with regard to the use and protection of flora and fauna, territories and objects of the nature-preserve fund, and the atmosphere;

labour relations;

financial relations with the participation of subjects of economic management arising in the process of forming and control over the execution of budgets of all levels;

administrative and other management relations with the participation of subjects of economic management in which an agency of State power or local self-government does not effectuate organizational-economic powers relative to a subject of economic management.

2. The peculiarities of the regulation of property relations of subjects of economic management shall be determined by the present Code.

3. The rules of the present Code shall apply to economic relations arising from merchant shipping and not regulated by the Merchant Shipping Code of Ukraine.

Article 5. Constitutional Foundations of Legal Order in Sphere of Economic Management

1. The legal economic order in Ukraine shall be formed on the basis of the optimal combining of market self-regulation of economic relations of subjects of economic management and State regulation of macroeconomic processes, proceeding from the constitutional requirement of the responsibility of the State to man for its activity and the definition of Ukraine as a sovereign and independent, democratic, social, and rule-of-law State.

2. The constitutional foundations of the legal economic order in Ukraine shall comprise: the right of ownership of the Ukrainian people to land, the subsoil thereof, atmosphere, water and other natural resources situated within the limits of the territory of Ukraine, natural resources of its continental shelf, exclusive (maritime) economic zone effectuated in the name of the Ukrainian people by agencies of State power and agencies of local self-government within the limits determined by the Constitution of Ukraine; the right of each citizen to use natural objects of the right of ownership of the people in accordance with a law; ensuring by the State of defense of the rights of all subjects of the right of ownership and economic management, social orientation of the economy, not permitting the use of ownership to the detriment of man and society; the right of each to possess, use, and dispose of his ownership, results of his intellectual and creative activity; deeming all subjects of the right of ownership to be equal before the law, indestructibility of the right of private ownership, not permitting the unlawful deprivation of ownership; economic diversity, the right of each to entrepreneurial activity not prohibited by a law, determined exclusively by a law of the legal foundations and guarantees of entrepreneurship; ensuring by the State of the defense of competition in entrepreneurial activity, not permitting abuse of a monopoly position on the market, unlawful limitation of competition and unfair competition, determination of the rules of competition and norms of antimonopoly regulation exclusively by a law; ensuring by the State of ecological security and maintenance of ecological equilibrium on the territory of Ukraine; ensuring by the State of proper, safe, and health conditions of

labour, defense of the rights of consumers; mutually-advantageous competition with other countries; recognition and operation in Ukraine of the principle of the sovereignty of law [jus].

3. Subjects of economic management and other participants of relations in the sphere of economic management shall effectuate their activity within the liits of the established legal economic order, complying with the requirements of legislation.

Article 6. General Principles of Economic Management

The general principles of economic management in Ukraine shall be:

ensuring economic diversity and equal defense by the State of all subjects of economic management;

freedom of entrepreneurial activity within the limits determined by a law;

free movement of capital, goods, and services on the territory of Ukraine;

limitation of State regulation of economic processes in connection with the need to ensure the social orientation of the economy, good-faith competition in entrepreneurship, ecological defense of the population, defense of the rights of consumers, and security of society and the State;

defense of national goods producer;

prohibition of illegal interference of agencies of State power and agencies of local self-government and officials thereof in economic relations.

Article 7. Normative-Legal Regulation of Economic Activity

1. Relations in the sphere of economic management shall be regulated by the Constitution of Ukraine, the present Code, laws of Ukraine, normative-legal acts of the President of Ukraine and Cabinet of Ministers of Ukraine, normative-legal acts of other agencies of State power and agencies of local self-government, and also other normative acts.

Chapter 2
Basic Orientations and Forms of Participation of State And Local Self-Government in Sphere of Economic Management

Article 8. Participation of State, Agencies of State Power, and Agencies of Local Self-Government in Economic Activity

1. The State, agencies of State power, and agencies of local self-government shall not be subjects of economic management.

2. Decisions of agencies of State power and agencies of local self-government with regard to financial questions arising in the process of forming and control over the execution of budgets of all levels, and also from administrative and other relations of management, except organizational-economic in which an agency of State power or agency of local self-government is a subject endowed with economic competence, shall be adopted in the name of this agency and within the limits of its governing powers.

3. Economic competence of agencies of State power and agencies of local self-government shall be realized in the name of the respective State or municipal institution. Direct participation of the State, agencies of State power, and agencies of local self-government in economic activity may be effectuated only on the basis and within the limits of powers and means which have been determined by the Constitution and laws of Ukraine.

Article 9. Forms of Realization of Economic Policy by State

1. In the sphere of economic management the State shall effectuate long-term (strategic) and current (tactical) economic and social policy directed towards the realization and optimal coordination of the interests of subjects of economic management and requirements of various social strata and the population as a whole.

2. Economic strategy is the course of economic policy selected

by the State for the long-term perspective and directed towards resolving large-scale economic and social tasks, the tasks of cultural development, ensuring the economic security of the State, preserving and multiplying its economic potential and national wealth, and enhancing the people's well-being. Economic strategy shall include the determination of priority aims of the national economy, the means and methods of their realization by proceeding from the content of objective processes and trends existing in the national and world economy, and taking into account the interests of subjects of economic management.

3. Economic tactics are the aggregate of imminent aims, tasks, means, and methods of their achievement for the realization of the strategic course of economic policy under specific conditions formed in the current period of development of the national economy.

4. The legal consolidation of economic policy shall be effectuated by means of determining the foundations of the domestic and foreign policies, in forecasts and programs of economic and social development of Ukraine and individual regions thereof, programs of activity of the Cabinet of Ministers of Ukraine, special-purpose programs of economic, scientific-technical, and social development, and also respective legislative acts.

Article 10. Basic Orientations of Economic Policy of State

1. The basic orientations of economic policy which are determined by the State shall be:
structural-branch policy directed towards the effectuation by the State of progressive changes in the structure of the national economy, improvement of inter-branch and intra-branch proportions, stimulation of the development of branches determining scientific-technical progress ensuring the competitiveness of fatherland products and the growth of the standard of living of the population. Industrial, agrarian, construction, and other spheres of economic policy under which the State effectuates a relatively autonomous complex of measures of stimulating impact shall comprise this policy;
investment policy directed towards the creation for subjects of

economic management of the necessary conditions to attract and concentrate means for the requirements of an expanded regeneration of the basic means of production, preferentially in branches whose development is determined as priorities of structural-branch policies, and also ensuring the effective and responsible use of these mans and effectuation of control over them;

amortization policy directed towards the creation for subjects of economic management of the most favorable and equal conditions for ensuring the process of simple regeneration of basic production and nonproduction funds preferentially on a qualitatively-new technical-technogenic basis;

policy of institutional transformations directed towards the forming of a rational, multi-tiered economic system by means of transforming relations of ownership, effectuation of destatization of the economy, privatization, and nationalization of production funds, ensuring on an own basis for the development of various forms of ownership and economic management, the equivalence of relations of exchange between subjects of economic management, State support, and defense of all forms of effective economic management and liquidation of any illegal economic structures;

price policy directed towards the regulation by the State of relations of exchange between subjects of the market for the purpose of ensuring equivalence in the process of the realization of the national product, compliance with the necessity parity of prices between branches and types of economic activity, and also ensure the stability of wholesale and retail prices;

anti-monopoly and competition policy directed towards the creation of an optimal competitive milieu of activity of subjects of economic management, ensuring their interaction onconditions of not permitting manifestation of discrimination against some subjects by others, above all in the sphere of monopoly price-formation and at the expense of a reduction of the quality of products and services, and promoting the growth of an efficient socially-orientated economy;

budget policy directed towards the optimization and rationalization of the forming of revenues and use of State financial resources, raising the effectiveness of State investments in the national economy, coordination of general-State and local interests in the sphere of inter-budgetary relations, regulation of the State debt, and ensuring social justness when redistributing national revenue;

tax policy directed towards ensuring the economically substantiated tax burden for subjects of economic management, stimulation of socially necessary economic activity of subjects, and also compliance with the principle of social justness and constitutional guarantees of the rights of citizens when taxing their revenues;

monetary-credit policy directed towards ensuring the national economy with the economically necessary volume of monetary mass, achievement of effective cash turnover, attraction of means of subjects of economic management and the population into the banking system, and stimulation of the use of credit resources for the requirements of the functioning and development of the economy;

hard currency policy directed towards the establishment and maintenance of a parity exchange rate of the national currency relative to foreign hard currencies and stimulation of the growth of State hard currency reserves and their effective use;

foreign currency policy directed towards the regulation by the State of relations of subjects of economic management with foreign subjects of economic management and defense of the national market and fatherland goods producer.

2. The State shall effectuate an economic policy ensuring the rational use and full-fledged regeneration of natural resources and the creation of safe conditions for the vital activity of the population.

3. In the socio-economic sphere the State shall effectuate a social policy of defense of the rights of consumers, policy of earnings and revenues of the population, policy of employment, and policy of social defense and social security.

Article 11. Forecasting and Planning of Economic and Social Development

1. The effectuation by the State of economic strategy and tactics in the sphere of economic management shall be directed towards the creation of economic, organizational, and legal conditions under which

subjects of economic management shall take into account in their activity the indicators of forecasting and program documents of economic and social development.

2. The principles of State forecasting and working out of programs of economic and social development of Ukraine, requirements for the content thereof, and also the general procedure for working out, confirming, and fulfillment of forecasting and program documents of economic and social development, the powers and responsibility of agencies of State power and agencies of local self-government with regard to these questions, shall be determined by a law.

3. The State Program of Economic and Social Development of Ukraine, State Budget of Ukraine, and also other State programs with reard to questions of economic and social development, procedure for working out, tasks, and realization of which are determined by a Law on State programs, shall be the basic forms of State planning of economic activity.

4. Agencies of power of the Autonomous Republic Crimea, local agencies of executive power, and agencies of local self-government shall in accordance with the Constitution of Ukraine be worked out and confirmed by programs of socio-economic and cultural development of the respective administrative-territorial entities and effectuate the planning of economic and social development of these entities.

5. Privileges and preferences in the effectuation of economic activity may not be granted to subjects of economic management that do not take into account public interests reflected in the program documents of economic and social development.

Article 12. Means of State Regulation of Economic Activity

1. The State shall in order to realize economic policy, fulfill special-purpose economic and other programs, and programs of economic and social development apply various means and mechanisms of regulating economic activity.

2. The principal means of regulating the impact of the State on the activity of subjects of economic management shall be:
the State order, State planning task;
licensing, patenting, and quotaing;
certification and standardization;
application of normative standards and ceilings;
regulation of prices and tariffs;
granting of investment, tax, and other privileges;
provision of donations, contributory compensation, special-purpose innovations, and subsidies.

3. The conditions, amounts, spheres, and procedure for the application of individual types of means of State regulation of economic activity shall be determined by the present Code, other legislative acts, and also programs of economic and social development. The establishment and repeal of privileges and preferences in economic activity of individual categories of subjects of economic management shall be effectuated in accordance with the present Code and other laws.

4. Limitations with regard to the effectuation of entrepreneurial activity, and also a List of types of activity in which entrepreneurship shall be prohibited, shall be established by the Constitution of Ukraine and by a law.

Article 13. State Order, State Planning Task

1. A State order shall be the means of State regulation of the economy by means of forming on a contractual basis the composition and amounts of products (or work, services) necessary for State needs, the placement of State contracts for delivery (or purchase) of these products (or fulfillment of work, rendering of services) among subjects of economic management, irrespective of their form of ownership.

2. The State contract is a contract concluded by a State customer in the name of the State with a subject of economic management-executor of the State order in which the economic and legal obligations of the parties are determined and their economic relations are regulated.

3. Deliveries of products for State needs shall be ensured at the expense of means of the State budget of Ukraine and other sources of financing attracted therefore in the procedure determined by a law.

4. In the instances provided for by the present Code and other laws, the Cabinet of Ministers of Ukraine and other agencies of executive power may establish State planning orders binding upon subjects of economic management.

5. The principles and general procedure for forming a State order for the delivery (or purchase) of a product, fulfillment of work, and rendering of services in order to satisfy State needs shall be determined by a law.

6. The peculiarities of relations arising in connection with deliveries (or purchase) for State needs of an agricultural product, provision, armament, and military technology, and also other specially-determined (or specific) goods, shall be regulated in accordance with a law.

Article 14. Licensing, Patenting, and Quotaing in Economic Activity

1. The licensing and patenting of determined types of economic activity and quotaing shall be means of State regulation in the sphere of economic management directed towards ensuring a unified State policy in this sphere and the defense of economic and social interests of the State, society, and individual consumers.

2. The legal foundations of licensing and patenting of individual types of economic activity and quotaing shall be determined by proceeding from the constitutional right of each to the effectuation of entrepreneurial activity not prohibited by a law, and also the principles of economic management established in Article 6 of the present Law.

3. A license shall be a document of the State model certifying the right of a subject of economic management-licensee to conduct the type of economic activity specified therein during a determined period on condition of fulfillment of the license conditions. Relations connected with licensing of determined

types of economic activity shall be regulated by a law.

4. In spheres connected with trade for monetary means (cash, cheques, and likewise with the use of other forms of settlement and payment cards on the territory of Ukraine), exchange of cash hard-currency valuables (including operations with cash means of payment expressed in foreign currency, and with payment cards), in the sphere of the gambling business and domestic services, and other spheres determined by a law may be effectuated by the patenting of entrepreneurial activity of subjects of economic management.

A trade patent shall be a State certificate certifying the right of a subject of economic management to engage in determined types of entrepreneurial activity during an established period. A special trade patent shall be a State certificate certifying the right of a subject of economic management to a special procedure of taxation in accordance with a law. The procedure for patenting of determined types of entrepreneurial activity shall be established by a law.

5. When necessary, the State shall apply quotaing, establishing a maximum amount (quota) of production or turnover of determined goods and services. The procedure for quotaing production and/or turnover (including export and import), and also the distribution of quotas, shall be established by the Cabinet of Ministers of Ukraine in accordance with a law.

Article 15. Standardization and Certification in Sphere of Economic Management

1. There shall apply in the sphere of economic management:
State standards of Ukraine;
codes of practice;
classification indexes;
technical conditions;
international, regional, and national standards of other countries (applied in Ukraine in accordance with prevailing international treaties of Ukraine).

2. The application of standards or individual provisions thereof shall be obligatory for:

subjects of economic management, if there are references to the standards in normative-legal acts;

participants of a transaction (or contract) concerning the working out, manufacture, or delivery of a product if there is a reference to determined references therein;

producer or supplier of a product, if it drew up a declaration concerning the conformity of the product to determined standards or applied the designation of these standards in the marking thereof;

producer or supplier, if its product has been certified according to the requirements of standards.

3. In the event of manufacture of a product for export, if other requirements have been determined by the transaction (or contract) than have been established by normative-legal acts of Ukraine, the application of the provisions of the transaction (or contract) shall be authorized if they are not contrary to legislation of Ukraine in the part of requirements for the procedure of manufacture of the product, keeping thereof, and transport on the territory of Ukraine.

4. For the purpose of preventing the rendering of services and realization of products dangerous to life, health, and property and citizens and the environment, assisting consumers in the choice of product, and creating conditions for the participation of subjects of economic management in international economic and scientific-technical cooperation and international trade, certification shall be effectuated, that is, confirmation of the conformity of the quality of the product and service to the requirements of standards.

5. The types and procedure of certification of products and services shall be established by a law.

Article 16. Donations and Other Means of State Support of Subjects of Economic Management

1. The State may grant donations to subjects of economic

management for: the support of the production of vitally important products of nourishment, the production of vitally important medicinal preparations and means of rehabilitation of disabled persons, import purchases of individual goods, transport services ensuring socially vital carriages, and also to subjects of economic management in a critical social-economic or ecological situation for the purpose of financing capital investments at a level necessary to maintain their activity, technical development which gives a significant economic effect, and also in other instances provided for by a law.

2. The State may effectuate contributory compensation or additional payments to agricultural goods-producers for an agricultural product being realized by them to the State.

3. The grounds and procedure for applying means of State support of subjects of economic management shall be determined by a law.

Article 17. Taxes in Mechanism of State Regulation of Economic Activity

1. The system of taxation in Ukraine and taxes and charges shall be established exclusively by laws of Ukraine. The system of taxation shall be built on principles of economic advisability, social justness, combining of the interests of society, State, territorial hromadas, subjects of economic management, and citizens.

2. For the purpose of resolving the most important economic and social tasks of the State, laws by which the taxation of subjects of economic management must make provision for:
optimal combining of fiscal and stimulant functions of taxation;
stability (or immutability) for several years of the general rules of taxation;
elimination of dual taxation;
coordination with tax systems of other countries.

3. Rates of taxes shall have a normative character and may not be established individually for an individual subject of economic management.

4. The system of taxation in Ukraine should provide for maximum amounts of taxes and charges which may be levied against subjects of economic management. In so doing taxes and other obligatory payments which in accordance with a law are incorporated in the prices of goods (or work, services) or relegated to their cost of production shall be paid by subjects of economic management irrespective of the results of their economic activity.

Article 18. Limitation of Monopolism and Promotion of Adversariality in Sphere of Economic Management

1. The State shall effectuate an antimonopoly-competition policy and promote the development of adversariality in the sphere of economic management on the basis of general-State programs confirmed by the Supreme Rada of Ukraine upon the recommendation of the Cabinet of Ministers of Ukraine.

2. State policy in the sphere of economic competition, limitation of monopolism in economic activity, and defense of subjects of economic management and consumers against unfair competition shall be effectuated by empowered agencies of State power and agencies of local self-government.

3. It shall be prohibited for agencies of State power and agencies of local self-government and officials thereof to adopt acts and perform actions which eliminate competition or without foundation assist individual competitors in entrepreneurial activity, or introduction a limitation on the market not provided for by legislation. Exceptions from this rule may be established by a law for the purpose of ensuring national security, defense. Or other social interests.

4. The rules of competition and norms of antimonopoly regulation shall be determined by the present Code and other laws.

Article 19. State Control and Supervision Over Economic Activity

1. Subjects of economic activity shall have the right without limitation to autonomously effectuate economic activity not contrary to legislation.

2. Subjects of economic activity shall be subject to State registration in accordance with the present Code and a law.

3. The State shall effectuate control and supervision over economic activity of subjects of economic management in the following spheres:

preservation and expenditure of means and material valuables by subjects of economic relations – with regard to the state and reliability of bookkeeping records and accounts;

financial and credit relations, hard currency regulation, and tax relations – with regard to compliance by subjects of economic management with credit obligations to the State and settlement discipline, compliance with the requirements of hard currency legislation and tax discipline;

prices and price-formation – with regard to questions of compliance by subjects of economic management with State prices for products and services;

monopolism and competition – with regard to questions of compliance with antimonopoly and competition legislation;

land relations – with regard to the use and protection of lands; water relations and forestry – with regard to the use and protection of waters and forests, and regeneration of water resources and forests;

production and labor – with regard to the safety of production and labor, compliance with legislation on labor; fire, ecological, and sanitary-epidemiological safety; compliance with standards, norms and rules by which obligatory requirements have been established relative to conditions for the effectuation of economic activity;

consumption – for the quality and safety of products and services;

foreign economic activity – with regard to questions of technological, economic, ecological, and social safety.

4. Agencies of State power and officials empowered to effectuate State control and State supervision over economic activity, the status thereof, general conditions, and the procedure for the effectuation of control and supervision shall be determined by laws.

5. Illegal interference and obstruction of economic activity of subjects of economic management on the part of agencies of State power and officials thereof in the event of the effectuation of State control and supervision by them shall be prohibited.

6. Agencies of State power and officials shall be obliged to effectuate inspecting and verification of the activity of subjects of economic management without warning, objectively, and efficiently, complying with the requirements of legislation and respecting the rights and legal interests of subjects of economic management.

7. A subject of economic management shall have the right to receive information concerning the results of inspecting and verifications of its activity not later than thirty days after the ending thereof, unless provided otherwise by a law. The actions and decisions of State agencies of control and supervision, and also officials thereof, which conducted the inspecting and verification may be appealed by the subject of economic activity in the procedure established by legislation.

8. All subjects of economic management shall be obliged to effectuate primary (or operational) and bookkeeping records of the results of their work, draw up statistical information, and also provide in accordance with the requirements of a law financial reports and statistical information concerning their economic activity and other data determined by a law. It shall be prohibited to demand from subjects of economic management the provision of statistical information and other data not provided for by a law or in violation of the procedure established by a law.

Article 20. Defense of Rights of Subjects of Economic Management and Consumers

1. The State shall ensure the defense of the rights and legal interests of subjects of economic management and consumers.

2. Each subject of economic management and consumer shall have the right to the defense of its rights and legal interests. The rights and legal interests of the said subjects shall be defended by means of:
recognition of the existence or absence of rights;
recognition fully or partially of the invalidity of acts of agencies of State power and agencies of local self-government and the acts of other subjects which are contrary to legislation, impinge the rights and legal interests of a subject of economic management or consumers;
recognize as invalid economic transactions on the grounds provided for by a law;
restoration of the position which existed before a violation of the rights and legal interests of subjects of economic management;
termination of actions violating the right or creating a threat of a violation thereof;
awarding of the fulfillment of a duty in kind;
compensation of losses;
application of fine sanctions;
application of operational-economic sanctions;
application of administrative-economic sanctions;
establishment, change, and termination of economic legal relations;
other means provided for by a law.

3. The procedure for the defense of rights of subjects of economic management and consumers shall be determined by the present Code and by other laws.

Article 21. Associations of Entrepreneurs

1. For the purposes of promoting the development of the national economy, integration thereof into the world economy, and also the

creation of favorable conditions for entrepreneurial activity in Ukraine, chambers of commerce and industry may be created as voluntary associations of entrepreneurs and organizations. A chamber of commerce and industry shall be a non-State self-governing charter organization created in the principles of membership and having the status of a juridical person.

2. The State shall assist chambers of commerce and industry in the fulfillment of charter tasks by them.

3. The procedure for the formation and activity of chambers of commerce and industry shall be established by a law.

4. Subjects of economic management-employers shall have the right of association in organizations of employers in order to realize and defend their rights.

5. Organizations of employers shall be self-governing charter organizations which are formed on the principles of voluntariness and equality for the purpose of the representation and defense of the legal interests of employers. Organizations of employers may associate in unions and other charter associations of employers.

6. The procedure for the formation and principles of activity of organizations and associations of employers shall be determined by a law.

Article 22. Peculiarities of Administration of Economic Activity in State Sector of Economy

1. The State shall effectuate the administration of the State sector of the economy in accordance with the foundations of internal and foreign policy.

2. Subjects operating on the basis of only State ownership, and also subjects whose State participatory share in the charter fund exceeds fifty per cent or comprises an amount ensuring to the State the right of decisive influence of the economic activity of these subjects, shall be

subjects of economic management of the State sector of the economy.

3. The powers of subjects of administration in the State sector of the economy – the Cabinet of Ministers of Ukraine, ministries, and other agencies of power and organizations relative to subjects of economic management — shall be determined by a law.

4. Types of economic activity which exclusively State enterprises, institutions, and organizations are authorized to effectuate may be determined by a law.

5. The State shall realize the right of State ownership in the State sector of the economy through a system of organizational-economic powers of respective agencies of administration relative to subjects of economic management relating to that sector and effectuating their activity on the basis of the right of economic jurisdiction or the right of operative management.

6. The legal status of an individual subject of economic management in the State sector of the economy shall be determined by empowered agencies of administration in accordance with the requirements of the present Code and other laws. The relations of the agencies of administration with the said subjects of economic management may in the instances provided for by a law be effectuated on contractual principles.

7. The State shall apply to subjects of economic management in the State sector of the economy all means of State regulation of economic activity provided for by the present Code, taking into account the peculiarities of the legal status of the said subjects.

8. The peculiarities of the effectuation of antimonopoly-competition policy and the development of adversariality in the State sector of the economy, which must be taken into account when forming the respective State programs, shall be established by a law.

9. The procedure for deeming bankrupt shall apply relative to

State enterprises, taking into account the requirements specified in Chapter 23 of the present Code.

10. Management organs effectuating the organizational-economic powers relative to subjects of economic management of the State sector of the economy shall be prohibited from delegating to other subjects the powers with regard to the disposition of State ownership and powers with regard to management of the activity of subjects of economic management, except for delegating the said powers in accordance with a law to agencies of local self-government and other instances provided for by the present Code and other laws.

Article 23. Relations of Subjects of Economic Management with Agencies of Local Self-Government

1. Agencies of local self-government shall effectuate their powers relating to subjects of economic management exclusively within the limits determined by the Constitution of Ukraine, laws on local self-government, other laws providing for the peculiarities of effectuation of local self-government in the cities of Kiev and Sevastopol, and other laws. Agencies of local self-government may effectuate also individual powers of agencies of executive power granted to them by a law relating to subjects of economic management.

2. Relations of agencies of local self-management with subjects of economic management in instances provided for by a law may be effectuated also on contractual principles.

3. Legal acts of agencies and officials of local self-government adopted within the limits of their powers shall be binding upon all participants of economic relations which are located or effectuated their activity on the respective territory.

4. Illegal interference of agencies and officials of local self-government in economic activity of subjects of economic management shall be prohibited. The issuance of legal acts of agencies of local self-government by which limitations are established not provided for by a

law with regard to the turnover of individual types of goods (or services) on the territory of the respective administrative-territorial entities shall be prohibited.

5. Agencies and officials of local self-government shall have the right to have recourse to a court concerning the deeming invalid of acts of enterprises and other subjects of economic management limiting the rights of territorial hromadas and powers of agencies of local self-government.

6. Agencies, officials, and employees of local self-government shall bear responsibility for their activity to subjects of economic management and the powers of agencies of local self-government.

7. Disputes concerning the restoration of violated rights of subjects of economic management and compensation of damage caused to them as a consequence of decisions, actions, or failure to act of agencies, officials, or employees of local self-government when effectuating their powers shall be settled in a judicial proceeding.

Article 24. Peculiarities of Administration of Economic Activity in Municipal Sector of Economy

1. The administration of economic activity in the municipal sector of the economy shall be effectuated through a system of organizational-economic powers of territorial hromadas and agencies of local self-government relating to subjects of economic management relegated to the municipal sector of the economy and effectuating their activity on the basis of the right of economic jurisdiction or the right of operative management.

2. The legal status of an individual subject of economic management in the municipal sector of the economy shall be determined by empowered management organs in accordance with the requirements of the present Code and other laws. Relations of management organs between the said subjects in instances provided for by a law may be effectuated on contractual principles.

3. Subjects operating on the basis of only municipal ownership, and also subjects in whose charter fund the participatory sare of municipal ownership exceeds fifty per cent or comprise an amount ensuring to agencies of local self-government the right of decisive impact on the economic activity of these subjects, shall be subjects of economic management of the municipal sector.

4. The peculiarities of the effectuation of antimonopoly-competition policy relative to the municipal sector of the economy, and also additional requirements and guarantees of the right of ownership of the Ukrainian people and right of municipal ownership when realizing procedures of bankruptcy relating to subjects of economic management of the municipal sector of the economy, may be established by a law.

5. Agencies of local self-government shall bear responsibility for the results of the activity of subjects of economic management relegated to the municipal sector of the economy on the grounds, within the limits, and in the procedure determined by a law.

Chapter 3
Limitation of Monopolism and Defense of Subjects of Economic Management and Consumers Against Unfair Competition

Article 25. Competition in Sphere of Economic Management

1. The State shall support competition as competitiveness between subjects of economic management ensuring, thanks to their own achievements, the receipt by them of determined economic preferences, as a result of which consumers and subjects of economic management receive the possibility of choice of a necessary good and in so doing individual subjects of economic management do not determine the conditions of realization of the good on the market.

2. Agencies of State power and agencies of local self-government regulating relations in the sphere of economic management shall be

prohibited to adopt acts or perform actions which determine the privileged position of subjects of economic management of a particular form of ownership, or place in an unequal position individual categories of subjects of economic management or by other means violate the rules of competition. In the event of a violation of this requirements, agencies of State power to whose powers are relegated control and supervision over compliance with antimonopoly-competition legislation, and also subjects of economic management, may contest such acts in the procedure established by a law.

3. Empowered agencies of State power and agencies of local self-government must effectuate an analysis of the state of the market and level of competition thereon and take the measures provided for by a law with regard to putting in order competition of subjects of economic management.

4. The State shall ensure the defense of commercial secrecy of subjects of economic management in accordance with the requirements of the present Code and other laws.

Article 26. Limitation of Competition

1. Decisions or actions of agencies of State power and agencies of local self-government which are directed towards the limitation of competition or may have such limitations as a consequence shall be deemed to be substantiated in instances of:

rendering assistance of a social character to individual subjects of economic management on condition that the assistance is rendered without discrimination to other subjects of economic management;

rendering assistance at the expense of State resources for the purpose of compensation of losses caused by a natural disaster or other extraordinary events on determined markets for goods and services, a List of which shall be established by legislation;

rendering assistance, including the creation of preferential economic conditions for individual regions for the purpose of contributory compensation of socio-economic losses caused by a grave economic situation;

effectuation of State regulation connected with the realization of drafts of general-national significance.

2. The conditions and procedure for the limitation of competition shall be established by a law in accordance with the present Law.

Article 27. Limitation of Monopolism in Economy

1. A dominant position of a subject of economic management which gives to it the possibility autonomously or together with other subjects to limit competition on the market of a determined good (or work, service) shall be deemed a monopoly [position].

2. A position of a subject of economic management whose participatory share on the market of a determined good exceeds the amount established by a law shall be deemed a monopoly [position].

3. A position of subjects of economic management on the market of a good when there are other conditions determined by a law also may be deemed to be a monopoly [position].

4. In the event of public need and for the purpose of eliminating the negative impact on competition, agencies of State power shall effectuate with respect to existing monopoly formations measures of antimonopoly regulation in accordance with the requirements of legislation and measures of demonopolization of the economy provided for by respective State programs, except for natural monopolies.

5. Agencies of State power and agencies of local self-government shall be prohibited to adopt acts or perform actions directed towards the economic intensification of existing subjects of economic management-monopolists and the formation without sufficient grounds of new monopoly formations, and also to adopt decisions concerning the exclusively centralized distribution of goods.

Article 28. Natural Monopolies

1. The state of the goods market under which the satisfaction of demand in that market is more efficient on condition of the absence of competition as a result of technological peculiarities of production (in connection with the material reduction of expenses of production per unit of product as the volumes of production increase), and goods (or services) produced by subjects of economic management may not be substituted in consumption by others in connection with the fact that demand on that goods market depends less on changes of prices for such goods than demand for other goods (or services) – shall be considered to be a natural monopoly.

2. Subjects of economic management of any form of ownership (monopoly formations) producing (or realizing) goods on the market that is in a state of natural monopoly may be subjects of a natural monopoly.

3. The spheres of activity of subjects of natural monopolies, agencies of State power, agencies of local self-government, and other agencies regulating the activity of the said subjects, and also other questions of the regulation of relations arising on goods markets of Ukraine which are in a state of natural monopoly, and on mixed markets with the participation of subjects of natural monopolies, shall be determined by a law on natural monopolies.

Article 29. Abuse of Monopoly Position on Market

There shall be considered to be an abuse of monopoly position:
foisting such conditions of a contract which place contracting parties in an unequal position or additional conditions not concerning the subject of the contract, including foisting a good not needed by the contracting party;
limitation or termination of production, and also removal of goods from turnover, for the purpose of creating or maintaining a shortage on the market or establishing monopoly prices;
other actions performed for the purpose of creating obstacles of

access to the market (or withdrawal from the market) of subjects of economic management;

establishment of monopoly high or discriminatory prices (or tariffs) on their goods, which leads to a violation of the rights of consumers or limits the rights of individual consumers;

establishment of monopoly low prices (or tariffs) on their goods, which leads to a limitation of competition.

Article 30. Unlawful Transactions Between Subjects of Economic Management

Unlawful transactions between subjects of economic management shall be deemed to be transactions or concordant actions directed towards:

the establishment (or maintenance) of monopoly prices (or tariffs), discounts, supplements (or additional payments), and price reductions;

the distribution of markets on the territorial principle, volume of realization or purchase of goods, assortment thereof, or by group of consumers or other indicators – for the purpose of monopolization thereof;

the elimination from the market or limitation of access thereto of sellers, purchasers, and other subjects of economic management.

Article 31. Discrimination Against Subjects of Economic Management

1. Discrimination against subjects of economic management by agencies of power in the present Code shall be deemed to be:

prohibition of the creation of new enterprises or other organizational forms of economic management in any sphere of economic activity, and also the establishment of limitations on the effectuation of individual types of economic activity or the production of determined types of goods for the purpose of the limitation of competition;

compelling subjects of economic management to conclude contracts in priority, the priority realization of goods to determined

enterprises, or entry into economic organizations and other associations;
adoption of decisions concerning the centralized distribution of goods leading to a monopoly position on the market;
establishment of a prohibition against the realization of goods from one region of Ukraine to another;
granting to individual entrepreneurs of tax and other privileges placing them in a privileged position relative to other subjects of economic management that leads to the monopolization of the market of a determined good;
limitation of rights of subjects of economic management with regard to the acquisition and realization of goods;
establishment of prohibitions or limitations relating to individual subjects of economic management or groups of entrepreneurs.

2. Discrimination against subjects of economic management shall not be permitted. Exceptions from the provisions of the present Article for the purpose of ensuring national security, defense, and public interests may be established by a law.

Article 32. Unfair Competition

1. Any actions in competition contrary to rules and to trade and other honorable customs in entrepreneurial activity shall be deemed to be unfair competition.

2. Unlawful use of the business reputation of a subject of economic management, creation of obstacles to subjects of economic management in the process of competition, and the achievement of unlawful preferences in competition, unlawful collection, divulgence and use of commercial secrecy, and also other actions classified in accordance with paragraph one of the present Article, shall be unfair competition.

3. Unfair competition shall entail the legal responsibility of persons if their actions have a negative impact on competition on the territory of Ukraine, irrespective of where such actions were committed.

Article 33. Unlawful Use of Business Reputation of Subject of Economic Management

1. There shall be deemed the unlawful use of business reputation of a subject of economic management: unlawful use of another's designations, advertising materials, packaging; unlawful use of the good of another producer; copying of the external appearance of a manufacture of another producer; comparative advertising.

2. The use without authorization of an empowered person of another's name, commercial name, trademark, other designations, and also advertising materials belonging to another person, and so on, which may lead to confusion with the activity of another subject of economic management having priority to the use thereos, shall be unlawful.

3. The use in a commercial name of the own name of a citizen shall be lawful if to the own name is added any distinguishing element which excludes confusion with the activity of another subject of economic management.

4. The introduction into economic turnover under its designation of a good of another producer by means of changes or removal of designations of the producer without the authorization of an empowered person shall be the unlawful use of the good of another producer.

5. Reproduction of the external appearance of the manufacture of another subject of economic management and introduction thereof into economic turnover without an unequivocal indication of the producer of the copy that may lead to confusion with the activity of another subject of economic management shall be copying the external appearance of a manufacture. The copying of the external appearance of a manufacture or parts thereof, if such copying was conditioned exclusively by the functional use thereof, shall not be deemed to be unlawful copying.

6. The operation of paragraph five of the present Article shall not extend to manufactures having protection as objects of the right of

intellectual property.

7. An advertisement containing a comparison with goods (or work, services) or the activity of another subject of economic management shall be comparative. Comparison in an advertisement in instances provided for by a law shall not be deemed to be unlawful.

Article 34. Creation of Obstacles to Subjects of Economic Management in Process of Competition

1. There shall be considered to be obstacles in the process of competition: discrediting the subject of economic management; foisting on consumers a compulsory assortment of goods (or work, services), inclining towards a boycott of a subject of economic management or discrimination against a purchaser (or customer), or towards dissolution of a contract with a competitor, bribery of a worker of a supplier or purchaser (or customer).

2. The dissemination in any form whatsoever of untrue, inaccurate, or incomplete information connected with a person or the activity of a subject of economic management which caused or might cause harm to the business reputation of a subject of economic management shall be discrediting a subject of economic management.

3. The purchase-sale of some goods, fulfillment of work, and rendering of services on condition of the purchase-sale of other goods, fulfillment of work, and rendering of services not necessary to the acquirer or contracting party shall be the purchase-sale of goods, fulfillment of work, and rendering of services with compulsory assortment.

4. Inclining to boycott of a subject of economic management shall be considered to be the urging by a competitor of another person directly or through an intermediary to refuse to establish contractual relations with this subject of economic management.

5. Inclining of a supplier to discriminate against a purchaser

shall be the urging, directly or through an intermediary, to provide by the supplier to a competitor of the purchaser determined preferences without sufficient grounds for this.

6. Inclining a subject of economic management to dissolve a contract with a competitor of another subject of economic management shall be the urging committed for mercenary motives or in the interests of third persons of a subject of economic management-participant of a contract for the failure to fulfill or improper fulfillment of contractual obligations to this competitor by means of providing or proposing to the subject of economic management-participant of a contract, directly or through an intermediary, material remuneration, contributory compensation, or other preferences.

7. The bribery of a worker of a supplier is the provision or proposal to him by a competitor of the purchaser (or customer), directly or through an intermediary, of material valuables, property or nonproperty benefits for the improper performance or failure to perform by the worker of the supplier of employment duties arising from a contract of delivery of goods concluded or connected with the conclusion between the supplier and purchaser, fulfillment of work, and rendering of services that entailed or could entail the receipt by the competitor of the purchaser (or customer) of determined preferences for the purchaser (or customer).

8. To the worker of a supplier shall be equated also another person who according to his powers adopts a decision in the name of the supplier concerning the delivery of a good, fulfillment of work, rendering of services, and influences the adoption of such a decision or otherwise is linked with it.

9. The bribery of a worker of a purchaser (or customer) is the provision or proposal to him by the contracting party of a supplier, directly or through an intermediary, of material valuables, property or nonproperty benefits for the improper performance or failure to perform by the worker of the purchaser (or customer) of employment duties arising from a contract for the delivery of goods concluded or connected

with the conclusion between the supplier and purchaser, fulfillment of work, and rendering of services that entailed or could entail the receipt by the competitor of the supplier of determined preferences to the supplier.

10. To the worker of a purchaser (or customer) shall also be equated another person who according to his powers adopts a decision in the name of the purchaser (or customer) concerning the acquisition of a good, fulfillment of work, rendering of services, or influences the adoption of such decision or otherwise is linked with it.

Article 35. Achievement of Unlawful Preferences in Competition

The achievement of unlawful preferences in competition shall be the receipt of determined preferences relative to another subject of economic management by means of a violation of legislation that is confirmed by a decision of the respective agency of State power.

Article 36. Unlawful Collection, Divulgence and Use of Information Which is Commercial Secret

1. Information connected with the production, technology, management, financial, and other activity of a subject of economic management that is not a state secret, the divulgence of which may cause damage to the interests of the subject of economic management may be deemed to be its commercial secret. The composition and amount of information comprising a commercial secret and the means of defense thereof shall be determined by the subject of economic management in accordance with a law.

2. The unlawful collection of information comprising a commercial secret shall be considered to be the extracting by unlawful means of the said information if this caused or might cause damage to the subject of economic management.

3. Divulgence of a commercial secret shall be the familiarization

of another person without the consent of the person empowered to do so with information which in accordance with a law comprises a commercial secret by a person to whom this information was entrusted in the established procedure or became known in connection with the performance of employment duties, if this caused or might cause damage to the subject of economic management.

4. Inclining to divulgence of commercial secret shall be the urging of a person to whom information was entrusted in the established procedure or became known in connection with the performance of employment duties which in accordance with a law comprises a commercial secret and to the disclosure of this information, if this caused or might cause damage to the subject of economic management.

5. Unlawful use of a commercial secret shall be the introduction into production or registration when planning or effectuating entrepreneurial activity without the authorization of the empowered person of information unlawfully extracted which comprises a commercial secret in accordance with a law.

6. For the unlawful collection, divulgence, or use of information that is a commercial secret the guilty persons shall bear the responsibility established by a law.

Article 37. Responsibility for Unfair Competition

The performance of actions determined as unfair competition shall entail the responsibility of the subject of economic management according to the present Code or administrative, civil, or criminal responsibility of the guilty persons in the instances provided for by a law.

Article 38. Rules of Professional Ethics in Competition

1. Subjects of economic management may when assisting interested organizations work out rules for professional ethics in competition for the respective spheres of economic activity, and also

for determined branches of the economy. The rules for professional ethics in competition shall be agreed with the Antimonopoly Committee of Ukraine.

2. The rules of professional ethics in competition may be used when concluding contracts and working out constitutive and other documents of subjects of economic management.

Article 39. Defense of Rights of Consumers

1. Consumers situated on the territory of Ukraine shall in the event of the acquisition, order, or use of goods (or work, services) for the purpose of satisfaction of their requirements have the right to:
State defense of their rights;
guaranteed level of consumption;
proper quality of goods (or work, services);
safety of goods (or work, services);
necessary, accessible, and reliable information concerning the quantity, quality, and assortment of goods (or work, services);
compensation of losses caused by goods (or work, services) of improper quality, and also harm caused by goods (or work, services) harmful to human life and health in the instances provided by a law;
recourse to a court and other empowered agencies of power for the defense of violated rights or legal interests.

For the purpose of defense of their rights and legal interests citizens may combine on a voluntary basis into social organizations of consumers (or consumer associations).

2. The State shall ensure to citizens the defense of their interests as consumers, provide the possibility of free choice of goods (or work, services), receive knowledge and skills necessary to take autonomous decisions when acquiring and using goods (or work, services) in accordance with their requirements, and guarantee the acquisition or receipt by other legal means of goods (or work, services) in the amounts ensuring a level of consumption sufficient for the maintenance of health and vital activity.

3. The rights of consumers, mechanism for the realization of the defense of these rights, and relations between consumers of goods (or work, services) and producers (or performers, sellers) shall be regulated by a law on the defense of the rights of consumers and other legislative acts.

4. If other rules have been established by an international treaty in force, consent to the bindingness of which has been given by the Supreme Rada of Ukraine, than those which there are in the legislation of Ukraine concerning the rights of consumers, the rules of the international treaty shall apply.

Article 40. State Control Over Compliance with Antimonopoly-Competition Legislation

1. State control over compliance with antimonopoly-competition legislation and defense of the interests of entrepreneurs and consumers against violations thereof shall be effectuated by the Antimonopoly Committee of Ukraine in accordance with its powers determined by a law.

2. For the purpose of the prevention of a monopoly position of individual subjects of economic management on the market, the creation, reorganization, and liquidation of subjects of economic management, acquisition of their assets and participatory shares (or stocks, shares) of economic societies, and also the formation of associations of enterprises or transformation of agencies of power into the said associations in instances provided for by legislation, shall be effectuated on condition of receiving consent for this of the Antimonopoly Committee of Ukraine. The grounds for giving consent to a concentration of subjects of economic management shall be determined by a law.

3. If subjects of economic management abuse a monopoly position on the market, the Antimonopoly Committee of Ukraine shall have the right to adopt a decision concerning the compulsory division of monopoly formations. The period for the fulfillment of such a decision may not be less than six months.

4. Compulsory division shall not apply in the event of:

the impossibility of organizational or territorial solitariness of enterprises or structural subdivisions;

the existence of a close technological link of enterprises and structural subdivisions, if the participatory share of internal turnover in the total volume of gross product of an enterprise (or association, and so forth) comprises less than 30 per cent.

5. Reorganization of a monopoly formation subject to compulsory division shall be effectuated at the discretion of the subject of economic management on condition of the elimination of the monopoly position of this formation on the market.

6. The Antimonopoly Committee of Ukraine and its territorial divisions shall in the procedure established by a law consider cases concerning unfair competition and other cases concerning a violation of antimonopoly-competition legislation provided for by a law.

7. Decisions of the Antimonopoly Committee of Ukraine and its territorial divisions may be appealed to a court. Losses caused by illegal decisions of the Antimonopoly Committee of Ukraine or its territorial divisions shall be compensated from the State budget of Ukraine upon the suit of interested persons in the procedure determined by a law.

Article 41. Antimonopoly-Competition Legislation

1. Legislation regulating relations arising in connection with unfair competition and the limitation and prevention of monopolism in economic activity shall consist of the present Code, the Law on the Antimonopoly Committee of Ukraine, and other legislative acts.

2. The provisions of the present Chapter of the Code shall not extend to relations in which subjects of economic management and other participants of economic relations take part if the result of their activity is manifested only beyond the limits of Ukraine, unless provided otherwise by an international treaty in force, consent to the bindingness of which was given by the Supreme Rada of Ukraine.

3. The peculiarities of the regulation of relations connected with unfair competition and monopolism on the financial markets and securities markets may be determined by a law.

Chapter 4
Economic Commercial Activity
(Entrepreneurship)

Article 42. Entrepreneurship as Type of Economic Activity

Entrepreneurship is autonomous, initiative, systematic economic activity at own risk effectuated by subjects of economic management (or entrepreneurs) for the purpose of achieving economic and social results and receiving profits.

Article 43. Freedom of Entrepreneurial Activity

1. Entrepreneurs shall have the right without limitations autonomously to effectuate an entrepreneurial activity not prohibited by a law.

2. The peculiarities of the effectuation of individual types of entrepreneurship shall be established by legislative acts.

3. A List of types of economic activity shall be subject to licensing, and also a List of types of activity in which entrepreneurship is prohibited, shall be established exclusively by a law.

4. The effectuation of entrepreneurial activity shall be prohibited to agencies of State power and agencies of local self-government.
Entrepreneurial activity of officials and employees of agencies of State power and agencies of local self-government shall be limited by a law in instances provided for by Article 64, paragraph two, of the Constitution of Ukraine.

Article 44. Principles of Entrepreneurial Activity

Entrepreneurship shall be effectuated on the basis of:

free choice by the entrepreneur of the types of entrepreneurial activity;

autonomous forming by the entrepreneur of the program of activity, choice of suppliers and consumers of the product to be produced, attraction of material-technical, financial, and other types of resources, the use of which is not limited by a law, establishment of prices for the product and services in accordance with a law;

free hire of workers by the entrepreneur;

commercial settlement of accounts and own commercial risk;

free disposition of profit remaining with the entrepreneur after the payment of taxes, charges, and other payments provided for by a law;

autonomous effectuation by the entrepreneur of foreign economic activity and use by an entrepreneur of the participatory share of hard currency receipts belonging to him at his discretion.

Article 45. Organizational Forms of Entrepreneurship

1. Entrepreneurship in Ukraine shall be effectuated in any organizational forms provided for by a law at the choice of the entrepreneur.

2. The procedure for the creation, State registration, activity, reorganization, and liquidation of subjects of entrepreneurship of individual organizational forms shall be determined by the present Code and other laws.

3. With respect to citizens and juridical persons for whom entrepreneurial activity is not basic, the provisions of the present Code shall extend to that part of their activity which by its character is entrepreneurial.

Article 46. Right to Hire Workers and Social Guarantees With Regard to Use of Their Labor

Entrepreneurs shall have the right to conclude contracts with citizens concerning the use of their labor. When concluding a labor contract (or agreement) an entrepreneur shall be obliged to ensure proper and safe conditions of labor, payment of labor not lower than determined by a law, and the timely receipt thereof by workers, and also other social guarantees, including social and medical insurance and social security in accordance with legislation of Ukraine.

Article 47. General Guarantees of Rights of Entrepreneurs

1. The State shall guarantee to all entrepreneurs, irrespective of the organizational forms of entrepreneurial activity selected by them, equal rights and equal possibilities in order to attract and use material-technical, financial, labor, informational, natural, and other resources.

2. The provision of an entrepreneur with material-technical and other resources which are distributed in a centralized procedure by the State shall be effectuated for the purpose of the fulfillment by an entrepreneur of deliveries, work, or services for State needs.

3. The State shall guarantee the inviolability of property and ensure the defense of property rights of an entrepreneur. The seizure by the State or agencies of local self-government from an entrepreneur of basic and circulating funds and other property shall be permitted in accordance with Article 41 of the Constitution of Ukraine on the grounds and in the procedure provided for by a law.

4. Losses caused to an entrepreneur as a consequence of a violation by citizens or juridical persons, agencies of State power, or agencies of local self-government of his property rights shall be compensated to the entrepreneur in accordance with the present Code and other laws.

5. An entrepreneur or citizen working for an entrepreneur by

hire may in the instances provided for by a law be enlisted to fulfill in work time State or social duties with compensation to the entrepreneur of respective losses by the agency which adopts such a decision. Disputes concerning compensation of losses shall be settled by a court.

Article 48. State Support of Entrepreneurship

1. For the purpose of creating favorable organizational and economic conditions for the development of entrepreneurship agencies of power, on the conditions and in the procedure provided for by a law, shall:

grant land plots to entrepreneurs, transfer State property necessary for the effectuation of entrepreneurial activity;

assist entrepreneurs in organizing material-technical provision and informational servicing of their activity and the training of personnel;

effectuate initial fitting out of undeveloped territories with objects of production and social infrastructure with the sale or transfer thereof to entrepreneurs in a procedure determined by a law;

stimulate the modernization of technology, innovation activity, and mastery by entrepreneurs of new types of products and services;

render other types of assistance to entrepreneurs.

2. The State shall promote the development of small entrepreneurship and create the necessary conditions for this.

Article 49. Responsibility of Subjects of Entrepreneurship

1. Entrepreneurs shall be obliged not to cause harm to the natural environment, not to violate the rights and legal interests of citizens and associations thereof, other subjects of economic management, institutions, organizations, and the rights of local self-government and the State.

2. An entrepreneur shall bear property and other responsibility established by a law for harm and losses caused.

Article 50. Activity of Foreign Entrepreneurs in Ukraine

1. The peculiarities of effectuating entrepreneurial activity on the territory of Ukraine, on its continental shelf, and in the exclusive (maritime) economic zone by foreign juridical persons and citizens shall be determined by the present Code and by other laws of Ukraine.

2. If other rules concerning entrepreneurship have been established by an international treaty in force, consent to the obligatoriness of which was given by the Supreme Rada of Ukraine than those which have been provided for by legislation of Ukraine, the rules of the international treaty shall apply. The rules of international treaties of Ukraine in force at the moment of the adoption of the Constitution of Ukraine shall apply in accordance with the Constitution of Ukraine in the procedure determined by those international treaties.

Article 51. Termination of Entrepreneurial Activity

1. Entrepreneurial activity shall terminate:
at own initiative of the entrepreneur;
in the event of the expiry of the period of operation of a license;
in the event of the termination of the existence of the entrepreneur;
on the basis of a decision of a court in instances provided for by the present Code and other laws.

2. The procedure for the termination of activity of an entrepreneur shall be established by a law in accordance with the requirements of the present Code.

Chapter 5
Noncommercial Economic Activity

Article 52. Noncommercial Commercial Management

1. Noncommercial economic management is autonomous systematic economic activity effectuated by subjects of economic

management directed towards the achievement of economic, social, and other results without the purpose of receiving a profit.

2. Noncommercial commercial activity shall be effectuated by subjects of economic management of State or municipal sectors of the economy in branches (or types of activity) in which in accordance with Article 12 of the present Code entrepreneurship is prohibited on the basis of the decision of a respective agency of State power or agency of local self-government. Noncommercial economic activity may also be effectuated by other subjects of economic management to which the effectuation of economic activity in the form of entrepreneurship is prohibited by a law.

3. Agencies of State power, agencies of local self-government, and officials thereof may not effectuate noncommercial economic activity.

Article 53. Organizational Forms of Effectuating Noncommercial Economic Activity

1. Noncommercial economic activity may be effectuated by subjects of economic management on the basis of the right of ownership or right of operative management in the organizational forms determined by the owner or respective management organ or agency of local self-government, taking into account the requirements provided for by the present Code and other laws.

2. The creation, State registration, activity, reorganization, and liquidation of subjects of economic management of individual organizational forms of noncommercial economic activity shall be determined by the present Code and other laws.

3. If economic activity of citizens or a juridical person registered as a subject of noncommercial economic management acquires the character of entrepreneurial activity, to it shall apply the provisions of the present Code and other laws by which entrepreneurship is regulated.

Article 54. Regulation of Noncommercial Economic Activity

1. The general requirements concerning the regulation of economic activity, taking into account the peculiarities of the effectuation thereof by various subjects of economic management which are determined by the present Code and other legislative acts, shall extend to subjects of economic management effectuating noncommercial economic activity.

2. When concluding a labor contract (or agreement) a subject of economic management effectuating noncommercial economic activity shall be obliged to ensure proper and safe conditions of labor, payment thereof not lower than the minimum amount determined by a law, and also ensure other social guarantees provided for by a law.

Section II
Subjects of Economic Management

Chapter 6
General Provisions

Article 55. Concept of Subject of Economic Management

1. Participants of economic relations which effectuate economic activity, realizing economic competence (aggregate of economic rights and duties), have solitary property and bear responsibility for their obligations within the limits of this property, except for instances provided for by legislation, shall be deemed to be subjects of economic management.

2. There shall be subjects of economic management:
(1) economic organizations – juridical persons created in accordance with the Civil Code of Ukraine, State, municipal, and other enterprises created in accordance with the present Code, and also other juridical persons effectuating economic activity and registered in the

procedure established by a law;

(2) citizens of Ukraine, foreigners, and stateless persons effectuating economic activity and registered in accordance with a law as entrepreneurs;

(3) branches, representations, other solitary subdivisions of economic organizations (structural entities) formed by them in order to effectuate economic activity.

3. Subjects of economic management shall realize their economic competence on the basis of the right of ownership, right of economic jurisdiction, right of operative management, and right of operational-economic use of property in accordance with the definition of this competence in the present Code and other laws.

4. Subjects of economic management are economic organizations operating on the basis of the right of ownership, right of economic jurisdiction or operative management, and having the status of a juridical person, which is determined by civil legislation and the present Code.

5. Subjects of economic management which are solitary subdivisions (structural entities) of economic organizations may operate only on the basis of the right of operational-economic use of property without the status of a juridical person.

Article 56. Formation of Subject of Economic Management

1. A subject of economic management may be formed by decision of the owner(s) of property or agency empowered by them, and in instances specially provided for by legislation, also by decision of other agencies, organizations, and citizens by means of founding a new, reorganization (merger, accession, separation, division, transformation) of an operating subject(s) of economic management in compliance with the requirements of legislation.

2. Subjects of economic management may be formed by means of the compulsory division (or separation) of an operating subject of economic management at the instruction of antimonopoly agencies in

accordance with antimonopoly-competition legislation of Ukraine.

3. The creation of subjects of economic management shall be effectuated in compliance with the requirements of antimonopoly-competition legislation.

Article 57. Constitutive Documents

1. The constitutive documents of a subject of economic management shall be the decision concerning its formation or constitutive contract, and in instances provided for by a law, the charter (or statute) of a subject of economic management.

2. In constitutive documents must be specified the name and location of the subject of economic management, purpose and subject of economic activity, composition and competence of its management organs, procedure for the adoption of decisions by them, procedure for forming property, distribution of profits and losses, and conditions of its reorganization and liquidation, unless provided otherwise by a law.

3. In a constitutive contract the founders shall be obliged to form the subject of economic management, determine the procedure for joint activity with regard to its formation, conditions of the transfer of their property to it, procedure for the distribution of profits and losses, management of the activity of the subject of economic management and participation of the founders therein, procedure for withdrawal of and entry of new founders, other conditions of activity of a subject of economic management provided for by a law, and also the procedure for its reorganization and liquidation in accordance with a law.

4. The charter of a subject of economic management must contain information concerning its name and location, purposes and subject of activity, amount and procedure for the formation of the charter and other funds, procedure for distribution of profits and losses, management and control organs, the competence thereof, conditions

of reorganization and liquidation of the subject of economic management, and also other information connected with the peculiarities of organizational form of the subject of economic management provided for by legislation. The charter may also contain other information not contrary to legislation.

The economic competence of agencies of State power, agencies of local self-government, or other subjects in instances determined by a law shall be determined by a statute.

5. The charter (or statute) shall be confirmed by the owner of property (founder) of the subject of economic management or representatives thereof, agencies, or other subjects in accordance with a law.

Article 58. State Registration of Subject of Economic Management

1. A subject of economic management shall be subject to State registration, except for instances established by the present Code.

2. State registration of subjects of economic management shall be conducted in the executive committee of a city or district in city soviet or in a district State administration at the location or place of residence of the particular subject unless provided otherwise by a law.

3. The following documents shall be filed for the State registration of a subject of economic management:

decision of the owner(s) of property or agency empowered by them in the instances provided for by a law;

constitutive documents provided for by a law for the respective type of juridical persons;

decision of the Antimonopoly Committee of Ukraine concerning consent to the creation or reorganization (merger, accession) of subjects of economic management in the instances provided for by a law;

document(s) certifying payment by the founder(s) of the contribution to the charter fund of the subject of economic management in the amount established by a law;

registration card of the established form;
document certifying the payment of means for State registration.

In the event of the creation in the process of privatization and/or corporatization of open joint-stock societies a report also must be submitted concerning the results of subscription to stocks, confirmed by the State Commission for Securities and the Stock Market.

4. Citizens having the intention to effectuate entrepreneurial activity without the creation of a juridical person shall file the registration card of the established form, which shall be simultaneously an application concerning State registration, a copy of the reference concerning the conferment of an identification number of a citizen-taxpayer and other obligatory payments, and a document certifying the making of payment for State registration.

5. The owner (or founder) or agencies empowered by him shall bear responsibility for the failure to conform to legislation and unreliability of documents filed for registration.

6. State registration of subjects of economic management shall be effectuated within a period of not more than ten days from the day of filing the documents specified in the present Article. The registering agency shall be obliged within that period to issue to the subject of economic management a certificate concerning the State registration thereof.

7. An identification code under which this subject is included in the State register of subjects of economic management, or the identification code of a citizen-entrepreneur, must be indicated on seals and stamps of the subject of economic management.

8. A certificate concerning State registration of a subject of economic management and copy of the document confirming the registration thereof in agencies of the State tax service shall be grounds for opening accounts in branches of banks.

9. Information concerning State registration of a subject of

economic management shall be included in the unified State register open for general familiarization.

10. Information concerning State registration of a subject of economic management and making changes therein shall be subject to publication by the registering agency in a special annex to the newspaper *Урядовий кур'єр* and/or official printed publication of the agency of State power or agency of local self-government at the location of the subject of economic management within ten days from the moment of conducting State registration of the subject of economic management (or making changes in information of the State registration) in the procedure established by the Cabinet of Ministers of Ukraine.

11. A violation of the procedure established by a law for the creation of a subject of economic management or unreliability or failure to conform to the requirements of legislation of documents to be filed for the registration thereof shall be grounds for a refusal of state registration of the subject of economic management. A refusal to register a subject of economic management for other reasons shall not be permitted.

12. A refusal of State registration of a subject of economic management may be appealed in a judicial proceeding.

13. The activity of an unregistered subject of economic management subject to State registration shall be prohibited. Revenues received by such subject shall be recovered to the State budget of Ukraine in the procedure established by a law.

14. The re-registration of a subject of economic management shall be conducted in the event of a change of the form of ownership on which the said subject is based, or the organizational form of economic management, or the name of the subject of economic management and shall be effectuated in the procedure established for his registration.

15. The revocation (or termination) of State registration of a

subject of economic management shall be effectuated upon his personal application, and also on the basis of a decision of a court in instances of deeming invalid or contrary to legislation of constitutive documents, or the effectuation of activity contrary to a law or constitutive documents, or in other instances provided for by a law.

The revocation of State registration shall terminate economic activity and shall be grounds for the effectuation of measures with regard to the liquidation of a subject of economic management.

16. Special rules for State registration of individual organizational forms of economic management may be established by legislation of Ukraine.

17. Subjects of economic management specified in Article 66, paragraph two, (1) of the present Code shall have the right to open their branches (or divisions) and representations without the creation of a juridical person. The opening of the said subdivisions shall not require their registration. A subject of economic management shall only notify their opening to the registering agency by means of submitting additional information on its registration card.

18. The Statute on the Procedure for the State Registration of Subjects of Economic Management shall be confirmed by the Cabinet of Ministers of Ukraine.

Article 59. Termination of Activity of Subject of Economic Management

1. Termination of the activity of a subject of economic management shall be effectuated by means of the reorganization (or merger, accession, division, transformation) thereof or liquidation – by decision of the owner(s) or agencies empowered by them, by decision of other persons-founders of a subject of economic management, or the legal successors thereof, and in instances provided for by the present Code – by decision of a court.

2. In the event of the merger of subjects of economic

management, all property rights and duties of each of them shall pass to the subject of economic management formed as a result of the merger.

3. In the event of accession of one or several subjects of economic management to another subject of economic management, to this last shall pass all property rights and duties of the acceding subjects of economic management.

4. In the event of the division of a subject of economic management, all of its property rights and duties shall pass under the act of division (or balance sheet) in respective participatory shares to each of the new subjects of economic management formed as a result of this division. In the event of separation of one or several new subjects of economic management to each of them shall pass under the act of division (or balance sheet) in respective participatory shares the property rights and duties of the reorganized subject.

5. In the event of transformation of one subject of economic management into another, to the newly formed subject of economic management shall pass all property rights and duties of the preceding subject of economic management.

6. A subject of economic management shall be liquidated:
at the initiative of the persons specified in paragraph one of the present Article;
in connection with the expiry of the period for which it was created, except for instances provided for by a law;
in the event of it being deemed to be bankrupt, except for instances provided for by a law;
in the event of the revocation of its State registration in instances provided for by a law.

7. Revocation of State registration shall deprive the subject of economic management of the status of a juridical person and be grounds for the removal thereof from the State register. A subject of economic management shall be considered to be liquidated from the day of making an entry in the State register concerning the termination of its activity.

Such entry shall be made after confirmation of the liquidation balance sheet in accordance with the requirements of the present Code.

8. An announcement concerning the reorganization or liquidation of an economic organization or termination of the activity of an individual entrepreneur shall be subject to publication by the registering agency in a special annex to the newspaper *Урядовий кур'єр* and/or official printed publication of the agency of State power or agency of local self-government at the location of the subject of economic management within ten days from the day of termination of the activity of the subject of economic management.

Article 60. General Procedure for Liquidation of Subject of Economic Management

1. The liquidation of a subject of economic management shall be effectuated by a liquidation commission, which shall be formed by the owner(s) of property of the subject of economic management or representatives (or agencies) thereof, or by another agency determined by a law, unless another procedure for the formation thereof has been provided by the present Code. The liquidation of a subject of economic management may also be placed on the management organ of the subject which is being liquidated.

2. The agency (or person) which adopted the decision concerning liquidation of a subject of economic management shall establish the procedure and determined the periods for conducting liquidation, and also the period for declaring of claims by creditors, which may not be less than two months from the day of the declaration concerning liquidation.

3. The liquidation commission or other agency which conducts the liquidation of a subject of economic management shall place in printed organs specified in Article 58, paragraph ten, of the present Code a communication concerning the liquidation thereof and the procedure and periods for the declaring of claims by creditors, and obvious (or known) creditors shall be informed personally in written

form within the periods established by the present Code or by a special law.

4. Simultaneously, the liquidation commission shall take necessary measures to recover debtor indebtedness of the subject of economic management being liquidated and elicit the demands of creditors, with the written notification of each of them concerning liquidation of the subject of economic management.

5. The liquidation commission shall value the existing property of the subject of economic management being liquidated and shall settle with creditors, draw up the liquidation balance sheet, and file it with the owner or agency designated by the liquidation commission. The reliability and comprehensiveness of the liquidation balance sheet must be verified in the procedure established by legislation.

Article 61. Procedure for Settlements with Creditors in Event of Liquidation of Subject of Economic Management

1. Claims of creditors against a subject of economic management being liquidated shall be satisfied from the property of this subject unless provided otherwise by the present Code and other laws.

2. The priority and procedure for the satisfaction of demands of creditors shall be determined in accordance with a law.

3. Claims not satisfied in view of the absence of property of a subject of economic management and claims not recognized by the liquidation commission, if the declarer thereof has not within a month's period after receipt of notification concerning full or partial rejection of the claim applied to a court with a respective suit, and also claims whose satisfaction has been refused by decision of a court to the creditor, shall be considered to be paid.

4. Property remaining after satisfaction of claims of creditors shall be used according to the instruction of the owner.

Chapter 7
Enterprise

Article 62. Enterprise as Organizational Form of Economic Management

1. An enterprise is an autonomous subject of economic management crated by a competent agency of State power or agency of local self-government, or other subjects in order to satisfy social and personal requirements by means of the systematic effectuation of production, scientific-research, trade, and other economic activity in the procedure provided for by the present Code and other laws.

2. Enterprises may be created both for the effectuation of entrepreneurship and for noncommercial economic activity.

3. An enterprise, unless established otherwise by a law, shall operate on the basis of a charter.

4. An enterprise shall be a juridical person, have solitary property, an autonomous balance sheet, accounts in branches of banks, a seal with its own name, and an identification code.

5. An enterprise shall not have other juridical persons within its composition.

Article 63. Types and Organizational Forms of Enterprises

1. Depending on the form of ownership provided for by a law, enterprises of the following types may operate in Ukraine:
private enterprise operating on the basis of private ownership of citizens or subject of economic management (juridical person);
enterprise operating on the basis of collective ownership (enterprise of collective ownership);
municipal enterprise operating on the basis of municipal ownership of territorial hromada;
State enterprise operting on the basis of State ownership;

Enterprise based on mixed form of ownership (on base of combining property of various forms of ownership).

In Ukraine other types of enterprises provided for by a law also may operate.

2. If in the charter fund of an enterprise foreign investment comprises not less than ten per cent, it shall be deemed to be an enterprise with foreign investments. An enterprise in whose charter fund foreign investment comprises one hundred per cent shall be considered to be a foreign enterprise.

3. Depending upon the means of formation (or founding) and forming of the charter fund, unitary and corporative enterprises shall operate in Ukraine.

4. A unitary enterprise shall be created by one founder, which shall allocate the property necessary for this, form the charter fund in accordance with a law that is not divided into participatory shares (or shares), confirm the charter, distribute revenues, directly or through an executive appointed by it direct the enterprise and form its labor collective on the bases of labor hire, decide questions of reorganization and liquidation of the enterprise. State, municipal, enterprises based on the ownership of an association of citizens, religious organization, or private ownership of the founder shall be unitary.

5. A corporative enterprise shall be formed, as a rule, by two or more founders by their joint decision (or contract), operate on the basis of combining the property and/or entrepreneurial or labor activity of the founders (or participants), the joint management of the affairs thereof, on the basis of corporative rights, including through organs created by them, the participation of the founders (or participants) in the distribution of revenues and risks of the enterprise. Cooperative enterprises, enterprises to be created in the form of an economic society, and also other enterprises, including based on the private ownership of two or more persons, shall be corporative.

6. The peculiarities of the legal status of unitary and corporative

enterprises shall be established by the present Code and other legislative acts.

7. Enterprises, depending upon the quantity of persons working and volume of gross revenue from the realization of products per year, may be relegated to small enterprises or to medium or large-scale enterprises.

Enterprises in which the average recorded number of persons working for each reporting (or financial) year does not exceed fifty persons, and the volume of gross revenue from the realization of products (or work, services) per year exceeds the amount equivalent to five hundred thousand euros at the average yearly exchange rate of the National Bank of Ukraine relative to the hrivna, shall be deemed to be small (irrespective of form of ownership).

Enterprises in which the average recorded number of persons working for each reporting (or financial) year exceeds a thousand persons, and the volume of gross revenue from the realization of products (or work, services) per year exceeds the amount equivalent to five million euros at the average yearly exchange rate of the National Bank of Ukraine relative to the hrivna, shall be deemed to be large-scale enterprises.

All other enterprises shall be deemed to be medium.

8. In instances of the existence of dependence on another enterprise provided for by Article 126 of the present Code an enterprise shall be deemed to be a subsidiary.

9. Peculiarities of economic management may be established for enterprises of a determined type and organizational forms by laws.

Article 64. Organizational Structure of Enterprise

1. An enterprise may consist of production structural subdivisions (production entities, shops, divisions, sectors, brigades, offices, laboratories, and so on), and also functional structural subdivisions of the management apparatus (administrations, sections, offices, services, and so on).

2. The functions, rights, and duties of structural subdivisions of an enterprise shall be determined by Statutes on them, which shall be confirmed in the procedure determined by the charter of the enterprise or other constitutive documents.

3. An enterprise autonomously shall determine its organizational structure and establish the numbers of workers and personnel establishment.

4. An enterprise shall have the right to create branches, representations, divisions, and other solitary subdivisions, agreeing questions concerning the siting of such subdivisions of an enterprise with respective agencies of local self-government in the procedure established by legislation. Such solitary subdivisions shall not have the status of a juridical person and shall operate on the basis of a Statute on them, confirmed by the enterprise. They may open accounts in branches of banks in accordance with a law.

5. The activity of solitary subdivisions located on the territory of Ukraine situated beyond its limits shall be regulated by the present Code and other laws.

Article 65. Management of Enterprise

1. The management of an enterprise shall be effectuated in accordance with its constitutive documents on the basis of combining the rights of the owner with regard to the economic use of its property and participation in management by the labor collective.

2. An owner shall effectuate its rights with regard to the management of an enterprise directly or through empowered agencies in accordance with the charter of the enterprise or other constitutive documents.

3. The owner(s) or organ empowered by it shall appoint (or elect) the executive of the enterprise in order to direct the economic activity of the enterprise.

4. When hiring an executive of an enterprise, a contract shall be concluded with him in which the period of hire, rights, duties, and responsibility of the executive, conditions of material provision, conditions of relieving him from office, and other conditions of hire by agreement of the parties are determined.

5. The executive of an enterprise shall operate without a power of attorney in the name of the enterprise, represent its interests in agencies of State power and agencies of local self-government, other organizations, relations with juridical persons and citizens, form the administration of the enterprise, and resolve questions of the activity of the enterprise within the limits and in the procedure determined by the constitutive documents.

6. The executive of an enterprise may be relieved from office before time on the grounds provided for by the contract in accordance with a law.

7. At all enterprises using hired labor a collective contract shall be concluded between the owner or organ empowered by it and the labor collective or organ empowered by it, which shall regulate production, labor, and social relations of the labor collective with the administration of the enterprise. Requirements for the content and procedure for the conclusion of collective contracts shall be determined by legislation on collective contracts.

8. The labor collective of an enterprise shall comprise all citizens who by their labor take part in its activity on the basis of a labor contract (or agreement) or other forms regulating labor relations of a worker with an enterprise. The powers of a labor collective with regard to its participation in the management of the enterprise shall be established by the charter or other constitutive documents in accordance with the requirements of the present Code, legislation on individual types of enterprises, and the law on labor collectives.

9. Decisions with regard to socio-economic questions concerning the activity of an enterprise shall be worked out and adopted

by its management organs with the participation of the labor collective and agencies empowered by it.

10. The peculiarities of the management of enterprises of individual types (or organizational forms of enterprises) shall be established by the present Code and by laws on such enterprises.

Article 66. Property of Enterprise

1. The property of an enterprise shall comprise production and nonproduction funds, and also other valuables whose cost is reflected on the autonomous balance sheet of the enterprise.

2. The sources of forming the property of an enterprise shall be:
monetary and material contributions of the founders;
revenues received from the realization of products, services, and other types of economic activity;
revenues from securities;
credits of banks and other creditors;
capital investments and donations from budgets;
property acquired from other subjects of economic management, organizations, and citizens in the procedure established by legislation;
other sources not prohibited by legislation of Ukraine.

3. The integral property complex of an enterprise shall be deemed to be an immoveable and may be an object of purchase-sale and other transactions on the conditions and in the procedure determined by the present Code and laws adopted in accordance therewith.

4. Realization of the property rights of an enterprise shall be effectuated in the procedure established by the present Code and other legislative acts of Ukraine.

5. The possession and use of natural resources an enterprise shall effectuate in the procedure established by legislation for payment and, in instances provided for by a law, on privileged conditions.

6. An enterprise shall issue, realize, and acquire securities in accordance with legislation of Ukraine.

7. The State shall guarantee the defense of property rights of an enterprise. The seizure by the State of property from an enterprise which it uses shall be effectuated only in the instances and in the procedure provided for by a law.

Article 67. Economic Relations of Enterprise with Other Enterprises, Organizations, and Citizens

1. Relations of an enterprise with other enterprises, organizations, and citizens in all spheres of economic activity shall be effectuated on the basis of contracts.

2. Enterprises shall be free in the choice of subject of a contract, determination of obligations, and other conditions of economic mutual relations which are not contrary to legislation of Ukraine.

3. An enterprise shall have the right to realize autonomously all products which are not within a State order or State planning task on the territory of Ukraine and beyond its limits unless provided otherwise by a law.

Article 68. Foreign Economic Activity of Enterprise

1. An enterprise autonomously shall effectuate foreign economic activity which is part of the foreign economic activity of Ukraine and shall be regulated by laws of Ukraine and other normative legal acts adopted in accordance therewith.

2. The procedure for the use of means of an enterprise in foreign currency shall be determined by the present Code and other laws.

3. An enterprise effectuating foreign economic activity may open its representations, branches, and production subdivisions beyond the limits of Ukraine, the maintenance of which shall be effectuated at the

means of the enterprise.

Article 69. Social Activity of Enterprise

1. Questions concerning the improvement of the conditions of labor, life, and health, guarantees of obligatory medical insurance of workers of an enterprise and their families, and also other questions of social development, shall be decided by the labor collective with the participation of the owner or organ empowered by it in accordance with legislation, constitutive documents of the enterprise, and the collective contract.

2. An enterprise shall ensure the training of skilled workers and specialists, their economic and vocational instruction both in own educational institutions and in other educational institutions according to a respective agreement. An enterprise shall provide privileges in accordance with a law to its workers who are studying without interruption of production.

3. Pensioners and disabled persons who worked before retirement on pension at an enterprise shall enjoy equally with its workers available possibilities of medical servicing, provision of housing, passes to recreational and prophylactic institutions, and other social services and privileges provided for by the charter of the enterprise.

4. The owner and management organs of an enterprise shall be obliged to ensure for all workers of the enterprise proper and safe conditions of labor. An enterprise shall bear responsibility in the procedure established by a law for harm caused to the health and labor capacity of its workers.

5. An enterprise shall be obliged to ensure favorable conditions of labor for women and minors, provide them with work preferentially in the day time; women having young children and pregnant women shall be transferred to lighter work with harmless conditions of labor, and grant them other privileges provided for by a law. An enterprise with harmful conditions of labor shall create individual shops and sectors

for provision to women, minors, and individual categories of workers with lighter work.

6. An enterprise autonomously shall establish for its workers additional leaves, a reduced work day, and other privileges, and also have the right to encourage workers of other enterprises, institutions, and organizations which service it.

7. An enterprise shall have the right to provide an additional pension, irrespective of the amounts of State pension, to a worker who became a disabled person at the particular enterprise as a consequence of an accident or vocational illness. In the event of the death of a worker of an enterprise when performing his employment duties, the owner or enterprise voluntarily or by decision of a court shall provide to the family of the worker a benefit in accordance with a law.

8. An enterprise with the right to hire a work force shall ensure a quantity of jobs determined in accordance with a law for the arrangement of employment for minors, disabled persons, and other categories of citizens needing social defense. The responsibility of an enterprise for the failure to fulfill this requirement shall be established by a law.

Article 70. Associations of Enterprises

1. Enterprises shall have the right on a voluntary basis to combine their economic activity (production, commercial, and other types of activity) on the conditions and in the procedure established by the present Code and other laws.

2. By decision of the Cabinet of Ministers of Ukraine or agencies to whose powers are relegated the administration of State or municipal enterprises, associations of enterprises may be formed on the conditions and in the procedure established by the present Code and other laws.

3. Types of associations of enterprise, their general status, and also the basic requirements with regard to the effectuation by them of

economic activity shall be determined by the present Code and other questions of their activity shall be regulated by legislation of Ukraine.

Article 71. Records and Reports of Enterprise

1. The records and reports of an enterprise shall be effectuated in accordance with the requirements of Article 19 of the present Code and other normative legal acts.

2. Information not provided for by a law an enterprise shall provide to agencies of State power, agencies of local self-government, other enterprises, institutions, and organizations on a contractual basis or in the procedure provided for by the constitutive documents of the enterprise.

Article 72. Legislation on Enterprises

1. Enterprises in Ukraine shall effectuate their activity in accordance with the requirements of Articles 62-71 of the present Code unless provided otherwise relative to enterprises of individual types by the present Code and other laws adopted in accordance with the present Code.

2. If other rules have been established an international treaty in force of Ukraine, consent to the bindingness of which was given by the Supreme Rada of Ukraine, than those that have been provided for by legislation on enterprises, the rules of the international treaty shall apply.

Chapter 8
State and Municipal Unitary Enterprises

Article 73. Concept of State Unitary Enterprise

1. A State unitary enterprise shall be formed by a competent agency of State power in a dispositive procedure on the base of a

solitary part of State ownership, as a rule, without the division thereof into participatory shares, and be within the sphere of its administration.

2. The agency of State power within those sphere of administration an enterprise is shall be the representative of the owner and fulfill its functions within the limits determined by the present Code and other legislative acts.

3. The property of a State unitary enterprise shall be in State ownership and shall be consolidated to that enterprise by right of economic jurisdiction or right of operative management.

4. The name of a State unitary enterprise must contain the words "State enterprise".

5. A State unitary enterprise shall not bear responsibility for obligations of the owner and agency of power within whose sphere of administration it is.

6. The executive of an enterprise appointed by the agency within whose sphere of administration the enterprise is and accountable to this agency shall be the management organ of the State unitary enterprise.

7. The peculiarities of the status of an executive of a State unitary enterprise, including increased responsibility of the executive established for the results of work of the enterprise, may be determined by a law.

8. State unitary enterprises shall operate as State commercial enterprises or treasury enterprises.

Article 74. State Commercial Enterprise

1. A State commercial enterprise shall be a subject of entrepreneurial activity, operate on the basis of a charter on the principles of entrepreneurship specified in Article 44 of the present Code, and bear responsibility for the results of its activity with all of the property belonging to it by right of economic jurisdiction according to the present

Code and other laws adopted in accordance with the present Code.

2. The property of a State commercial enterprise shall be consolidated to it by right of economic jurisdiction.

3. The charter fund of a State commercial enterprise shall be formed by an empowered agency within whose sphere of administration it is before the registration of this enterprise as a subject of economic management. The minimum amount of the charter fund of a State commercial enterprise shall be established by a law.

4. If the value of assets of a State commercial enterprise with regard to the results of its activity proved to be less than the amount of the charter fund provided for by the charter of the enterprise, the agency within whose sphere of administration the particular enterprise is shall be obliged to conduct a reduction of its charter fund in the procedure established by legislation, but not lower than the established minimum amount of the charter fund.

5. The State and agency within whose sphere of administration is a State commercial enterprise shall not bear responsibility for its obligations except for instances provided for by the present Code and other laws.

6. Losses caused to a State commercial enterprise as a consequence of the fulfillment of decisions of agencies of State power or agencies of local self-government which were deemed by a court to be unconstitutional or invalid shall be subject to compensation by the said agencies voluntarily or by decision of a court.

7. A State unitary commercial enterprise may be transformed in the instances and in the procedure provided for by a law into a corporatized enterprise (State joint-stock society). The peculiarities of the activity of corporatized enterprises shall be determined by the present Code and other laws.

Article 75. Peculiarities of Economic Activity of State Commercial Enterprises

1. A State commercial enterprise shall be obliged to accept and to fulfill State orders and State planning tasks brought to it in the procedure established by legislation, and also to take them into account when forming a production program, determining the prospects for its economic and social development, and choosing contracting parties.

2. A State commercial enterprise shall not have the right without compensation to transfer property belonging to it to other juridical persons or citizens, except for instances provided for by a law. A State commercial enterprise shall have the right to alienate and pledge out property objects relegated to basic funds, and lease out integral property complexes of structural entities and subdivisions only with the prior consent of the agency within whose sphere of administration it is and, as a rule, on a competitive basis.

3. Means received from the sale of property objects relegated to basic funds of a State commercial enterprise shall be sent for investing in the production activity of this enterprise.

4. Withdrawing from the balance sheet basic funds not completely amortized, and also accelerated amortization of basic funds of a State commercial enterprise, may be conducted only with the consent of the agency within whose sphere of administration is the particular enterprise.

5. State commercial enterprises shall form at the expense of profit (or revenue) special (or special-purpose) funds intended to cover expenses connected with their activity:
    amortization fund;
    production development fund;
    consumption fund (or payment of labor);
    reserve fund;
    other funds provided by the charter of an enterprise.

6. The procedure for determining the normative standards of

deductions to special-purpose funds of State commercial enterprises, the maximum amounts thereof, and the procedure for the forming and use of these funds, shall be established by a law.

7. In the event of a change of executive of a State commercial enterprise, the conducting of an internal audit of the financial-economic activity of the enterprise in the procedure provided for by a law shall be obligatory.

8. Other peculiarities of the economic and social activity of State commercial enterprises shall be determined by a law.

Article 76. Treasury Enterprise

1. Treasury enterprises shall be created in branches of the national economy in which:
the effectuation of economic activity has been authorized by a law only to State enterprises;
the State is the principal (in excess of fifty per cent) consumer of the products (or work, services);
the free competition of goods producers or consumers is impossible under the conditions of economic management;
the production of socially necessary products (or work, services) which according to the conditions and character of requirements satisfied by it may, as a rule, not be profitable is predominant (in excess of fifty per cent);
the privatization of property complexes of State enterprises is prohibited by a law.

2. A treasury enterprise shall be created by decision of the Cabinet of Ministers of Ukraine. The volume and character of basic activity of the enterprise, and also the agency within whose sphere of economic management the enterprise is created, shall be determined in the decision concerning the creation of a treasury enterprise. The reorganization and liquidation of a treasury enterprise shall be conducted in accordance with the requirements of the present Code by decision of the agency to whose competence is relegated the creation of the particular enterprise.

3. The property of a treasury enterprise shall be consolidated to it by right of operative management in the amount specified in the charter of the enterprise.

4. A treasury enterprise shall be a juridical person and have respective accounts in branches of the State bank and a seal with its own name.

5. The agency within whose sphere of administration is a treasury enterprise shall confirm the charter of the enterprise, appoint its executive, give authorization for the effectuation of economy activity by the treasury enterprise, determined the types of products (or work, services) to whose production and realization the said authorization extends.

6. The name of a treasury enterprise must contain the words "treasury enterprise".

Article 77. Peculiarities of Economic Activity of Treasury Enterprises

1. A treasury enterprise shall effectuate economic activity in accordance with production tasks of the agency within whose sphere of administration it is.

2. A treasury enterprise shall autonomously organize the production of products (or work, services) and realize it at prices (or tariffs) which are determined in the procedure established by the Cabinet of Ministers of Ukraine, unless provided otherwise by a law.

3. The agency within whose administration a treasury enterprise is shall effectuate control over the use and preservation of property belonging to the enterprise and shall have the right to remove property from the treasury enterprise not being used or being used not for designation and shall dispose of it within the limits of its powers.

4. A treasury enterprise shall not have the right to alienate or by other means dispose of property consolidated to it, which shall be

relegated to the basic funds, without the prior consent of the agency within whose sphere of administration it is.

5. The sources of forming the property of a treasury enterprise shall be:
    State property transferred to the enterprise in accordance with a decision concerning the creation thereof;
    monetary means and other property received from the realization of products (or work, services) of the enterprise;
    special-purpose means allocated from the State Budget of Ukraine;
    credits of banks;
    part of the revenues of the enterprise received by it with regard to results of economic activity provided by the charter;
    other sources not prohibited by a law.

6. A treasury enterprise shall receive credits in order to fulfill charter tasks under guarantee of the aency within whose sphere of administration the enterprise is.

7. A treasury enterprise shall be liable for its obligations only with means which are at its disposition. In the event of the insufficiency of the said means the State, in the person of the agency within whose sphere of administration the enterprise is shall bear full subsidiary responsibility for obligations of the treasury enterprise.

8. The procedure for the distribution and use of profit of a treasury enterprise shall be determined by its charter in accordance with the procedure established by the Cabinet of Ministers of Ukraine in accordance with a law.

9. Other peculiarities of economic and social activity of treasury enterprises shall be determined by the present Code, the Law on State Enterprises, and other legislative acts.

Article 78. Municipal Unitary Enterprises

1. A municipal unitary enterprise shall be formed by a competence

agency of local self-government by way of disposition on the base of a solitary part of municipal ownership and shall be within the sphere of its administration.

2. The agency within whose sphere of administration a municipal unitary enterprise is shall be the representative of the owner – respective territorial hromada – and shall fulfill its functions within the limits determined by the present Code and other legislative acts.

3. The property of a municipal unitary enterprise shall be in municipal ownership and shall be consolidated to such enterprise by right of economic jurisdiction (municipal commercial enterprise) or by right of operative management (municipal noncommercial enterprise).

4. The charter fund of a municipal unitary enterprise shall be formed by the agency in whose sphere of administration it is before the registration thereof as a subject of economic management. The minimum amount of the charter fund of a municipal unitary enterprise shall be established by the respective local soviet.

5. The name of a municipal unitary enterprise must contain the words "municipal enterprise" and an indication of the agency of local self-government within whose sphere of administration the enterprise is.

6. A municipal unitary enterprise shall not bear responsibility for obligations of the owner and agency of local self-government within whose sphere of administration it is.

7. An executive of a municipal unitary enterprise shall head the enterprise appointed by the agency within whose sphere of administration it is and shall be accountable to that agency.

8. Losses caused to a municipal unitary enterprise as a result of the execution of decisions of agencies of State power or agencies of local self-government shall be subject to compensation by the said agencies voluntarily or by decision of a court.

9. The peculiarities of economic activity of municipal unitary enterprises shall be determined in accordance with the requirements established by the present Code relating to the activity of State commercial or treasury enterprises, and also by other requirements provided for by a law.

Chapter 9
Economic Societies

Article 79. Concept of Economic Society

1. Enterprises or other subjects of economic management created by juridical persons and/or citizens by means of combining their property and participation in entrepreneurial activity of the society for the purpose of receiving profit shall be deemed to be economic societies. In instances provided for by the present Code, an economic society may operate composed of one participant.

2. Subjects of economic management and other participants of economic relations specified in Article 2 of the present Code, and also citizens who are not subjects of economic management, may be founders and participants of a society. Limitations with regard to founding and participation in economic societies of subjects of economic management or other persons shall be established by the present Code and by other laws.

3. Economic societies shall be juridical persons.

4. Subjects of economic management-juridical persons which have become founders or participants of an economic society shall retain the status of a juridical person.

5. Economic societies may effectuate any entrepreneurial activity unless provided otherwise by a law.

Article 80. Types of Economic Societies

1. To economic societies shall be relegated: joint-stock societies, limited responsibility societies, additional responsibility societies, full societies, kommandit societies.

2. An economic society having a charter fund divided into a determined quantity of stocks of identical par value shall be a joint-stock society and shall bear responsibility for obligations only with property of the society, and stockholders shall bear the risk of losses connected with activity of the society within the limits of the value of the stocks belonging to them.

3. A limited responsibility society shall be an economic society having a charter fund divided into participatory shares, the amount of which is determined by the constitutive documents and bearing responsibility for its obligations only with its property. The participants of a society who have fully paid up their contributions shall bear the risk of losses connected with the activity of the society within the limits of their contributions.

4. An additional responsibility society shall be an economic society whose charter fund is divided into participatory shares determined by constitutive documents and which bears responsibility for its obligations with own property, and in the event of the insufficiency thereof the participants of this society shall bear additional joint and several responsibility within an identical multiple determined by the constitutive documents to the contribution of each participant.

5. A full society shall be an economic society, all the participants of which in accordance with a contract concluded among them shall effectuate entrepreneurial activity in the name of the society and bear additional joint and several responsibility for obligations of the society with all of their property.

6. A kommandit society shall be an economic society in which one or several participants effectuate entrepreneurial activity in the name

of the society and bear additional joint and several responsibility for its obligations with all of their property against which according to a law execution may be levied (full participants), and other participants present in the activity of the society only with their contributions (contributors).

7. Only persons registered as subjects of entrepreneurship may be participants of a full society or full participants of a kommandit society.

Article 81. Joint-Stock Societies

1. Joint-stock societies may be open or closed.

2. Stocks of an open joint-stock society may be distributed by means of open subscription and purchase-sale on stock exchanges. Stockholders of an open society may alienate stocks belonging to them without the consent of other stockholders and the society.

3. Stocks of a closed joint-stock society shall be distributed among te founders or among a previously determined group of persons and may not be distributed by subscription or purchased and sold on a stock exchange. The stockholders of a closed society shall have a preferential right to acquire stocks which are sold by other stockholders of the society.

4. In order to create a joint-stock society the founders must make a communication concerning an intention to create a joint-stock society, effectuate a subscription for stocks, conduct a constitutive meeting, and State registration of the joint-stock society.

5. The total par value of issued stocks must be equal to the amount of the charter fund of the joint-stock society, which may not be less than an amount determined by a law.

6. The founders of a joint-stock society shall conclude between themselves a contract which determines the procedure for the effectuation by them of joint activity with regard to the creation of the

joint-stock society and responsibility to persons who have subscribed for stocks and third persons. If citizens take part in the creation of the society, the contract may be notarially certified.

7. The founders shall bear joint and several responsibility for obligations which arose in accordance with the constitutive contract.

8. An open subscription for stocks when creating a joint-stock society shall be organized by the founders. The founders in any event shall be obliged to be the holders of stocks in an amount of not less than 25% of the charter fund and for a period of not less than two years.

9. The procedure for the creation of joint-stock societies, including conducting a constitutive meeting, shall be determined by a law.

10. A closed joint-stock society may be reorganized into an open in the procedure provided for by a law.

11. The peculiarities of the creation and activity of State joint-stock societies shall be determined by the present Code, the Law on State Enterprises, and other laws.

12. Other peculiarities of the activity of joint-stock societies shall be determined by the present Code, the Law on Economic Societies, and other laws.

Article 82. Constitutive Documents of Economic Society

1. A constitutive contract shall be the constitutive document of a full society or kommandit society. A charter shall be the constitutive document of a joint-stock society, limited responsibility society, and additional responsibility society.

2. Constitutive documents of an economic society must contain information concerning the type of society, subjects and purposes of

its activity, composition of the founders and participants, composition and competence of organs of the society and the procedure for the adoption of decisions by them, including a List of questions under which unanimity or a qualified majority of votes is necessary provided for by Article 57 of the present Code.

3. A charter of a joint-stock society, besides the information specified in paragraph two of the present Article, must contain also information concerning the types of stocks to be issued, their par value, the correlation of stocks of various types, the quantity of stocks which the founders are purchasing, and the consequences of the failure to fulfill obligations with regard to the purchase of stocks.

4. A charter of a limited responsibility society, besides the information specified in paragraph two of the present Article, must contain information concerning the amount of participatory shares of each participant, and the amount, composition, and procedure for the making of contributions by them.
The procedure for determining the amount of participatory shares of participants depending upon a change of the value of property submitted as a contribution and additional contributions of participants may be established by the charter.

5. The constitutive contract of a full society and kommandit society, besides the information specified in paragraph two of the present Article, must determine the amount of participatory share of each participant, the form of their participation in the affairs of the society, the amount, composition, and procedure for the making of contributions by them. Only the aggregate amount of their participatory shares in the property of the society and the amount, composition, and procedure for making contributions by them shall be specified in the constitituve contract relative to the contributors of a kommandit society.

6. The name of an economic society must contain an indication of the type of society, for full societies and kommandit societies – the surname (or name) of the participants of the society who bear additional responsibility for obligations of the society with all of their property,

and also other necessary information. The name of an economic society may not specify the affiliation of the society to agencies of State power or agencies of local self-government.

7. Information also may be included in constitutive documents concerning other conditions of activity of the economic society which are not contrary to a law. Unless the period of activity of an economic society has been specified in the constitutive documents, it shall be considered to be created for an indeterminate period.

8. Constitutive documents of an economic society shall in the instances provided for by a law be agreed with the Antimonopoly Committee of Ukraine.

9. A violation of the requirements established by the present Article for the content of constitutive documents of an economic society shall be grounds for a refusal of the State registration thereof.

Article 83. State Registration of Economic Society

1. State registration of an economic society shall be effectuated in the procedure provided for by Article 58 of the present Code.

2. The peculiarities of the registration of economic societies effectuating banking and insurance activity, and als professional activity on the securities market, shall be determined by the present Code and respective laws.

3. An economic society shall receive the status of a juridical person from the day of its State registration.

4. Changes which have occurred in constitutive documents of an economic society and which are entered in the State register shall be subject to State registration according to the same rules which have been established for State registration of the society. An economic society shall be obliged within a five-day period to inform the agency which effectuated the registration about changes in the constitutive documents

of the society.

Article 84. Consequences of Conclusion of Transactions Before Registration of Economic Society

1. An economic society may open accounts in a bank, and also conclude contracts and other transactions, only after the State registration thereof. Transactions concluded by the founders of a society before the day of its registration shall be deemed to be concluded with the society only on condition of their subsequent approval by the society in the procedure determined by a law and the constitutive documents.

2. Transactions concluded by founders before the day of registration of the society and thereafter not approved by the society shall entail legal consequences only for persons who have concluded these transaction.

Article 85. Ownership of Economic Society

An economic society shall be the owner of:
property transferred to it in ownership by the founders and participants as contributions;
products produced as a result of economic activity of the society;
revenues received from economic activity of the society;
other property acquired by the society on grounds not prohibited by a law.

Article 86. Contributions of Participants and Founders of Economic Society

1. Buildings, installations, equipment and other material valuables, securities, rights of use of land, water, and other natural resources, buildings, installations, and also other property rights (including property rights to objects of intellectual property), monetary means, including foreign currency, may be contributions of participants and founders of an economic society.

2. A contribution valued in hrivnas shall comprise the participatory share of a participant and founder in the charter fund of a society. The procedure for valuing contributions shall be determined in the constitutive documents of an economic society, unless provided otherwise by a law.

3. It shall be prohibited to use for forming the charter fund of a society budgetary means and means received on credit and under pledge. The financial status of founders-juridical persons relative to their possibility to effectuate respective contributions to the charter fund of an economic society in instances provided for by a law must be verified by a proper auditor (or auditing organization) in the established procedure, and the property status of founders-citizens must be confirmed by a declaration concerning their revenues and property certified by a respective tax agency.

Article 87. Funds of Economic Society

1. The amount of contributions of founders and participants of an economic society shall comprise the charter fund of the society.

2. A society shall have the right to change (to increase or to reduce) the amount of the charter fund in the procedure established by the present Code and by a law adopted in accordance with it.

3. A decision of a society concerning a change of the amount of charter capital shall enter into force from the day of making these changes in the State register.

4. A reserve (or insurance) fund shall be created in an economic society in an amount established by the constitutive documents, but not less than twenty-five per cent of the charter fund, and also other funds provided for by legislation of Ukraine or the constitutive documents of the society. The amount of annual deductions to the reserve (or insurance) fund shall be provided for by the constitutive documents, but may not be less than five per cent of the amount of profit of the society.

5. The profit of an economic society shall be formed from the proceeds from its economic activity after the covering of material expenses and those equated thereto and expenses for the payment of labor. From economic profit of a society shall be paid the taxes and other obligatory payments provided for by a law, and also interest on the credits of banks and bonds. Profit received after the said settlements shall remain at the disposition of the society, which shall determine the orientations of its use in accordance with the constitutive documents of the society.

Article 88. Rights and Duties of Participants of Economic Society

1. Participants of an economic society shall have the right to:

take part in the management of affairs of the society in the procedure determined in the constitutive documents, except for instances provided for by the present Code and other laws;

take part in the distribution of the profit of the society and receive a participatory share thereof (or dividends);

receive information concerning the activity of the society. At the demand of a participant, the society shall be obliged to provide to him for familiarization the yearly balance sheets, reports concerning the financial-economic activity of the society, protocols of the internal audit commission, protocols of meetings of management organs of the society, and so on;

withdraw from the society in the procedure provided for by the constitutive documents.

2. Participants of a society also shall have other rights provided for by the present Code, other laws, and constitutive documents of the society.

3. Participants of an economic society shall be obliged to:

comply with the requirements of constitutive documents of the society and fulfill decisions of its management organs;

make contributions (or pay up stocks) in the amount, in the procedure, and with the means provided for by the constitutive documents in accordance with the present Code and the Law on Economic Societies;

bear other duties provided for by the present Code, other laws, and constitutive documents of the society.

Article 90. Records and Reports of Economic Society

1. Records and accounts of economic societies shall be effectuated in accordance with the requirements of Article 19 of the present Code and other normative-legal acts.

2. Verifications of the financial activity of the society shall be effectuated by State tax agencies, other agencies of State power within the limits of the powers determined by a law, internal audit commission (or internal auditor) of the economic society, and/or auditors.

3. The reliability and comprehensiveness of the yearly balance sheet and reports of an economic societies must in instances determined by a law be confirmed by an auditor (or auditing organization).

Article 91. Termination of Activity of Economic Society

1. The termination of the activity of an economic society shall occur by means of its liquidation or reorganization in accordance with Article 59 of the present Code.

2. An economic society shall be liquidated by a liquidation commission appointed by its highest organ, and in the event of the termination of the activity of the society by decision of a court – by a liquidation commission formed in accordance with the decision of the court.

3. From the day of formation of the liquidation commission to it shall pass the powers with regard to the management of affairs of the economic society. The liquidation commission shall within a three-day period from the moment of its formation publish information concerning the liquidation of the economic society and effectuate other actions in

accordance with the requirements of Articles 58-61 of the present Code and other laws.

4. Settlements with creditors in the event of the liquidation of an economic society shall be effectuated in accordance with Article 61 of the present Code, taking into account the following peculiarities:

means belonging to the economic society, including from the sale of its property during the liquidation, after the settlement of accounts with regard to payment for labor of persons who work on conditions of hire, fulfillment of obligations to the budget, banks, possessors of bonds issued by the society, and other creditors, shall be distributed among the participants of the society in the procedure and on the conditions provided for by the present Code, the Law on Economic Societies, and constitutive documents of the society within a six-month period after publication of the information concerning its liquidation;

property transferred to the society by its founders or participants for use shall be returned in kind without remuneration. In the event disputes arise with regard to payment of indebtedness of the society, its means shall not be subject to distribution between the participants of the society until the settlement of that dispute or until receipt by the creditors of respective guarantees of repayment of the indebtedness.

5. The liquidation of an economic society shall be considered to be completed, and the society to have terminated its activity, from the day of making an entry concerning its liquidation in the State register.

Article 92. Legislation on Economic Societies

The procedure for the creation and the procedure for activity of individual types of economic societies shall be regulated by the present Code, Civil Code of Ukraine, and other laws.

Chapter 10
Enterprises of Collective Ownership

Article 93. Concept of Enterprise of Collective Ownership

1. A corporative or unitary enterprise operating on the basis of collective ownership of the founder(s) shall be an enterprise of collective ownership.

2. Production cooperatives, enterprises of a consumer cooperative society, enterprises of social and religious organizations, and other enterprises provided for by a law shall be enterprises of collective ownership.

Article 94. Economic Activity of Cooperatives

1. Cooperatives as voluntary associations of citizens for the purpose of the joint resolution by them of economic, socio-domestic, and other questions may be created in various branches (production, consumer, housing, and so on). The activity of various types of cooperatives shall be regulated by a law.

2. Economic activity of cooperatives must be effectuated in accordance with the requirements of the present Code and other legislative acts.
For the purpose of the effectuation of economic activity on the principles of entrepreneurship citizens may form production cooperatives (or cooperative enterprises).

Article 95. Production Cooperative

1. A voluntary association of citizens on the basis of membership for the purpose of joint production or other economic activity which is based on their personal labor participation and combining of property share contributions, participation in the management of the enterprise, and distribution of revenue among the members of the cooperative in accordance with their participation in its activity shall be deemed to be

a production cooperative.

2. Production cooperatives may effectuate production, processing, procurement-sale, supply, service, and any other entrepreneurial activity not prohibited by a law.

3. A production cooperative shall be a juridical person and operate on the basis of a charter.

4. The name of a production cooperative must contain the words "production cooperative" or "cooperative enterprise".

Article 96. Principles of Activity of Production Cooperative

Production cooperatives shall be created and effectuate their activity on the following principles:
voluntariness of membership of citizens in the cooperative and free withdrawal therefrom;
personal labor participation of members of the cooperative in the activity of the enterprise;
openness and accessibility to membership for those who recognize the charter of the cooperative, and wish to take part in its activity on conditions established by the charter of the cooperative;
democratic character of management of the cooperative, and equal rights of members of the cooperative when adopting decisions;
distribution of revenue among members of the cooperative in accordance with their labor and property participation in the activity of the cooperative;
control of members of the cooperative over its work in the procedure determined by the charter.

Article 97. General Conditions of Creation of Production Cooperative

1. Citizens, foreigners, and stateless persons may be founders (or members) of a production cooperative. The number of members of a production cooperative may not be less than three persons.

2. A decision concerning the creation of a production cooperative shall be adopted by its constitutive meeting.

3. A production cooperative shall be considered to be created and acquire the status of a juridical person from the day of its State registration in accordance with the requirements of the present Code.

Article 98. Membership in Production Cooperative

1. Citizens who have attained 16 years of age, recognize the charter of the cooperative, and comply with its requirements, and take property and labor participation in the activity of the cooperative may be members of a production cooperative.

2. Citizens may be simultaneously members of production cooperatives, and also members of cooperatives of other types (consumer, housing, and so on).

3. Joining a production cooperative shall be effectuated on the basis of the written application of a citizen. A member of a cooperative shall make an entry and share contribution in the procedure determined by the charter of the production cooperative. The decision of the board (or chairman) of the cooperative concerning the admission to membership of the cooperative shall be subject to confirmation by the general meeting. The procedure for taking such a decision and confirmation thereof shall be determined by the charter of the cooperative.

4. Membership in a production cooperative shall be terminated in the event of:
voluntary withdrawal from the cooperative;
termination of labor participation in the activity of the cooperative;
expulsion from the cooperation in the instances and in the procedure determined by the charter;
failure of the general meeting of members of the cooperative to confirm the decision of the board (or chairman) concerning admission to the cooperative;

death of the member of the cooperative.

5. The procedure and property consequences of termination of membership in a production cooperative shall be determined by the present Code and charter of the cooperative.

6. Expulsion from the production cooperative (or dismissal of members of the cooperative from a cooperative enterprise) may be appealed to a court.

Article 99. Rights and Duties of Members of Production Cooperative

1. The basic rights of members of a production cooperative shall be:
participation in the management of the cooperative, right to vote at a general meeting of members of the cooperative, riht to elect and be elected to management organs of the cooperative;
use of services of the cooperative;
receipt of cooperative payments and participatory share of the revenue per share;
receipt of reliable and complete information concerning the financial-economic activity of the cooperative;
receipt of a share in the event of withdrawal from the cooperative in the procedure and within the periods determined by its charter.

2. The basic duties of members of a production cooperative shall be compliance with the charter and fulfillment of decisions of management organs of the cooperative.

3. Other rights and duties of members of a cooperative also may be provided for by the charter of a production cooperative.

Article 100. Property of Production Cooperative

1. Property of a production cooperative shall comprise collective ownership of the cooperative. A production cooperative shall be the

possessor of buildings, structures, property contributions of its members, products manufactured by them, revenues received from its realization and other activity provided for by the charter of the cooperative, and other property acquired on grounds not prohibited by a law.

2. Members of a cooperative may transfer as a share contribution the right to use a land plot belonging to them in the procedure determined by land legislation. Payment may be recovered from the cooperative in amounts determined by the general meeting of members of the cooperative for a land plot transferred to a production cooperative for use.

3. In order to effectuate economic and other activity, respective funds shall be formed by the production cooperative at the expense of own property.

4. The property of a production cooperative shall in accordance with its charter be divided into share and indivisible funds. The indivisible fund shall be formed at the expense of entry contributions and property of the cooperative (except for land). Share contributions of members of the cooperative shall not be included therein. The procedure for forming and the amounts of the indivisible fund shall be established by the charter.

5. The amounts of share contributions in a cooperative shall be established in equal parts and/or in proportion to the anticipated participation of a member of the cooperative in its economic activity.

6. Financial resources of a production cooperative shall be formed at the expense of revenue from the realization of products (or work, services), share and other contributions of members of the cooperative, credits, and other proceeds not prohibited by legislation.

Article 101. Management of Production Cooperative

1. The management of a production cooperative shall be effectuated on

the basis of self-government, glasnost, and participation of its members in deciding questions of activity of the cooperative.

2. The highest management organ of a production cooperative shall be the general meeting of members of the cooperative. The board (or chairman) of the cooperative and internal audit commission (or internal auditor) of the cooperative shall be relegated to management organs of the cooperative.

3. A supervisory council of the cooperative may be provided for by the charter of a production cooperative. Members of the internal audit commission (or internal auditor) of the cooperative may not be members of its board (or chairman of the cooperative) or supervisory council.

Article 102. General Meeting of Members of Production Cooperative

1. A general meeting shall:
make changes in the charter of the cooperative;
elect by means of direct secret ballot the chairman of the cooperative, members of the board of the cooperative, members of the internal audit commission (or internal auditor), and members of the supervisory council of the cooperative;
confirm the orientations of development of the cooperative;
hear reports of the management organs of the cooperative concerning their activity;
determine the types and amounts of funds of the cooperative and the procedure of their formation and use;
confirm the rules of internal order of the cooperative enterprise, yearly report and balance sheet of the cooperative, procedure for forming and distributing revenue of the cooperative, decisions of the board (or chairman) of the cooperative concerning the admission of new members;
decide questions concerning the entry of a cooperative enterprise into an association of enterprises (or cooperatives) and participation of the cooperative in founding other subjects of economic management;
adopt a decision concerning the reorganization or liquidation of

the cooperative.

2. A general meeting shall have the right to adopt any other decision connected with charter activity of the production cooperative.

3. A general meeting of members of a cooperative shall be conducted annually after the end of the financial year. It may also be convoked at any time by decision of the board (or chairman) of the cooperative or at the initiative of not less than a third of the members of the cooperative, unless provided otherwise by the charter.

4. A general meeting shall be empowered to adopt decisions if more than half the members of the production cooperative are present at it. Decisions with regard to questions specified in paragraph one of the present Article shall be adopted by a majority of votes of the total number of members of the cooperative.

Article 103. Board of Production Cooperative

1. A board of a production cooperative shall be created in a cooperative composed of not less than ten members.

2. The board of a cooperative shall:
work out and submit for confirmation of the general meeting the orientations of development of the cooperative;
convoke the general meeting of members of the cooperative and control the fulfillment of decisions adopted by it;
submit for confirmation of the general meeting a decision concerning the acceptance of new members into the cooperative and the termination of membership;
ensure the preservation of property of the cooperative;
organize the conducting of independent auditor verifications of the activity of the cooperative;
decide questions of the training of members of the cooperative and cooperative with fatherland and foreign organizations;
delegate to the executive director of a cooperative the right to adopt respective decisions with regard to questions of the competence

of the board if this has been provided for by the charter of the cooperative;

decide other questions of activity of the cooperative.

3. The board shall be headed by the chairman of the cooperative, which shall be elected by the general meeting of the production cooperative. The functions of chairman of the cooperative and procedure for the recall thereof shall be determined by the charter of the cooperative.

4. Members of the board may elect from their composition the deputy chairman and secretary of the board in accordance with the charter of the cooperative.

5. Members of the board of a cooperative shall work primarily on social principles. Remuneration for work of members of the board may be provided for in the charter of a cooperative.

6. The periodicity of conducting sessions of the board of a cooperative shall be determined by the charter of a cooperative. The decision shall be adopted by a majority of votes when not less than two-thirds of the members of the board of the cooperative are present at the session.

7. If there are less than ten members in the composition of a production cooperative, the functions and powers of the board shall be effectuated by the general meeting and chairman of the cooperative in accordance with the charter.

Article 104. Executive Director of Production Cooperative

1. The board of a production cooperative may hire an executive director for the operative management of the activity of the enterprise. An executive director may not be a member of the cooperative.

2. An executive director shall effectuate his activity on conditions of a contract which the board of the cooperative shall conclude with

him and shall fulfill functions in accordance with the charter.

3. An executive director shall bear responsibility for his activity to the cooperative.

4. In the absence in a production cooperative of the post of executive director, the chairman of the cooperative shall direct the work of the cooperative enterprise.

Article 105. Supervisory Council of Production Cooperative

1. If the number of members of a production cooperative comprises more than fifty persons, a supervisory council may be formed in the cooperative in order to control the activity of the executive director of the cooperative enterprise.

2. The supervisory council shall be elected by the general meeting from among the members of the cooperative, composed of from three to five persons. A member of the supervisory council may not be a member of the board of internal audit commission.

3. The procedure for the election of a supervisory council and chairman thereof, and also the procedure for the activity of the supervisory council, shall be established by the charter of the cooperative.

Article 106. Internal Audit Commission (or Internal Auditor) of Production Cooperative

1. For the purposes of control over the financial-economic activity of a production cooperative, an internal audit commission shall be elected, and in a cooperative in which there are less than ten members – an internal auditor.

2. An internal audit commission (or internal auditor) shall be elected by the general meeting from among members of the cooperative in accordance with its charter. Members of the internal audit commission (or internal auditor) may not be members of the board or supervisory

council of a production cooperative.

Article 107. Economic Activity of Production Cooperative

1. A production cooperative shall in accordance with its charter autonomously determine the basic orientations of economic activity and effectuate its planning and organization.

2. A production cooperative shall realize its products and render services at prices and tariffs which are established autonomously by it or on a contractual basis, and in the instances provided for by legislation – at State prices and tariffs.

3. Relations of a production cooperative with other enterprises, institutions, organizations, and citizens in all spheres of economic activity shall be established on the basis of contracts.

4. Revenue of a production cooperative shall be formed from proceeds from economic activity after covering material expenses and those equated thereto and expenses for the payment of labor of hired personnel. Revenue shall be directed to the payment of taxes and other obligatory payments, the repayment of credits, covering of losses, conducting of deductions to funds of the cooperative, cooperative payments, payment of participatory shares of revenues per share, and so on.

5. Cooperative payments are part of the revenue of a production cooperative distributed between members of the cooperative, taking into account their labor and other participation in the activity of the cooperative. The calculation and payment of participatory shares of the revenue per share shall be effectuated according to the results of the financial year from revenue remaining at the disposition of the cooperative, taking into account the need to form its funds. By decision of the general meeting of member of the cooperative, the payment of participatory shares of revenue per share may be effectuated in monetary form, by goods, securities, and so on.

6. The procedure for the use of revenue of a production cooperative shall be determined by the charter of the cooperative in accordance with a law.

7. A production cooperative autonomously shall effectuate foreign economic activity in accordance with a law. The procedure for the use of means of a cooperative in foreign currency shall be established by a law and by the charter of the cooperative.

8. Property relations of members of a production cooperative with the cooperative in the event of termination of membership in the cooperative and relative to the transfer of the share shall be regulated by civil legislation.

Article 108. Property Responsibility of Production Cooperative

1. A production cooperative shall be liable for its obligations with all of the property belonging to it. Members of a production cooperative shall bear with regard to obligations of the cooperative subsidiary (or additional) responsibility with their property in the amount not less than their share contribution unless a larger amount of responsibility has been provided for by a law or by the charter of the cooperative. The production cooperative shall not bear responsibility for obligations of members of the cooperative.

2. A production cooperative may insure its property and property rights by decision of the general meeting of members of the cooperative unless another procedure has been established by a law.

Article 109. Termination of Activity of Production Cooperative

1. A production cooperative may by decision of the general meeting of members of the cooperative be reorganized into an enterprise of other forms of economic management in the procedure determined by the charter of the cooperative in accordance with the requirements

of the present Code.

2. A production cooperative shall be liquidated in the general procedure of liquidation of a subject of economic management provided for by the present Code, taking into account the following:

the liquidation of a production cooperative shall be effectuated by the liquidation commission appointed by the general meeting of members of the cooperative, and in the event of its liquidation by decision of a court – the liquidation commission formed in accordance with that decision;

disposition of the land of a production cooperative being liquidated shall be effectuated in the procedure and on the conditions provided for by land legislation. The property of a cooperative remaining after the settlement of accounts with the budget and creditors shall be distributed among the members of the production cooperative in proportion to the value of their shares.

Article 110. Other Questions of Activity of Production Cooperative

Other questions of the activity of a production cooperative shall be regulated by the present Code and by other laws.

Article 111. Consumer Cooperative Society. Enterprises of Consumer Cooperative Society

1. A consumer cooperative society in Ukraine is a system of self-governing organizations of citizens (or consumer societies, unions thereof, associations), and also of enterprises and institutions of these organizations, being an autonomous organizational form of the cooperative movement.

2. The primary link of a consumer cooperative society shall be the consumer society – a self-governing organization of citizens who on the basis of voluntariness of membership, property participation, and mutual assistance combine for joint economic activity for the purpose of the collective organized ensuring of their economic and social

interests. Each member of a consumer society shall have his own participatory share in its property.

3. A consumer society shall be a juridical person and shall operate on the basis of a charter.

4. Consumer societies may on voluntary principles combine into unions and other forms of association provided for by a law, unified union of consumer societies of Ukraine, and shall have the right of free withdrawal therefrom.

5. The ownership of a consumer cooperative society shall consist of the ownership of consumer societies, unions (or associations), and their joint ownership and shall be one of the forms of collective ownership. The possession, use, and disposition of ownership of a consumer cooperative society shall be effectuated by its organs in accordance with the constitutive documents of the societies or unions (or associations).

Objects of the right of ownership of a consumer cooperative society may be in the joint ownership of consumer societies and unions (or associations). Their participatory share in ownership shall be determined by a contract.

6. The legal foundations of the organization and activity of a consumer cooperative society shall be determined by a law.

7. Consumer societies and unions (or associations) thereof may be formed for the effectuation of their charter purposes enterprises, institutions, and other subjects of economic management in accordance with the requirements of the present Code and other laws.

8. Unitary or corporative enterprises formed by a consumer society(ies) or a union (or association) of consumer societies in accordance with the requirements of the present Code and other legislative acts for the purposes of the effectuation of charter purposes of these societies and unions (or associations) shall be deemed to be enterprises of a consumer cooperative society.

Article 112. Enterprises of Associations of Citizens, Religious Organizations

1. A unitary enterprise founded on the ownership of an association of citizens (or social organization, political party) or the ownership of a religious organization for the effectuation of economic activity with a view to the fulfillment of their charter tasks shall be an enterprise of an association of citizens or a religious organization.

2. The right of ownership of associations of citizens shall be realized by their highest charter management organs in the procedure provided for by a law and charter documents. The right of ownership of religious organizations shall be realized by their management organs in accordance with a law.

3. The respective association of citizens having the status of a juridical person, and also an association (or union) of social organizations, if the right of founding enterprises has been provided for by its charter, shall be the founder of an enterprise of an association of citizens. It shall be prohibited for political parties and juridical persons by which they are created to found enterprises, except for mass media, enterprises effectuating the sale of socio-political literature, and other propaganda-agitation materials, manufactures with own symbols, conducting exhibitions, lectures, festivals, and other socio-political measures.

4. Religious organizations shall have the right to found publishing, printing, production, restoration-construction, agricultural, and other enterprises necessary in order to ensure the activity of these organizations.

5. An enterprise of an association of citizens and religious organization shall operate on the basis of a charter and shall be a juridical person effectuating its activity by right of operative management or economic jurisdiction in accordance with the requirements of the present Code.

6. Limitations with regard to the creation and activity of individual types of enterprises of an association of citizens and religious organization shall be established by laws.

Chapter 11
Private Enterprises. Other Types of Enterprises

Article 113. Private Enterprises

1. An enterprise operating on the basis of private ownership of one or several citizens, foreigners, stateless persons and the labor thereof or with the use of hired labor shall be deemed to be a private enterprise. An enterprise operating on the basis of private ownership of a subject of economic management-juridical person also shall be deemed to be private.

2. The procedure for the organization and activity of private enterprises shall be determined by the present Code and other laws.

Article 114. Peasant (or Farmer) Economy

1. A peasant (or farmer) economy shall be a form of entrepreneurship of citizens for the purposes of production, processing, and realization of goods agricultural products.

2. Persons working on it under a labor contract (or agreement) may not be members of a peasant (or farmer) economy.

3. Relations connected with the creation and activity of peasant (or farmer) economies shall be regulated by the present Code, and also by the Law on a Peasant (or Farmer) Economy, and other laws.

Article 115. Lease Enterprise

1. An enterprise created by a lessee on the basis of a lease of an integral property complex of an existing State or municipal enterprise

or property complex of a production structural subdivision (or structural entity) of this enterprise for the purpose of the effectuation of entrepreneurial activity shall be deemed to be a lease enterprise.

2. The juridical person formed by members of the labor collective of an enterprise or subdivision thereof, whose property complex is an object of lease, shall be the lessee.

3. The organization of members of the labor collective registered as a juridical person shall have a preferential right to conclude a contract of lease of the property of that enterprise (or structural subdivision) where this organization is created.

4. The State Property Fund of Ukraine and its regional subdivisions, and also agencies empowered by the Supreme Rada of the Autonomous Republic Crimea and local soviets to administer property which belongs respectively to the Autonomous Republic Crimea or is in municipal ownership, shall be the lessors with respect to property complexes relegated to State or municipal ownership.

5. Objects of State and municipal ownership on the basis of which lease enterprises may not be created shall be determined by a law.

6. The transfer on lease of property complexes shall not terminate the right of ownership to this property. It shall be prohibited to transfer integral property complexes on sublease.

7. A lessee shall bear responsibility for ensuring the integrity and preservation of property received on lease and upon the demand of the lessor must compensate the losses caused to it.

8. A leased enterprise may be deemed to be bankrupt in the procedure established by a law.

9. The procedure for the conclusion of a contract of lease of a property complex and other questions of the creation and activity of a

lease enterprise shall be regulated by the present Code and other laws.

Article 116. Enterprise With Foreign Investments

1. An enterprise created in accordance with the requirements of the present Code in whose charter fund not less than ten per cent comprises a foreign investment shall be deemed to be an enterprise with foreign investments. An enterprise shall acquire the status of an enterprise with foreign investments from the day of crediting the foreign investment on its balance sheet.

2. Valuables contributed by foreign investors to objects of investment activity in accordance with legislation of Ukraine for the purpose of the receipt of profit or achievement of a social effect shall be a foreign investment.

3. Foreign investments may be contributed to objects in which investing is not prohibited by laws of Ukraine.

4. Enterprises with foreign investments shall have the right to be founders of subsidiary enterprises, create branches and representations on the territory of Ukraine and beyond its limits in compliance with the requirements of legislation of Ukraine and legislation of the respective States.

5. Branches of economic management and/or territories in which the total amount of participation of a foreign investor is established, and also territories to which the activity of enterprises with foreign investments are limited or prohibited, may be determined by a law, proceeding from the requirements of ensuring national security.

6. The legal status and procedure for activity of enterprises with foreign investments shall be determined by the present Code, law on the regime of foreign investing in Ukraine, and other legislative acts.

Article 117. Foreign Enterprise

1. A unitary or corporative enterprise created according to legislation of Ukraine operating exclusively on the basis of ownership of foreigners or foreign juridical persons, or an operating enterprise acquired wholly in the ownership of these persons, shall be a foreign enterprise.

2. Foreign enterprises may not be created in branches determined by a law which have strategic significance for the security of the State.

3. Activity of branches, representations, and other solitary subdivisions of enterprises formed according to the legislation of other States shall be effectuated on the territory of Ukraine in accordance with the legislation of Ukraine.

4. The conditions and procedure for the creation, and the requirements for the organization and activity of foreign enterprises shall be determined by the present Code, the Law on the Regime of Foreign Investing, and other laws.

Chapter 12
Associations of Enterprises

Article 118. Concept of Association of Enterprises

1. An economic organization formed of two or more enterprises for the purpose of the coordination of their production, scientific, and other activity in order to resolve common economic and social tasks shall be an association of enterprises.

2. Associations of enterprises shall be formed by enterprises on a voluntary basis or by decision of agencies which in accordance with the present Code and other laws of Ukraine shall have the right to form associations of enterprises. Enterprises formed according to the legislation of other States may join as association of enterprises, and

enterprises of Ukraine may join associations of enterprises formed on the territory of other States.

3. Associations of enterprises shall be formed for an indefinite period or as temporary associations.

4. Associations of enterprises shall be a juridical person.

5. State registration of associations of enterprises shall be effectuated in accordance with Article 58 of the present Code.

Article 119. Types of Associations of Enterprises

1. Depending upon the procedure of founding, associations of enterprises may be formed as economic associations or as State or municipal economic associations.

2. An economic association is an association of enterprises formed at the initiative of enterprises, irrespective of the type thereof, which on a voluntary basis have combined their economic activity.

3. Economic associations shall operate on the basis of a constitutive contract and/or charter which shall be confirmed by their founders.

4. A State (or municipal) economic association is an association of enterprises formed by State (or municipal) enterprises by decision of the Cabinet of Ministers of Ukraine or, in instances determined by a law, decision of ministries (or other agencies within whose sphere of management are the enterprises forming the association), or by decision of competent agencies of local self-government.

5. A State (or municipal) economic association shall operate on the basis of a decision concerning its formation and charter, which shall be confirmed by the agency that adopted the decision concerning the formation of the association.

6. The provisions of the present Chapter also shall apply to associations of other subjects of economic management-juridical persons or associations of enterprises with the participation of such persons, unless provided otherwise by the present Code and other laws.

Article 120. Organizational-Legal Forms of Associations of Enterprises

1. Economic associations shall be formed as associations, corporations, consortiums, concerns, and other associations of enterprises provided for by a law.

2. An association shall be a contractual association created for the purposes of the coordination of economic activity of the enterprises which have combined by means of the centralization of one or several production and management functions, development of specialization and cooperation of production, organization of joint production entities on the basis of an association by participants of financial and material resources in order to satisfy primarily economic requirements of the participants of the association. In the charter of an association it must be indicated that it is an economic association. An association shall not have the right to interfere in the economic of the activity of enterprises-participants of the association. By decision of the participants, an association may be empowered to represent their interests in relations with agencies of power and other enterprises and organizations.

3. A contractual association created on the basis of the combining of production, scientific, and commercial interests of the enterprises which have combined with the delegating by them of individual powers of centralized regulation of activity of each of the participants to the management organs of the corporation shall be deemed to be a corporation.

4. A temporary charter association of enterprises in order to achieve a determined common economic purpose by the participants thereof (realization of special-purpose programs, scientific and construction projects, and so on) shall be a consortium. A consortium

shall use the means with which the participants endow it, centralized resources allotted for the financing of the respective program, and also means received from other sources, in the procedure determined by its charter. In the event of attaining the purpose of its creation the consortium shall terminate its activity.

5. A charter association of enterprises, and also other organizations, on the basis of their financial dependence on one or a group or participants of the association with the centralization of the functions of scientific-technical and production development, investment, financial, foreign economic, and other activity, shall be deemed to be a concern. The participants of the concern shall endow it with part of their powers, including the right to represent their interests in relations with agencies of power and other enterprises and organizations. The participants of a concern may not be simultaneously participants of another concern.

6. State and municipal economic associations shall be formed preferentially in the form of a corporation or concern, irrespective of the name of the association (kombinat, trust, and so on).

Article 121. Status of Enterprise-Participant of Association of Enterprises

1. Enterprises-participants of an association of enterprises shall retain the status of a juridical person irrespective of the organizational-legal form of association, and to them shall extend the provisions of the present Code and other laws with regard to the regulation of the activity of enterprises.

2. An enterprise-participant of an economic association shall have the right to:
voluntarily withdraw from the association on the conditions and in the procedure determined by the constitutive contract concerning its formation or charter of the economic association;
be a member of other associations of enterprises unless otherwise by a law, constitutive contract, or charter of the economic association;

receive information connected with the interests of the enterprise from the economic association in the established procedure;

receive part of the profit from the activity of an economic association in accordance with its charter. An enterprise may also have other rights provided for by the constitutive contract or charter of the economic association in accordance with legislation.

3. An enterprise which joins a State or municipal economic association shall not have the right without the consent of the association to withdrawn therefrom the composition thereof, and also combine on a voluntary basis its activity with other subjects of economic management and adopt a decision concerning the termination of its activity.

4. The decision concerning the formation of an association of enterprises (or constitutive contract) and the charter of the association shall be agreed with the Antimonopoly Committee of Ukraine in the procedure established by legislation.

Article 122. Management of Association of Enterprises

1. Economic associations shall have a highest management organ (or general meeting of participants) and form executive organs provided for by the charter of the economic association.

2. The highest organ of an economic association shall:

confirm the charter of the economic association and make changes therein;

decide questions concerning the admission of new participants in the economic association and expulsion of participants from the composition thereof;

form the executive organ of the economic association in accordance with its charter or a contract;

decide financial and other questions in accordance with the constitutive documents of the economic association.

3. The executive organ of an economic association (collegial or one-man) shall decide questions of current activity which in accordance

with the charter or contract have been relegated to its competence.

4. The board of the association and general director of the association, which shall be appointed to and relieved from office, having adopted the decision concerning the formation of the association, shall be the management of a State (or municipal) economic association. The composition of the board shall be determined by the charter of the association. The procedure for the management of a State (or municipal) economic association shall be determined by the charter of the association in accordance with a law.

5. The effectuation of the management of current activity of an association of enterprises may be entrusted to the administration of one of the enterprises (or head enterprise of the association) on conditions provided for by the constitutive documents of the respective association.

6. Disputes arising between participants of an association shall be settled in the procedure provided for by the charter of the association or in a judicial proceeding in accordance with a law.

Article 123. Property Relations in Association of Enterprises

1. The participants of an association of enterprises may make on the conditions and in the procedure provided for by the constitutive documents thereof property contributions (entry, membership, special-purpose, and so on).

2. The property shall be transferred to an association by the participants thereof in economic jurisdiction or operative management on the basis of a constitutive contract or decision concerning the formation of the association. The value of the property of the association shall be reflected on its balance sheet.

3. An economic association shall have the right to form by decision of its highest management organ unitary enterprises, branches, representations, and also be a participant (or founder) of economic societies. Enterprises formed by an economic association shall operate

in accordance with the provisions of the present Code, other laws, and the charter of the enterprise confirmed by the association.

4. An association of enterprises shall not be liable for obligations of its participants, and enterprises-participants shall not be liable for obligations of the association unless provided otherwise by the constitutive contract or charter of an association.

Article 124. Withdrawal of Participant from Association. Termination of Association of Enterprises

1. Enterprises-participants of an association may withdraw from the composition thereof with the preservation of mutual obligations and concluded contracts with other subjects of economic management.

2. The withdrawal of an enterprise from the composition of a State (or municipal) economic association shall be effectuated by decision of the organ which adopted the decision concerning formation of the association.

3. The termination of an association of enterprises shall occur as a result of its reorganization into another association or liquidation.

4. The reorganization of an economic association shall be effectuated by decision of enterprises-participants, and the reorganization of a State (or municipal) economic association – by decision of the organ which adopted the decision concerning formation of the association.

5. Liquidation of an economic association shall be effectuated by decision of enterprises-participants, and liquidation of a State (or municipal) association – by decision of the organ which adopted the decision concerning formation of the association. Liquidation of an association of enterprises shall be effectuated in the procedure established by the present Code relative to liquidation of the enterprise. Property remaining after the liquidation of an enterprise shall be distributed among the participants according to the charter of the association of enterprises or a contract.

Article 125. Industrial-Financial Groups

1. An enterprise may be a participant of an industrial-financial group (or transnational industrial-financial group if Ukrainian and foreign juridical persons are within the composition of the group).

2. An industrial-financial group shall be an association which is created by decision of the Cabinet of Ministers of Ukraine for a determined period for the purpose of the realization of State programs for the development of priority branches of production and structural restructuring of the economy of Ukraine, including programs according to international treaties of Ukraine, and also for the purpose of the production of a final product.

3. Industrial and other enterprises, scientific and design institutions, other institutions and organizations of all forms of ownership may join an industrial-financial group. The head enterprise shall be determined within the industrial-financial group, which shall have the exclusive right to operate in the name of the industrial financial group as a participant of economic relations.

4. An industrial-financial group shall not be a juridical person and shall not be subject to State registration as a subject of economic management.

5. The procedure for the formation and other questions of activity of industrial-financial groups shall be determined by a law on industrial-financial groups and other normative legal acts.

Article 126. Associated Enterprises. Holding Companies

1. Associated enterprises (or economic organizations) are a group of subjects of economic management-juridical persons connected between themselves by relations of economic and/or organizational dependence in the form of participation in the charter fund and/or management. Dependence between associated enterprises may be simple and decisive.

2. Simple dependence between associated enterprises shall arise if one of them has the possibility to block the adoption of decisions by another (dependent) enterprise which must be adopted in accordance with a law and/or constitutive documents of this enterprise by a qualified majority of votes.

3. Decisive dependence between associated enterprises shall arise if relations are established between enterprises of control-subordination at the expense of preferential participation of the controlling enterprise in the charter fund and/or general meeting or other management organs of another (subsidiary) enterprises, in particular the possession of a control packet of stocks. Relations of decisive dependence may be established on condition of receipt of consent of the respective agencies of the Antimonopoly Committee of Ukraine.

4. The existence of simple and decisive dependence must be specified in the information of State registration of a dependent (or subsidiary) enterprise and published in press organs in accordance with Article 58 of the present Code.

5. A subject of economic management possessing a control packet of stocks of a subsidiary enterprise(s) shall be deemed to be a holding company. Relations of control-subordination shall be established between a holding company and its subsidiary enterprises in accordance with the requirements of the present Article of the Code and other laws.

6. If through the fault of the controlling enterprise transactions or operations were concluded (or effectuated) disadvantageous for it by a subsidiary enterprise, then the controlling enterprise must contributorily compensate the losses caused to the subsidiary enterprise.

7. If a subsidiary enterprise through the fault of the controlling enterprise proves to be in a state of insolvency and will be deemed bankrupt, the controlling enterprise shall bear subsidiary responsibility to creditors of the subsidiary enterprise.

Article 127. Other Forms of Association of Interests of Enterprises

Other forms of association of interests of enterprises (or unions, partnerships, associations of entrepreneurs, and so on) not provided for in Article 120 of the present Code also may be determined by a law.

Chapter 13
Citizen as Subject of Economic Management. Peculiarities of Status of Other Subjects of Economic Management

Article 128. Citizen in Sphere of Economic Management

1. A citizen shall be deemed to be a subject of economic management when effectuating entrepreneurial activity on condition of State registration thereof as an entrepreneur without the status of a juridical person in accordance with Article 58 of the present Code.

2. A citizen-entrepreneur shall be liable for its obligations with all of its property against which in accordance with a law execution may be levied.

3. A citizen may effectuate entrepreneurial activity:
directly as an entrepreneur or through a private enterprise created by him;
with or without the enlistment of hired labor;
autonomously or jointly with other persons.

4. A citizen shall effectuate the management of a private enterprise founded by him directly or through an executed hired under a contract. When effectuating entrepreneurial activity jointly with other citizens or juridical persons, a citizen shall have the rights and duties respectively of a founder and/or participant of an economic society, member of a cooperative, and so on or the rights and duties determined by a contract concluded with his participation concerning joint activity without the

creation of a juridical person.

5. A citizen-entrepreneur shall effectuate his activity on the basis of freedom of entrepreneurship and in accordance with the principles provided in Article 44 of the present Code.

6. A citizen-entrepreneur shall be obliged to:

receive a license in the instances and procedure provided for by a law for the effectuation of determined types of economic activity;

inform agencies of State registration about a change of his address specified in the registration documents, subject of activity, other material conditions of his entrepreneurial activity subject to reflection in registration documents;

comply with the rights and legal interests of consumers, ensure the property quality of goods (or work, services) manufactured by him, comply with rules for obligatory certification of a product established by legislation;

not permit unfair competition and other violations of antimonopoly legislation;

keep a record of the results of his entrepreneurial activity in accordance with the requirements of legislation;

provide in a timely way to tax agencies a declaration on revenues and other necessary information for the calculation of taxes and other obligatory payments; pay taxes and other obligatory payments in the procedure and amounts established by a law.

7. A citizen-entrepreneur shall be obliged to comply with the requirements provided for by Articles 46 and 47 of the present Code, and also other legislative acts, and shall bear property and other responsibility established by a law for the damage and losses caused by him.

A citizen-entrepreneur may be deemed bankrupt by a court in accordance with the requirements of the present Code and other laws.

Article 129. Peculiarities of Status of Foreign Subjects of Economic Management

1. Foreigners and stateless persons shall when effectuating economic activity in Ukraine enjoy the same rights and have the same duties as citizens of Ukraine unless provided otherwise by the present Code and by other laws.

2. Foreign juridical persons when effectuating economic activity in Ukraine shall have the same status as juridical persons of Ukraine with the peculiarities provided by the present Code and by other laws, and also by international treaties, consent to the obligatoriness of which has been given by the Supreme Rada of Ukraine.

Article 130. Credit Unions in Sphere of Economic Management

1. Citizens permanently residing on the territory of Ukraine may combine into credit unions.

2. A nonprofit organization founded by citizens in the procedure established by a law on the basis of the voluntary combining of monetary contributions for the purpose of the satisfaction of the requirements of its members in the mutual granting of credits and rendering of other financial services shall be a credit union. The credit union shall be a juridical person. It shall acquire the status of a juridical person from the day of State registration thereof.

3. A credit union shall operate on the basis of a charter, which shall be confirmed by the general meeting of members of the credit union.

4. Property of a credit union shall be its ownership and consist of funds of the credit union, means of revenue, and other property.

5. A credit union may not be a founder or participant of subjects of entrepreneurial activity.

6. The status, procedure of organization, and effectuation of economic activity of a credit union shall be determined by the present Code, law on credit unions, and other laws.

Article 131. Peculiarities of Status of Philanthropic and Other Nonprofit Organizations in Sphere of Economic Management

1. Juridical persons, irrespective of forms of ownership, and also citizens who have reached majority, may form philanthropic organizations (philanthropic foundations, membership philanthropic organizations, philanthropic institutions, and so on).

2. A non-State organization effectuating philanthropic activity in the interests of society or individual categories of persons without the purpose of receiving profit from this activity shall be deemed to be a philanthropic organization. Philanthropic organizations shall be formed and operate on the territorial principle.

3. Agencies of State power and agencies of local self-government, and also State and municipal enterprises, institutions, and organizations which are wholly or partially financed from the budget may not be founder(s) and/or members of a philanthropic organization.

4. A philanthropic organization shall operate on the basis of a charter (or statute), which shall be confirmed by the highest management organ of the philanthropic organization, and shall be a juridical person.

5. A philanthropic organization shall have the right to effectuate nonprofit economic activity directed towards the fulfillment of its charter purposes and tasks. The effectuation by philanthropic organizations of activity in the form of rendering determined services (or fulfillment of work) which is subject to obligatory certification or licensing shall be permitted after such certification or licensing in the procedure established by a law.

6. Additional requirements for the creation, State registration,

and effectuation of economic activity and other questions of the activity of philanthropic organizations shall be established by the present Code, law on philanthropy and philanthropic organizations, and other laws.

7. The peculiarities of the status of other juridical persons effectuating nonprofit economic activity shall be determined by respective laws, by which the procedure for the activity of these subjects shall be regulated.

Article 132. Peculiarities of Status of Solitary Subdivisions (or Structural Entities) of Economic Organizations

1. Solitary subdivisions (or structural entities) of economic organizations shall be deemed to be subjects of economic management effectuating their activity in the name of these economic organizations without the status of a juridical person.

2. Branches, representations, divisions, and other structural subdivisions which are endowed with part of the property of economic organizations, effectuating relative to this property the right of operative use or other right to a thing provided for by a law shall be solitary subdivisions (or structural entities). They may have an account(s) in branches of a bank.

3. Branches, representations, and other solitary subdivisions of an economic organization shall operate on the basis of a Statute confirmed by this organization.

Section III
Property Basis of Economic Management

Chapter 14
Property of Subjects of Economic Management

Article 133. Legal Regime of Property of Subjects of Economic Management

1. The right of ownership and other rights to a thing – the right of economic jurisdiction, right of operative management, and also the right of operative use of property – shall constitute the basis of the legal regime of property of subjects of economic management on which their economic activity is based.

Economic activity also may be effectuated on the basis of other rights to a thing (right of possession, right of use, and so on) provided for by the Civil Code of Ukraine.

2. The property of subjects of economic management may be consolidated by another right in accordance with the conditions of a contract with the owner of the property.

3. Subjects of economic management effectuating economic activity on the basis of the right of operative use of property may not have the status of a juridical person and shall realize their economic competence within the limits of the status determined by an economic organization within whose composition it is.

4. The State shall ensure the right of equal defense of property rights of all subjects of economic management.

Article 134. Right of Ownership – Basic Right to Thing in Sphere of Economic Management

1. A subject of economic management effectuating economic activity on the basis of the right of ownership shall, at its discretion,

alone or jointly with other subjects, possess, use, and dispose of property belonging to it (or to them), including have the right to grant property to other subjects for use thereof by right of ownership, right of economic jurisdiction, or right of operative management, or on the basis of other forms of the legal regime of property provided for by the present Code.

2. Property to be used in economic activity may be in the joint ownership of two or more owners.

3. The legal regime of ownership and legal forms of the realization of the right of ownership in the sphere of economic management shall be determined by the present Code and a law.

Article 135. Organizational-Constitutive Powers of Owner

1. An owner of property shall have the right alone or jointly with other owners on the basis of property belonging to it (or to them) to found economic organizations or to effectuate economic activity in other organizational-legal forms of economic management not prohibited by a law at its discretion, determining the purpose and subject of economic activity, structure of the subject of economic management formed by it, composition and competence of management organs thereof, procedure for the use of property, and other questions of management of the activity of the subject of economic management, and also adopt a decision concerning the termination of economic activity of subjects of economic management founded by it in accordance with legislation.

2. An owner shall have the right personally or through agencies empowered by it for the purpose of the effectuation of economic activity to found economic organizations, consolidating to them property belonging to it by right of ownership and right of economic jurisdiction, and in order to effectuate noncommercial economic activity – by right of operative management, to determine the purpose and subject of activity of such organizations, the composition and competence of their management organs, procedure for the adoption by them of decisions, the composition and procedure for the use of property, and to determine

other conditions of economic management in the constitutive documents of the economic organization confirmed by the owner (or agency empowered by it), and also to effectuate directly or through agencies empowered by it within the limits established by a law other management powers relative to the founded organization and to terminate its activity in accordance with the present Law and other laws.

3. An owner shall have the right to effectuate organizational-constitutive powers also on the basis of corporative rights belonging to it in accordance with the present Code and other laws.

4. State and municipal enterprises may be combined by decision of the owner (or agency empowered by it) into State (or municipal) economic associations provided for by the present Code.

Article 136. Right of Economic Jurisdiction

1. The right of economic jurisdiction is a right to a thing of a subject of entrepreneurship which possesses, uses, and disposes of property consolidated to it by the owner (or agency empowered by it) with a limitation of the power of disposition relative to individual types of property with the consent of the owner in instances provided for by the present Code and other laws.

2. An owner of property consolidated by right of economic jurisdiction to a subject of entrepreneurship shall effectuate control over the use and preservation of property belonging to it directly or through an agency empowered by it without interfering in the operational-economic activity of the enterprise.

3. The provisions of a law established for the defense of the right of ownership shall apply relative to the defense of the right of economic jurisdiction. A subject of entrepreneurship effectuating economic activity on the basis of the right of economic jurisdiction shall have the right to defense of its property rights also against the owner.

Article 137. Right of Operative Management

1. The right to a thing of a subject of economic management which possesses, uses, and disposes of property consolidated to it by the owner (or agency empowered by it) for the effectuation of noncommercial economic activity within the limits established by the present Code and other laws, and also by the owner of the property (or agency empowered by it), shall be deemed to be the right of operative management.

2. An owner of property consolidated by right of operative management to a subject of economic management shall effectuate control over the use and preservation of property transferred on operative management directly or through an agency empowered by it and shall have the right to withdraw surplus property from the subject of economic management, and also property not being used and property being used by it not for designation.

3. The right of operative management shall be protected by a law in accordance with the provisions established for defense of the right of ownership.

Article 138. Right of Operative Use of Property

1. A subject of economic management — a solitary subdivision (or structural entity) of an economic organization – shall use property granted to it in order to effectuate economic activity by right of operative use of property.

2. The amount of property powers of a subject of economic management within the limits of the right of operative use of property shall be determined by the economic organization within whose composition the said subject is, in accordance with a law.

Article 139. Property in Sphere of Economic Management

1. The aggregate of things and other valuables (including

nonmaterial assets) which have a value determination, are produced or used in the activity of subjects of economic management, and reflected on the balance sheet thereof or taking into account in other forms of recording of property of these subjects provided for by a law, shall be deemed to be property in the present Code.

2. Depending upon the economic form acquired by property in the process of the effectuation of economic activity, property valuables shall be relegated to basic funds, circulating means, monetary means, and goods.

3. Buildings, structures, vehicles and fitting out, equipment, tools, production inventory and appurtenances, economic inventory, and other durable property which is relegated by legislation to basic funds shall be basic funds of production and nonproduction designation.

4. Raw material, fuel, materials, low-value articles and nondurable articles, and other property of production and nonproduction designation which is relegated by legislation to circulating means shall be circulating means.

5. Money in national and foreign currency intended for the effectuation of goods relations of these subjects with other subjects, and also financial relations in accordance with legislation, shall be monetary means within the composition of property of subjects of economic management.

6. Products produced (or goods stocks) and work and services fulfilled shall be deemed to be goods within the composition of property of subjects of economic management.

7. Securities shall be a special type of property of subjects of economic management.

Article 140. Sources of Forming Property of Subjects of Economic Management

1. There shall be sources of forming the property of subjects of economic management:
monetary and material contributions of founders;
revenues from the realization of products (or work, services);
revenues from securities;
capital investments and donations from budgets;
proceeds from the sale (or leasing out) of property objects (or complexes) belonging to them, and acquisition of property of other subjects;
credits of banks and other creditors;
uncompensated and philanthropic contributions, donations of organizations and citizens;
other sources not prohibited by a law.

2. The legal regime of property of subjects of economic management shall be established by the present Code and other laws, taking into account the types of property specified in Article 139 of the present Code.

Article 141. Peculiarities of Legal Regime of State Property in Sphere of Economic Management

1. Integral property complexes of State enterprises or their structural subdivisions, immoveable property, other separate individually-determined property of State enterprises, stocks (participatory shares, shares) of the State in the property of subjects of economic management of various forms of ownership, and also property consolidated to State institutions and organizations for the purpose of the effectuation of necessary economic activity and property transferred for uncompensated use to self-governing institutions and organizations or on lease for use thereof in economic activity, shall be relegated to State property in the sphere of economic management. The State through empowered agencies of State power shall effectuate the rights of owner also relative to objects of the right of ownership of the Ukrainian people

specified in Article 148, paragraph one, of the present Code.

2. The Cabinet of Ministers of Ukraine and, upon its empowerment, central and local agencies of executive power, shall effectuated the management of objects of State ownership in accordance with a law. In instances provided for by a law, other subjects also shall effectuate the management of State property.

3. The Cabinet of Ministers of Ukraine shall establish a List of State property to be transferred without compensation to the ownership of respective territorial hromadas (municipal ownership). The transfer of objects of economic designation from State to municipal ownership shall be effectuated in the procedure established by a law.

4. Enterprises effectuating activity which is authorized to be effectuated exclusively by State enterprises, institutions, and organizations may not be objects of transfer from State to municipal ownership.

5. Types of property which may be exclusively in State ownership, the alienation of which to non-State subjects of economic management is not permitted, and also additional limitations with regard to the disposition of individual types of property relegated to basic funds of State enterprises, institutions and organizations, shall be determined by a law.

Article 142. Profit (or Revenue) of Subject of Economic Management

1. The profit (or revenue) of a subject of economic management shall be an indicator of the financial results of its economic activity, which shall be determined by means of a reduction of the amount of gross revenue of the subject of economic management for a determined period by the amount of gross expenses and the amount of amortization deductions.

2. The composition of gross revenue and gross expenses of

subjects of economic management shall be determined by legislation. For the purposes of taxation a special procedure may be established by a law in order to determine revenue as an object of taxation.

3. The procedure for the use of profit (or revenue) of subjects of economic management shall be determined by the owner(s) or agency empowered by it in accordance with legislation and the constitutive documents. The procedure for the use of profit of State enterprises shall be established in accordance with a law.

4. The State may influence the choice by subjects of economic management of orientations and amounts of the use of profit (or revenue) through normative standards, taxes, tax privileges, and economic sanctions in accordance with a law.

Article 143. Securities Within Composition of Property of Subjects of Economic Management

A subject of economic management shall have the right to issue own securities, to realize them to citizens and juridical persons, and also to acquire securities of other subjects. Types of securities, the conditions and procedure for the issuance thereof, realization, and acquisition by subjects of economic management shall be established by the present Code and other laws.

Article 144. Grounds for Arising of Property Rights and Duties of Subject of Economic Management

1. Property rights and property duties of a subject of economic management may arise:

with regard to transactions provided for by a law, and also transactions not provided for by a law but not contrary thereto;

with regard to acts of agencies of State power and agencies of local self-government, and officials thereof in instances provided for by a law;

as a result of the creation and acquisition of property on grounds not prohibited by a law;

as a consequence of the causing of damage to another person, or the acquisition or preservation of property at the expense of another person without sufficient grounds;

as a consequence of a violation of the requirements of a law when effectuating economic activity;

with regard to other circumstances with which a law links the arising of property rights and duties of subjects of economic management.

2. The right to property subject to State registration shall arise from the day of registration of this property or respective rights thereto, unless established otherwise by a law.

Article 145. Property Status and Recording of Property of Subject of Economic Management

1. The property status of a subject of economic management shall be determined by the aggregate of property rights and property obligations belonging to it and reflected in bookkeeping records of its economic activity in accordance with the requirements of a law.

2. A change of the legal regime of property of a subject of economic management shall be effectuated by decision of the owner(s) of property by the means provided for by the present Code and other laws adopted in accordance therewith, except for instances when such change is prohibited by a law.

3. The legal regime of property of a subject of economic management fonded on State (or municipal) ownership may be changed by means of privatization of the property of the State (or municipal) enterprise in accordance with a law.

4. The legal regime of property of a subject of economic management founded on State (or municipal) ownership may be changed by means of leasing out an integral property complex of an enterprise or property complex of its structural subdivision.

5. Other grounds of the legal regime of property of a subject of economic management also may be determined by a law.

6. Subjects of economic management on the basis of the said bookkeeping records shall be obliged to draw up a financial report according to the forms provided for by legislation, conduct the inventorying of property belonging to it in order to ensure the reliability of the said bookkeeping records and report, and provide the financial report in accordance with the requirements of a law and constitutive documents thereof.

Article 146. Privatization of State and Municipal Enterprises

1. The property of a unified integral property complex of a State (or municipal) enterprise or individual subdivisions thereof which are unified (or integral) property complexes and are separated out into autonomous enterprises, and also objects of uncompleted construction and stocks (or participatory shares, shares) belonging to the State in the property of other subjects of economic management, may be alienated to the benefit of citizens or non-State juridical persons and have been privatized by these persons in accordance with a law.

2. The privatization of State (or municipal) enterprises shall be effectuated not otherwise than in execution of State programs for privatization, which shall determine the purposes, priorities, and conditions of privatization, and in the procedure established by a law.

3. The privatization of State (or municipal) enterprises or property thereof shall be effectuated by means of:

the purchase-sale of objects of privatization at auction, under a competition, and by other means which provide for a competition of purchasers;

the buying up of an integral property complex of a State (or municipal) enterprise leased out in the instances and procedure provided for by a law;

the buying up of property of a State (or municipal) enterprise in other instances provided for by a law.

4. Each citizen of Ukraine shall have the right to acquire State property in the process of privatization in the procedure established by a law.

5. The general conditions and procedure for the effectuation of privatization of State (or municipal) enterprises or property thereof shall be determined by a law.

6. In individual branches of the national economy peculiarities of privatization of the property of State enterprises may be determined by a law.

7. In the process of privatization of a State (or municipal) enterprise the rights of workers of a privatized enterprise shall be guaranteed by a law.

Article 147. Guarantees and Defense of Property Rights of Subjects of Economic Management

1. Property rights of subjects of economic management shall be protected by a law.

2. The withdrawal by the State from a subject of economic management of its property shall be permitted not otherwise than in the instances, on the grounds, and in the procedure provided for by a law.

3. Losses caused to a subject of economic management by a violation of its property rights by citizens or juridical persons, and also by agencies of State power or agencies of local self-government, shall be compensated to it in accordance with a law.

4. The right of ownership and other property rights of a subject of economic management shall be protected by a means specified in Article 20 of the present Code.

Chapter 15
Use of Natural Resources in Sphere of Economic Management

Article 148. Peculiarities of Legal Regime of Use of Natural Resources in Sphere of Economic Management

1. In accordance with the Constitution of Ukraine, land, the subsoil thereof, atmospheric air, water and other natural resources situated within the limits of the territory of Ukraine, the natural resources of its continental shelf, exclusive (maritime) economic zone shall be objects of the right of ownership of the Ukrainian people. Agencies of State power and agencies of local self-government within the limits determined by the Constitution of Ukraine shall effectuate the rights of ownership in the name of the people.

2. Each citizen shall have the right to use natural objects of the right of ownership of the Ukrainian people in accordance with a law.

3. Land shall be the principal national wealth, being under the special protection of the State. The right of ownership to land shall be guaranteed. The right shall be acquired and realized by citizens, juridical persons, and the State in accordance with the Land Code of Ukraine and other laws.

4. The legal regime of the use of individual types of natural resources (land, waters, forests, subsoil, atmospheric air, fauna) shall be established by a law.

5. Natural resources may be granted to subjects of economic management for use or to be acquired by them in ownership only in the instances and procedure provided for by a law.

Article 149. Use of Natural Resources by Subjects of Economic Management

1. Subjects of economic management shall use natural resources in economic activity by way of special or common nature use in

accordance with the present Code and other laws.

2. The Cabinet of Ministers of Ukraine shall ensure the State recording of natural resources which are relegated to State ownership, are in the management of the Autonomous Republic Crimea, are relegated to municipal ownership and may be used in economic activity.

Article 150. Use of Natural Resources by Right of Ownership

1. Land with enclosed water reservoirs, forest plots, generally-distributed minerals situated therein, may be transferred in ownership to subjects of economic management, including to citizens for conducting a peasant (or farmer) economy, and also to agricultural enterprises – for economic activity.

2. The procedure for the granting of land in ownership shall be determined exclusively by a law, taking into account the necessity of determining guarantees of effective use of the land by subjects of economic management and the prevention of the uneconomic use and spoilage thereof.

Article 151. Use of Natural Resources by Right of Use

1. Land and other natural resources (including for payment or on other conditions) shall be granted for use on the basis of special authorizations (or decisions) of agencies empowered by the State to subjects of economic management in order to effectuate economic activity.

2. The procedure of granting natural resources for use to citizens and juridical persons for the effectuation of economic activity shall be established by land, water, forestry, and other special legislation.

Article 152. Rights of Subjects of Economic Management With Regard to Use of Natural Resources

A subject of economic management effectuating economic

activity shall have the right to:

exploit the useful properties of natural resources granted thereto;

use minerals of local significance for economic requirements in the procedure established by legislation, water objects, and forestry resources situated on the land plot granted to it;

receive revenues from the results of economic activity connected with the use of natural resources;

receive preferential short-term and long-term credits for the realization of measures with regard to the effective use, regeneration, and protection of natural resources, and also use tax privileges when effectuating the said measures;

demand contributory compensation for damage caused to natural resources belonging thereto by other subjects, and also the elimination of obstacles in the effectuation of economic activity connected with the use of natural resources.

Article 153. Duties of Subjects of Economic Management With Regard to Use of Natural Resources

1. A subject of economic management effectuating economic activity shall be obliged to:

use natural resources in accordance with the special-purpose designation determined when granting (or acquiring) them for use in economic activity;

effectively and economically use natural resources on the basis of the application of the newest technologies in production activity;

effectuate measures with regard to the timely regeneration and prevention of spoilage, pollution, littering, and depletion of natural resources and not permit the reduction of their quality in the process of economic management;

make respective payment in a timely way for the use of natural resources;

effectuate economic activity without a violation of the rights of other owners and users of natural resources;

compensate losses caused by them to the owners or primary users of natural resources.

2. Other duties of a subject of economic management with regard to the use of natural resources in economic activity also may be determined by a law.

Chapter 16
Use in Economic Activity of Rights of Intellectual Property

Article 154. Regulation of Relations With Regard to Use in Economic Activity of Rights of Intellectual Property

1. Relations connected with the use in economic activity and protection of rights of intellectual ownership shall be regulated by the present Code and other laws.

2. The provisions of the Civil Code of Ukraine, taking into account the peculiarities provided for by the present Code and other laws, shall apply to relations connected with the use in economic activity of intellectual property rights.

Article 155. Objects of Intellectual Property Rights

1. There shall be deemed to be intellectual property rights in the sphere of economic management:
inventions and utility models;
industrial designs;
strains of flora and species of fauna;
trademarks (or marks for goods and services);
commercial (or firm) name;
geographic indication;
commercial secret;
computer programs;
other objects provided for by a law.

2. The general conditions for the defense of intellectual property rights on objects specified in the present Article shall be determined by the Civil Code of Ukraine.

Article 156. Powers With Regard to Use of Invention, Utility Model, and Industrial Design

1. The right of intellectual property in an invention, utility model, and industrial design shall be certified by a patent in accordance with legislation of Ukraine.

2. Relations of a subject of economic management who is an employer of the inventor(s) or author(s) of objects specified in paragraph one of the present Article relative to the rights to receive a patent and right of use of the said objects of intellectual property shall be regulated by the Civil Code of Ukraine and other laws.

3. The use of an invention, utility model, or industrial design in the sphere of economic management shall be:
manufacture, proposal for sale, introduction into economic (or commercial) turnover, application, carrying in or keeping for the said purpose of a product protected in accordance with a law;
application of a means protected in accordance with a law or proposal thereof for application in Ukraine on the conditions provided for by the Civil Code of Ukraine;
proposal for sale, introduction into economic (or commercial) turnover, application, carrying in or keeping for the said purpose of a product manufacture directly by a means which is protected in accordance with a law.

4. The right of prior use of an invention, utility model, or industrial design on the conditions provided for by the Civil Code of Ukraine shall belong to subjects of economic management.

5. The possessor of a patent may transfer his rights with regard to use of an invention, utility model, or industrial design as a contribution to the charter fund of an enterprise.

6. The rules of the present Article also shall apply to the regulation of relations arising in connection with the realization in the sphere of economic management of rights to a variety of flora and species of fauna.

Article 157. Powers With Regard to Use of Trademark

1. The right of intellectual property in a trademark shall be certified by a certified in the instances and procedure provided for by a law.

2. The use of a trademark in the sphere of economic management shall be deemed to be the application thereof on goods and when rendering services for which it has been registered, on packaging of goods, in an advertisement, printed publications, on signboards, when showing exhibits at exhibitions and fairs held in Ukraine, in prospectuses, accounts, stationary, and other documentation connected with the introduction of the said goods and services into economic (or commercial) turnover.

3. A certificate shall grant the right to the possessor thereof to prohibit other persons from using a registered trademark without the authorization thereof, except for instances of lawful use of the trademark without the authorization thereof.

4. Subjects of the right to a trademark may place a precautionary marking specifying that the trademark being applied is registered in Ukraine.

5. Subjects of the right to a trademark effectuating intermediary activity may on the basis of a contract with the producer of a good (or service) use its trademark with the trademark of the producer, and also instead of its trademark.

6. The right of intellectual property in a trademark may be transferred as a contribution to the charter fund of a subject of economic management.

7. In the event of bankruptcy of a subject of economic management the right to a trademark shall be valued together with other property of this subject.

Article 158. Powers With Regard to Use of Trademark, Right to Which Belongs to Several Persons

1. A trademark, the right to which belongs to several persons, is a mark distinguishing goods and services of participations of an association of enterprises (trade mark of an association, common trademark) from homogeneous goods and services of other subjects of economic management, or used jointly by several subjects in other instances provided for by a law.

2. Registration of a trademark, the right to which belongs to several persons, shall be effectuated in the procedure established by a law.

Article 159. Powers of Subjects of Economic Management With Regard to Commercial Name

1. A subject of economic management-juridical person or citizen-entrepreneur may have a commercial name.
A citizen-entrepreneur shall have the right to declare his own surname or forename as a commercial name.

2. Information concerning a commercial name of a subject of economic management shall be entered upon the submission thereof in registers, the procedure for keeping which shall be established by a law. A subject of economic management whose commercial name was included in a registered previously shall have a priority right to defend against any other subject an identical commercial name which has been included in the register later.

3. Both the full and abbreviated commercial name of a subject of economic management, if it is actually used by it in economic turnover, shall be subject to legal protection.

4. If a commercial name of a subject of economic management is an element of its trademark, the legal protection of both the commercial name and the trademark shall be effectuated.

5. A person using another's commercial name shall upon the demand of the owner thereof, be obliged to terminate such use and compensate the losses caused.

Article 160. Powers With Regard to Use of Geographic Indication

1. Only subjects of economic management producing goods (or rendering services) with regard to which State registration of the respective geographic indication has been effectuated shall have the right to use a geographic indication.

2. The use of a geographic indication shall by a subject of economic management shall be considered to be: application thereof on goods for which this geographic indication has been registered, and also on packaging; application in an advertisement, prospectuses, invoices, printed publications, official stationary, signboards, and so on.

3. Subject of economic management effectuating intermediary activity may use their trademark together with the geographic indication of a good of the producer not otherwise than on the basis of a contract.

4. The conditions of granting legal protection to a geographic indication shall be determined by a law.

Article 161. Use of Name of Country of Origin of Good

1. Manufactures of foreign origin or the packaging thereof in instances established by legislation, and also manufactures of fatherland production or the packaging thereof, intended for export must contain information concerning the country of their origin.

2. Information concerning the country of origin must be situated on an accessible place of the manufacture (or packaging) and affixed by a means which meets established requirements.

3. The use by subjects of economic management of an inscription (or brand) "Manufactured in Ukraine" or analogous in meaning relative to goods having foreign origin shall be prohibited.

4. Empowered agencies of State power shall control compliance with the said requirements in accordance with a law.

Article 162. Powers of Subjects of Economic Management With Regard to Commercial Secret

1. A subject of economic management which is the possessor of technical, organizational, or other commercial information shall have the right of defense against illegal use of this information by third persons on condition that this information has commercial value in connection with the fact that it is unknown to third persons and there is no free access thereto by other persons on legal grounds, and the possessor of the information takes proper measures with regard to the protection of its confidentiality.

2. The period of legal protection of a commercial secret shall be limited by the time of operation of the aggregate of the conditions specified in paragraph one of the present Article.

3. A person who unlawfully uses commercial information which belongs to a subject of economic management shall be obliged to compensate the losses caused to it by such actions in accordance with a law. A person who autonomously and in good faith received information which is a commercial secret shall have the right to use this information at its discretion.

4. The respective provisions of the Civil Code of Ukraine and other laws shall apply to relations connected with a commercial secret not regulated by the present Code.

Chapter 17
Securities in Economic Activity

Article 163. Securities and Types Thereof

1. Subjects of economic management may within the limits of their competence and in accordance with the procedure established by legislation issue and realize securities, and also acquire securities of other subjects of economic management.

A security shall be a document of the established form with the respective requisites certifying a monetary or other property right and determining relations between a subject of economic management which issue (or published) it and the possessor, providing for the fulfillment of obligations according to the conditions of the issue thereof, and also the possibility of the transfer of rights arising from this document to other persons.

2. Share, debt, and other securities may be issue and be in turnover in Ukraine. In the sphere of economic management in the instances provided for by a law the following types of securities shall be used: stocks, bonds of internal and external State loans, bonds of local loans, bonds of enterprises, treasury obligations, savings certificates, bills of exchange, and other types of securities provided for by the present Code and other laws.

3. Securities may be inscribed and bearer. Inscribed securities shall be transferred by means of the full endorsement (or inscription of transfer which certifies the transfer of the rights with regard to the security to another person) unless provided otherwise by a law or specially indicated on them that they are not subject to transfer. Bearer securities shall circulate freely.

The procedure for an inscribed identification of securities in paperless form shall be established by a law.

4. The legal regime of securities shall be determined by the present Code and by other laws.

Article 164. Conditions and Procedure for Issue of Securities by Subjects of Economic Management

1. A subject of economic management-juridical person shall in the instances and procedure provided for by a law have the right to issue in its own name stocks and bonds of an enterprise and realize them to citizens and juridical persons.

2. The right to issue stocks and bonds of an enterprise shall arise with a subject of economic management from the day of registration of this issue at the respective agency of State power.

3. It shall be prohibited for a subject of economic management to issue stocks and bonds of an enterprise in order to cover losses connected with its economic activity.

4. Subjects of economic management whose exclusive activity is activity connected with the issue and turnover of securities shall have the right to issue investment certificates.

5. Branches of banks which accept for deposit means from juridical persons and citizens shall issue them written certificates certifying the right of depositors to receive upon the expiry of the established period of a deposit and interest with regard thereto (savings certificates).

6. Subjects of economic management shall have the right in the procedure established by the Cabinet of Ministers of Ukraine and to issue into turnover bills of exchange-securities certifying the unconditional monetary obligation of the issuer of the bill of exchange to pay the determined amount of money to the possessor of the bill of exchange.

7. Securities (or sheets thereof) shall be manufactured only at State enterprises which have a license of the Ministry of Finances of Ukraine and shall be protected.

8. The peculiarities of the issue of securities in paperless form shall be determined by a law.

Article 165. Acquisition of Securities by Subjects of Economic Management

1. Subjects of economic management may acquire stocks and other securities specified in the present Code at the expense of means coming to the disposition thereof after payment of taxes and interest for a bank credit, unless established otherwise by a law.

2. Securities shall be paid up by subjects of economic management in hrivnas, and in instances provided for by a law and conditions of the issue thereof into turnover, — in foreign currency. Irrespective of the type of currency by which the securities have been paid up, the value thereof shall be expressed in hrivnas.

3. Purchase-sale operations of securities shall be effectuated by the emittents thereof, possessors, and also securities traders-intermediaries in the sphere of the issue and turnover of securities. The types and procedure for the effectuation of the said activity shall be determined by the present Code and other laws.

Article 166. State Regulation of Securities Market

1. State regulation of the securities market shall be effectuated for the purpose of realization of a unified State policy in the sphere of the issue and turnover of securities, creation of conditions for the effective mobilization and placement by subjects of economic management of financial resources, taking into account the interests of society and defense of the rights of participants of the stock market.

2. State regulation of the securities market shall be effectuated by the State Commission for Securities and the Stock Market, the status, procedure of organization, and activity of which shall be determined by a law.

3. Other agencies of State power shall effectuate control over the activity of participants of the securities market within the limits of powers determined by a law.

4. The forms of State regulation of the securities market, procedure for the effectuation of professional activity on the securities market by subjects of economic management, and responsibility of these subjects for a violation of the rules for the said activity shall be determined by the present Code and by other legislative acts adopted in accordance with it.

Chapter 18
Corporative Rights

Article 167. Content of Corporative Rights

1. Corporative rights are the rights of a person whose participatory share is determined in the charter fund (or property) of an economic organization which includes powers for the participation of this person in the management of the economic organization, receipt of a determined participatory share of profit (or dividends) of the particular organization, and assets in the event of the liquidation of the last in accordance with a law, and also other powers provided for by a law and the charter documents.

2. The possession of corporative rights shall not be considered to be entrepreneurship. Limitations may be established by a law for determined persons with regard to the possession of corporative rights and/or the effectuation thereof.

Article 168. Effectuation of Corporative Rights of State

1. Corporative rights of the State shall be effectuated by central agencies of executive power determined by a law and by empowered persons in the procedure established by the Cabinet of Ministers of Ukraine.

2. Central agencies of executive power and empowered persons shall:

effectuate powers with regard to participation in the management of an economic organization in accordance with the participatory share (or stocks, shares) of the State in the charter fund of this organization;

keep the register of State corporative rights;

conduct a valuation of State corporative rights;

effectuate control over the effectiveness of the work of the economic organization with regard to the realization of corporative rights belonging to the State.

3. Powers with regard to the management of corporative rights of the State shall be effectuated directly by the respective agencies of executive power if:

the State has one hundred percent of the participatory shares (or stocks) in the charter fund of an economic organization;

the subject of economic management with respect to which corporative rights of the State are effectuated takes part in State and regional programs financed from the State Budget of Ukraine;

a competition is not held with regard to appointment of an empowered person in view of the absence of applicants or if the proposals of competition participants do not correspond to the conditions of the competition;

in other instances provided by a law.

In remaining instances the management of the corporative rights of the State shall be effectuated by enlisting an empowered person.

4. The conditions for the transfer of powers and tasks with regard to the management of corporative rights of the State, including relative to legal responsibility of empowered persons, shall be an obligatory part of the respective decision of the Cabinet of Ministers of Ukraine and the contract with the empowered person.

5. The management of corporative rights of territorial hromadas shall be effectuated in accordance with the provisions of the present Article unless established otherwise by a law.

Article 169. Valuation of Corporative Rights of State

Corporative rights of the State and assets of subjects of economic management in those charter fund a participatory share of the State has been determined shall be subject to valuation according to a methodology confirmed by the Cabinet of Ministers of Ukraine in accordance with the requirements of a law.

Article 170. Determination of Empowered Person With Regard to Management of Corporative Rights of State

1. An empowered person with regard to the management of corporative rights of the State may be a citizen or juridical person, which has been determined according to the results of a competition, with whom the respective central agency of executive power concludes a contract of commission with regard to the management of corporative rights of the State.

2. The procedure for conducting the competition with regard to determining the empowered person for the fulfillment of functions with regard to corporative rights of the State shall be established by the Cabinet of Ministers of Ukraine.

Article 171. Register of Corporative Rights of State

A central agency of executive power empowered by the Cabinet of Ministers of Ukraine to effectuate necessary measures with regard to the management of corporative rights of the State, coordinate the activity of agencies of executive power in this sphere, and provide necessary information to other agencies of State power in accordance with legislation shall form and keep the register of corporative rights of the State.

Article 172. Legislation on Corporative Rights of State

Relations connected with the management of corporative rights of the State shall be regulated by the present Code, other laws, and normative legal acts adopted in accordance with the present Code.

Section IV
Economic Obligations

Chapter 19
General Provisions on Economic Obligations

Article 173. Economic Obligation

1. An obligation which arises between a subject of economic management and another participant(s) of relations in the sphere of economic management on the grounds provided for by the present Code by virtue of which one subject (the obliged party, including a debtor) shall be obliged to perform a determined action of an economic or administrative-economic character to the benefit of another subject (to fulfill work, transfer property, pay money, provide information, and so on) or refrain from determined actions, and the other subject (empowered party, including a creditor) has the right to demand performance from the obliged party the performance of its duty, shall be deemed to be an economic [obligation].

2. Property-economic obligations and organizational-economic obligations shall be the basic types of economic obligations.

3. The parties may by mutual consent concretize or expand the content of an economic obligation in the process of the fulfillment thereof unless established otherwise by a law.

Article 174. Grounds for Arising of Economic Obligations

Economic obligations may arise:
directly from a law or other normative-legal act regulating economic activity;
from an act of the administration of economic activity;

from an economic contract and other transactions provided for by a law, and also from transactions not provided for by a law but not contrary thereto;

as a consequence of the causing of damage to a subject or by a subject of economic management, the acquisition or preservation of property of a subject or by a subject of economic management at the expense of another person without sufficient grounds for this;

as a result of the creation of objects of intellectual property and other actions of subjects, and also as a consequence of events with which the law connects the ensuing of legal consequences in the sphere of economic management.

Article 175. Property-Economic Obligations

1. Civil-law obligations arising between participants of economic relations when effectuating economic activity, by virtue of which the obliged party must perform a determined economic action to the benefit of the other party or refrain from a determined action, and the empowered party has the right to demand from the obliged party the performance of the duty thereof, shall be a property-economic [obligation].

Property obligations arising between participants of economic relations shall be regulated by the Civil Code of Ukraine, taking into account the peculiarities provided for by the present Code.

2. Subjects of economic management specified in Article 55 of the present Code, noneconomic subjects-juridical persons, and also agencies of State power and agencies of local self-government endowed with economic competence, may be subjects of property-economic obligations. If a property-economic obligation arises between subjects of economic management or between subjects of economic management and noneconomic subjects-juridical persons the obliged and empowered parties shall be respectively the debtor and creditor.

3. Obligations of a property character arising between subjects of economic management and noneconomic subjects-citizens shall not be economic and shall be regulated by other acts of legislation.

4. Subjects of economic management in the instances provided for by the present Code and other laws may voluntarily assume obligations of a property character to the benefit of other participants of economic relations (philanthropy and so on). Such obligation shall not be grounds for demands with regard to their obligatory fulfillment.

Article 176. Organizational-Economic Obligations

1. Economic obligations arising in the process of the management of economic activity between a subject of economic management and a subject of organizational-economic powers, by virtue of which the obliged party must effectuate to the benefit of the other party a determined administrative-economic (or organizational) activity or refrain from a determined action, and the empowered party has the right to demand from the obliged party performance of its duty, shall be deemed to be organizational-economic [obligations].

2. Organizational-economic obligations may arise:
between a subject of economic management and the owner which is the founder of the said subject, or an agency of State power or agency of local self-government endowed with economic competence relative to this subject;
between a subject of economic management which jointly organizes an association of enterprises or economic society and the management organs of these associations or societies;
between subjects of economic management, and if one of them is a subsidiary enterprise with respect to the other;
in other instances provided for by the present Code, other legislative acts, or the constitutive documents of the subject of economic management.

3. Organizational-economic obligations of subjects may arise from a contract and acquire the form of a contract.

4. Subjects of economic management shall have the right jointly to effectuate economic activity in order to achieve a common purpose without the formation of a unified subject of economic management on

conditions determined by a contract on joint activity. If the participations of a contract on joint activity charge the direction of joint activity to one of the participants, on it may be placed the duty to conduct common affairs. Such participant shall effectuate organizational-administrative powers on the basis of a commission signed by the other participants.

Article 177. Socio-Municipal Obligations of Subjects of Economic Management

1. Subjects of economic management shall be obliged by decision of the local soviet at the expense of own means in accordance with a law to create special jobs for persons with limited labor capacity and to organize their vocational training.

2. Subjects of economic management may, in accordance with Article 175, paragraph four, of the present Code, irrespective of the charter purpose of their activity, assume obligations concerning economic assistance in deciding questions of social development of population centers of there whereabouts, in construction, and in maintenance of socio-cultural objects and objects of municipal economy and domestic servicing, and render other economic assistance for the purpose of resolving local problems. Subjects of economic management shall have the right to participate in the forming of respective funds of local soviets unless established otherwise by a law and in the fulfillment of work with regard to the integrated economic and social development of the territories.

Article 178. Public Obligations of Subjects of Economic Management

1. A subject of economic management which in accordance with a law and its constitutive documents is obliged to effectuate the fulfillment of work, rendering of services, or sale of goods to everyone who applies to it on legal grounds shall not have the right to refuse the fulfillment of work, rendering of services, or sale of a good when it has such possibility or to give preference to one consumer over another, except for instances provided for by legislation.

2. A subject of economic management which groundlessly evades the fulfillment of a public obligation must compensate the other party for losses caused by this in the procedure determined by a law.

3. The Cabinet of Ministers of Ukraine may in the instances determined by a law issue rules binding upon the parties to a public obligation, including with regard to the establishment of or regulation of prices. The conditions of the obligation not meeting these rules or established prices shall be invalid.

Chapter 20
Economic Contracts

Article 179. General Conditions of Conclusion of Contracts Giving Rise to Economic Obligations

1. Property-economic obligations arising between subjects of economic management or between subjects of economic management and noneconomic subjects-juridical persons on the basis of economic contracts shall be economic-contractual obligations.

2. The Cabinet of Ministers of Ukraine and agencies of executive power empowered by it may recommend to subjects of economic management orientation conditions for economic contracts (model contracts), and in instances determined by a law – confirm standard contracts.

3. The conclusion of an economic contract shall be binding for the parties if it was based on a State order, the fulfillment of which is a duty for the subject of economic management in instances provided for by a law, or there is a direct indication of a law relative to the obligatoriness of the conclusion of a contract for determined categories of subjects of economic management, or agencies of State power or agencies of local self-government.

4. When concluding economic contracts the parties may

determine the content of the contract on the basis of:

free expression of will when the parties have the right to agree at their discretion any conditions of a contract not contrary to legislation;

a model contract recommended by the management organ to subjects of economic management for use when concluding contracts and the parties have the right by mutual consent to change individual conditions provided for by the model contract or to supplement the content thereof;

a standard contract confirmed by the Cabinet of Ministers of Ukraine, or in instances provided for by a law, by another agency of State power, when the parties may not deviate from the content of the standard contract but have the right to clarify the provisions thereof;

of a contract of accession proposed by one party to other possible subjects, when these subjects entering into a contract do not have the right to insist upon a change of the content thereof.

5. The content of a contract concluded on the basis of a State order must correspond to this order.

6. Subjects of economic management providing consumers specified in paragraph one of the present Article with electric power, communications, services of railway and other types of transport, and in instances provided for by a law, also other subjects, shall be obliged to conclude contracts with all consumers of their products (or services). Obligatory conditions of such contracts may e provided for by legislation.

7. Economic contracts shall be concluded according to rules established by the Civil Code of Ukraine, taking into account the peculiarities provided for by the present Code and other normative-legal acts with regard to individual types of contracts.

Article 180. Material Conditions of Economic Contract

1. The content of an economic contract shall comprise the conditions of a contract determined by an agreement of the parties thereto directed towards the establishment, change, or termination of economic obligations both agreed by the parties and accepted by them

as obligatory conditions of the contract in accordance with legislation.

2. An economic contract shall be considered to be concluded if between the parties in the procedure established by a law and in form agreement has been reached with regard to all of its material conditions. Conditions deemed as such according to a law or necessary for contracts of the particular type, and also conditions with regard to which at the demand of one of the parties agreement must be reached, shall be material.

3. When concluding an economic contract the parties shall be obliged in any event to agree the subject, price, and period of operation of the contract.

4. Conditions concerning the subject in an economic contract must determine the name (or nomenclature, assortment) and quantity of products (or work, services), and also requirements for the quality thereof. Requirements relative to quality of the subject of a contract shall be determined in accordance with normative documents binding upon the parties specified in Article 15 of the present Code, and in the absence thereof, in an independent-work contract, in compliance with conditions ensuring the defense of the interests of the ultimate consumers of the goods and services.

5. Price in an economic contract shall be determined in the procedure established by the present Code, other laws, and acts of the Cabinet of Ministers of Ukraine. With the consent of the parties, supplementary payments to the established price for a product (or work, services) for higher quality or the fulfillment of work within shorter periods in comparison with normative standards may be provided for in an economic contract.

6. When prices agreed by the parties to a contract are deemed to violate the requirements of antimonopoly-competition legislation, the antimonopoly agency shall have the right to demand changes from the parties of the conditions of the contract with regard to price.

7. The time during which economic obligations of the parties exist which arose on the basis of this contract shall be the period of operation of the economic contract. Conditions of a concluded contract shall not extend to obligations which arose with the parties before the conclusion of the economic contract by them unless provided otherwise by the contract. The expiry of the period of operation of an economic contract shall not relieve the parties from responsibility for a violation thereof which occurred during the operation of the contract.

Article 181. General Procedure for Conclusion of Economic Contracts

1. An economic contract shall as a general rule be drawn up in the form of a single document signed by the parties and affixed with seals. The conclusion of economic contracts by simplified means, that is, by means of an exchange of letters, faxes, telegrams, telephonograms, and so on, and also by means of confirmation of acceptance to fulfill orders, unless special requirements have been established by a law for the form and procedure of the conclusion of a particular type of contracts, shall be permitted.

2. A draft contract may be proposed by any of the parties. If the draft contract has been drawn up as a single document, he shall be provided to the other party in two examples.

3. The party who has received a draft contract shall when agreeing with its conditions formalize the contract in accordance with the requirements of paragraph one of the present Article and return one example of the contract to the other party or send the reply in a letter, fax, and so on within a twenty-day period after receipt of the contract.

4. When there are objections with regard to individual conditions of the contract, the party which has received the draft contract shall drawn up a protocol of disagreements, concerning which a reservation shall be made in the contract, and within a twenty-day period shall send two examples of the protocol of disagreements to the other party together with the signed contract.

5. The party which has received a protocol of disagreements to the contract shall be obliged within twenty days to consider it, within this period take measures to settle the disagreements with the other party, and incorporate in the contract all proposals accepted, and the disagreements which remain unsettled to transfer to a court if the other party consents to this.

6. In the event of the parties reaching agreement with regard to all or individual conditions specified in the protocol of disagreements, such consent must be confirmed in written form (or by the protocol concerning the agreement of disagreements, letters, telegrams, teletypegrams, and so on).

7. If the party which has received a protocol of disagreements with regard to conditions of a contract based on a State order or such, the conclusion of which is obligatory for the parties on the basis of a law, or the party-executor under the contract deemed a monopolist in the established procedure on a determined market for goods (or work, services) which received the protocol of disagreements does not transfer the disagreements that remain unsettled to a court within the twenty-day period, the proposals of the other party shall be considered to be accepted.

8. If the parties have not reached agreement with regard to all material conditions of an economic contract, such contract shall be considered to be non concluded (or unconstituted). If one of the parties has effectuated actual actions with regard to the fulfillment thereof, the legal consequences of such actions shall be determined by norms of the Civil Code of Ukraine.

Article 182. Peculiarities of Conclusion of Preliminary Contracts

1. Under a preliminary contract a subject of economic management shall be obliged within a determined period, but not later than one year from the moment of conclusion of the preliminary contract, to conclude the basic economic contract on the conditions provided

for by the preliminary contract.

2. A preliminary contract must contain conditions enabling the subject to be determined, and also other materials conditions of the basic contract. The general procedure for the conclusion of economic contracts shall not apply to the conclusion of preliminary contracts.

3. If a part which has concluded a preliminary contract, having received the draft contract from the other party, evades the conclusion of the basic contract, the other party shall have the right to demand the conclusion of such contract in a judicial proceeding.

4. An obligation to conclude the basic contract provided for by the preliminary contract shall terminate if before the expiry of the period within which the parties should have concluded the basic contract, one of the parties does not send the draft of such contract to the other party.

5. Relations with regard to the conclusion of preliminary contracts shall be regulated by the Civil Code of Ukraine, taking into account the peculiarities provided for by the present Code.

6. An agreement of the parties concerning intentions (protocol of intent, and so on) shall not be deemed to be a preliminary contract and shall not give rise to legal consequences.

Article 183. Peculiarities of Conclusion of Economic Contracts With Regard to State Order

1. Contracts with regard to a State order shall be concluded between subjects of economic management-executors of the State order and State customers determined by a law who are empowered in the name of the State to conclude contracts (or State contracts) in which the economic obligations of the parties are determined and relations of the customer are regulated with the executor with regard to the fulfillment of the State order.

2. The State in the person of the Cabinet of Ministers of Ukraine shall act as the guarantor with regard to obligations of State customers.

3. The conclusion by the parties of a contract with regard to a State order (or State contract) shall be effectuated in the procedure provided for by Article 181 of the present Code, taking into account the peculiarities provided for by legislation. A State contract shall be concluded by means of signature by the parties of a single document.

4. Evasion of the conclusion of a contract with regard to a State order shall be a violation of economic legislation and entail the responsibility provided for by the present Code and other laws. Disputes connected with the conclusion of a contract with regard to a State order, including evasion of the conclusion of a contract by one or both parties, shall be settled in a judicial proceeding.

5. The executor of a State order shall be relieved from the duty to conclude a State contract on the conditions determined by the State order in the event of the State order being deemed to be invalid in a judicial proceeding.

Article 184. Peculiarities of Conclusion of Economic Contracts on Basis of Free Expression of Will of Parties and Model and Standard Contracts

1. When concluding an economic contract on the basis of free expression of will of the parties, the draft contract may be worked out at the initiative of any of the parties within the periods agreed by the parties themselves.

2. The conclusion of a contract on the basis of free expression of will of the parties may occur by simplified means or in the form of a single document in compliance with the general procedure for the conclusion of contracts established by Article 181 of the present Code.

3. The conclusion of economic contracts on the basis of model and standard contracts must be effectuated in compliance with the

conditions provided for by Article 179 of the present Code not other than by means of drawing up the contract in the form of a single document formalized according to the requirements of Article 181 of the present Code and in accordance with the rules established by normative legal acts with regard to the application of a model or standard contract.

Article 185. Peculiarities of Conclusion of Economic Contracts at Stock Exchanges, Fairs, and Public Sales

The general rules for the conclusion of contracts on the basis of free expression of will, taking into account normative legal acts by which the activity of respective stock exchanges, fairs, and public sales is regulated shall apply to the conclusion of economic contracts at stock exchanges, wholesale fairs, and public sales.

Article 186. Conclusion of Organizational-Economic Contracts

The contractual formalization of organizational-economic obligations may be effectuated by participants of economic relations either on the basis of the free expression of will of the parties or on the basis of model contracts, if the conclusion of such contracts is provided for by respective normative-legal acts. The simplified means of conclusion of organizational-economic contracts shall not be permitted.

Article 187. Conclusion of Economic Contracts by Decision of Court

1. Disputes arising when concluding economic contracts with regard to a State order or contracts whose conclusion is obligatory on the basis of a law and in other instances established by a law shall be considered by a court. Other precontractual disputes may be the subject of consideration of a court if this is provided for by an agreement of the parties or if the parties are obliged to conclude a determined economic contract on the basis of a preliminary contract concluded between them.

2. The day of entry into force of a decision of a court which has settled the question concerning a precontractual dispute shall be considered to be the day of conclusion of the respective economic contract unless determined otherwise by decision of the court.

Article 188. Procedure for Change of and Dissolution of Economic Contracts

1. The change or dissolution of economic contracts unilaterally shall not be permitted unless provided otherwise by a law or contract.

2. The party to a contract, considering it necessary to change or dissolve a contract, must send a proposal concerning this to the other party under the contract.

3. The party to a contract who has received a proposal concerning the change or dissolution of a contract shall within a twenty-day period after receipt of the proposal inform the other party about the results of consideration thereof.

4. If the parties have not reached agreement concerning a change (or dissolution) of a contract or in the event of the failure to receive a reply within the established period, taking into account the time of postal turnover, the interested party shall have the right to transfer the dispute for settlement of a court.

5. If a contract has been changed or dissolved by judicial decision, the contract shall be considered to be changed or dissolved from the day of entry into force of the particular decision unless another period for entry into force has been established by decision of the court.

Chapter 21
Prices and Price-Formation in Sphere of Economic Management

Article 189. Price in Economic Obligations

1. A price (or tariff) in the present Code shall be a form of monetary determination of the cost of a produce (or work, services) to be realized by subjects of economic management.

2. A price shall be a material condition of an economic contract. A price shall be specified in a contract in hrivnas. Prices with regard to foreign economic contracts may be determined in a foreign currency by agreement of the parties.

3. Subjects of economic management may use free prices in economic activity, State-fixed prices, and regulated prices – maximum levels of prices or maximum deviations from State-fixed prices.

4. When effectuating export and import operations contract (or foreign trade) prices which are formulated in accordance with prices and conditions of the world market and indicative prices shall be applied in settlements with foreign contracting parties.

Article 190. Free Prices

1. Free prices shall be determined for all types or products (or work, services), except for those for which State prices have been established.

2. Free prices shall be determined by subjects of economic management autonomously by agreement of the parties, and in intra-economic relations – also by decision of the subject of economic management.

Article 191. State and Municipal Prices

1. State-fixed and regulated prices shall be established for

resources exerting a determinative impact on the general level and dynamics of prices, and also for products and services which have material social significance for the population. The List of the said resources, products, and services shall be confirmed by the Cabinet of Ministers of Ukraine.

2. In accordance with a law State prices shall be established for a product (or service) of economic management-natural monopolists. Lists of types of products (or services) of the said subjects shall be confirmed by the Cabinet of Ministers of Ukraine.

3. State prices shall be established for import goods acquired at the expense of means of the State budget of Ukraine.

4. The establishment of municipal prices for a product and service whose production is effectuated by municipal enterprises may be provided for by a law.

5. State regulation of prices shall be effectuated by means of the establishment of fixed State and municipal prices, maximum levels of prices, maximum levels of trade increments and supply remuneration, maximum normative standards of profitability or by means of the introduction of the obligatory declaration of a change of prices.

6. Agencies of executive power and agencies of local self-government shall, when establishing fixed prices whose application makes impossible the receipt of profit for subjects of entrepreneurship, be obliged to grant to these subjects a donation in accordance with a law.

Article 192. Legislation on Prices and Price-Formation

The policy of price-formation, procedure for the establishment and application of prices, powers of agencies of State power and agencies of local self-government with regard to the establishment and regulation of prices, and also control over prices and price-formation, shall be determined by a law on prices and price-formation and by other legislative acts.

Chapter 22
Fulfillment of Economic Obligations. Termination of Obligations

Article 193. General Conditions of Fulfillment of Economic Obligations

1. Subjects of economic management and other participants of economic relations must duly fulfill economic obligations in accordance with a law, other legal acts, contract, and in the absence of specific requirements with regard to the fulfillment of an obligation – in accordance with the requirements which are advanced usually in determined conditions.

The respective provisions of the Civil Code of Ukraine, taking into account the peculiarities provided for by the present Code, shall apply to the fulfillment of economic contracts.

2. Each party must take all measures necessary for the proper fulfillment of its obligation, taking into account the interests of the other party and ensuring the general economic interest. A violation of obligations shall be grounds for the application of economic sanctions provided for by the present Code, other laws, or the contract.

3. The application of economic sanctions to a subject who has violated an obligation shall not relieve this subject from the duty to fulfill an obligation in kind, except for instances when provided otherwise by a law or contract or an empowered party refuses to accept the fulfillment of the obligation.

4. An empowered party shall have the right to fulfill an obligation before time unless provided otherwise by a law, other normative legal act, or contract, or does not arise from the content of the obligation.

5. An obliged party shall have the right to fulfill an obligation before time unless provided otherwise by a law, other normative legal act, or contract, or does not arise from the content of the obligation.

6. An obliged party shall have the right to refuse the fulfillment of an obligation in the event of the improper fulfillment by the other party of duties which are a necessary condition of fulfillment.

7. A unilateral refusal of the fulfillment of obligations shall not be permitted except for instances provided for by a law, and also a refusal of the fulfillment or of the fulfillment before time for the reason that an obligation of another party under another contract was not duly fulfilled.

8. An empowered party accepting the fulfillment of an economic obligation must at the request of the obliged party issue a written certification of the fulfillment of the obligation wholly or in part thereof.

Article 194. Fulfillment of Economic Obligation by Third Person

1. The fulfillment of an obligation may be placed as a whole or in part on a third person who is not a party to the obligation. The empowered party shall be obliged to accept the fulfillment proposed by the third person-direct performer unless from a law, economic contract, or character of the obligation the duty arises of the party to fulfill the obligation personally.

2. The improper fulfillment of an obligation by a third person shall not relieve the parties from the duty to fulfill the obligation in kind, except for instances provided for by Article 193, paragraph three, of the present Code.

Article 195. Transfer (or Delegation) of Rights in Economic Obligations

1. An empowered subject of an economic obligation, unless provided otherwise by a law, may transfer to another party with the consent thereof rights to receive property from a third person under a law, charter, or contract for the purpose of deciding determined questions with regard to the management of property or to delegate the rights to effectuate economic-management powers. The transfer (or delegation)

of such rights may be conditioned by a determined period.

2. The act of transfer of rights shall be considered to be in force from the day of receipt of notification concerning this by the obliged party, and an act of delegation of economic-management powers to another subject – from the day of official publication of this act.

Article 196. Fulfillment of Economic Obligations in Which Several Empowered or Several Obliged Subject Take Part

1. If several empowered or several obliged subjects take part in an economic obligation, each of the empowered subjects shall have the right to demand the fulfillment of, and each of the obliged subjects must fulfill, the obligation in accordance with the participatory share of this subject determined by the obligation.

2. If this has been provided for by legislation or contract, an obligation must be fulfilled jointly and severally. In the event of the joint and several fulfillment of economic obligatons, the respective provisions of the Civil Code of Ukraine shall apply, unless provided otherwise by a law.

Article 197. Place of Fulfillment of Economic Obligation

1. An economic obligation shall be subject to fulfillment at the place determined by a law, economic contract, or place which has been determined by the content of the obligation.

2. If the place of fulfillment of an obligation has not been determined, the obligation must be fulfilled with regard to:

obligations whose content is the transfer of rights to a structure or land plot and other immoveable property – at the location of the structure or land plot or other immoveable property;

monetary obligations – at the place of the site of the empowered party at the moment of the arising of the obligation, or at a new place of the site thereof on condition that the empowered party has informed the obliged party in a timely way thereof;

other obligations – at the location of the permanently operating management organ (or place of residence) of the obliged party, unless provided otherwise by a law.

In the absence of the empowered party, evasion by it of the acceptance of the fulfillment or other delay by it of fulfillment, the obliged party with regard to a monetary obligation shall have the right to deposit the money due from it or transfer securities with regard to the obligation with a notarial office, which shall inform the empowered party thereof. The deposit of money (or securities) with a notarial office shall be considered to be fulfillment of the obligation.

Article 198. Fulfillment of Monetary Obligations

1. Payments with regard to monetary obligations arising in economic relations shall be effectuated in noncash form or cash through branches of banks unless established otherwise by a law.

2. Monetary obligations of participants of economic relations must be expressed and shall be subject to payment in hrivnas. Monetary obligations may be expressed in foreign currency only in instances when subjects of economic management have the right to conduct settlements between themselves in foreign currency in accordance with legislation. The fulfillment of obligations expressed in foreign currency shall be effectuated in accordance with a law.

3. Interest with regard to monetary obligations of participants of economic relations shall be applied in the instances, amounts, and procedure determined by a law or by a contract.

Article 199. Securing Fulfillment of Economic Obligations

1. The fulfillment of economic obligations shall be secured by measures with regard to the defense of rights and responsibility of participants of economic relations provided for by the present Code and other laws. By agreement of the parties, types of securing the fulfillment of obligations which are usually applied in economic (or business) turnover provided for by a law or not contrary to it may be applied.

To relations with regard to securing the fulfillment of obligations of the participants of economic relations shall apply the respective provisions of the Civil Code of Ukraine.

2. Obligations of subjects of economic management relegated to the State sector of the economy may be secured by a State guarantee in the instances and by the means provided for by a law.

Article 200. Bank Guarantee of Securing Fulfillment of Economic Obligations

1. A guarantee shall be a specific means of securing the fulfillment of economic obligations by means of the written confirmation (letter of guarantee) concerning the satisfaction of demands by the empowered party in the amount of the full monetary amount specified in the written confirmation if a third person (obliged party) does not fulfill the determined obligation specified therein, or other conditions ensue provided for in the respective confirmation.

2. An obligation under a bank guarantee shall be fulfilled only upon the written demand of the empowered party.

3. A guarantor shall have the right to advance against the empowered party those claims, the advancement of which is permitted by the letter of guarantee. An obliged party shall not have the right to advance against the guarantor objections might be advanced against the empowered party if its contract with the guarantor does not contain obligations of the guarantor to insert in the letter of guarantee a clause concerning the advancement of such objections.

4. The respective provisions of the Civil Code of Ukraine shall apply to relations of the bank guarantee in the part not regulated by the present Code.

Article 201. General-Economic (Public) Guarantees of Fulfillment of Obligations

1. For the purpose of the neutralization of unfavorable consequences

from economic crimes the duty of commercial banks, insurers, joint-stock societies, and other subjects of economic management attracting means or securities of citizens and juridical persons to transfer part of their means in order to form a unified insurance fund of public pledge may be provided for by a law.

Article 202. General Conditions of Termination of Economic Obligations

1. An economic obligation shall be terminated by: fulfillment duly conducted; set-off of a counter homogeneous demand or insurance obligation; combining of an empowered and an obliged party into one person; with the consent of the parties; in view of the impossibility of fulfillment, and in other instances provided for by the present Code or other laws.

2. An economic obligation shall terminate also in the event of the dissolution thereof or deeming invalid by decision of a court.

3. To relations with regard to the termination of economic obligations shall apply the respective provisions of the Civil Code of Ukraine, taking into account the peculiarities provided for by the present Code.

Article 203. Termination of Economic Obligation by Fulfillment or Set-Off

1. An economic obligation, all conditions of which have been fulfilled properly, shall terminate if the fulfillment has been accepted by the empowered party.

2. If the obliged party duly fulfilled one of two or several obligations under which it had the right of choice (alternative obligation), the economic obligation shall be terminated by fulfillment.

3. An economic obligation shall be terminated by set-off of a homogeneous demand, the period of which has ensued or the period of

which was not specified, or was determined by the moment of demanding and obtaining. The declaration of one party shall be sufficient for set-off.

4. An economic obligation may be terminated by set-off of an insurance obligation unless arises otherwise from a law or the content of the principal or insurance obligation.

5. Set-off of demands to which according to the declaration of another party the period of limitation should apply and this period has lapsed, and also in other instances provided for by a law, shall not be permitted.

Article 204. Termination of Economic Obligation with Consent of Parties or in Event of Parties Thereof Combining into One Person

1. An economic obligation may be terminated with the consent of the parties, in particular, by an agreement to substitute one obligation with another between the same parties, if such substitution is not contrary to an obligatory act on the basis of which the preceding obligation arose.

2. An economic obligation shall terminate in the event of the combining of an empowered and obliged parties into one person. The obligation shall arise anew if this combination is terminated.

Article 205. Termination of Economic Obligation in Event of Impossibility of Fulfillment

1. An economic obligation shall be terminated by the impossibility of fulfillment when circumstances arise for which neither of the parties is liable, unless provided otherwise by a law.

2. In the event of the impossibility to fulfill obligations fully or partially, the obliged party must for the purpose of preventing property and other consequences disadvantageous for the parties immediately

inform the empowered party thereof, which must take necessary measures with regard to reducing the said consequences. Such informing shall not relieve the obliged party from the responsibility for the failure to fulfill an obligation in accordance with the requirements of a law.

3. An economic obligation shall be terminated by the impossibility to fulfill in the event of liquidation of the subject of economic management if legal succession with regard to this obligation is not permitted.

4. In the event of the insolvency of a subject of economic management in view of the insufficiency of its property to satisfy demands of creditors, it may be declared bankrupt by decision of a court. The conditions, procedure, and consequences of declaring subjects of economic management to be bankrupt shall be established by the present Code andother laws. Liquidation of the subject of economic management-bankrupt shall be grounds for termination of obligations with the participation thereof.

Article 206. Dissolution of Economic Obligation

1. An economic obligation may be dissolved by the parties in accordance with the rules established by Article 188 of the present Code.

2. A State contract shall be subject to dissolution in the event of a change or revocation of the State order by which termination of the operation of the contract was provided from the moment when the obligation about this became known to the parties. The consequences of dissolution of a State contract for the parties thereof shall be determined in accordance with a law.

Article 207. Invalidity of Economic Obligation

1. An economic obligation not meeting the requirements of a law, or concluded for a purpose known to be contrary to the interests of the State and society, or concluded by participants of economic relations with a violation of economic competence (or special legal

personality) by even one of them, may at the demand of one of the parties or respective agency of State power be deemed by a court to be invalid wholly or in part.

2. A useless condition of an economic obligation which autonomously or in combination with other conditions of an obligation violates the rights and legal interests of another party or third persons may be deemed to be invalid. Such conditions of standard contracts and contracts of accession shall be deemed, in particular, to be needless which:

exclude or limit the responsibility of the producer of products and performer of work (or services) or in general do not place on the obliged party determined duties;

permit the unilateral renunciation of an obligation on the part of the performer or unilateral change by the performer of its conditions;

require from the recipient of the good (or service) the payment disproportionately of a large amount of sanctions in the event of its renunciation of the contract and do not establish an analogous sanction for the performer.

3. The fulfillment of an economic obligation deemed by a court to be invalid wholly or in part shall terminate wholly or in part from the day of entry of the decision of the court into legal force as such, which shall be considered to be invalid from the moment of the arising thereof. If it may be terminated with regard to the content of the obligation only in future, such obligation shall be deemed to be invalid and shall terminate in future.

Article 208. Consequences of Deeming Economic Obligation to be Invalid

1. If an economic obligation has been deemed to be invalid as such, which was concluded for a purpose known to be contrary to the interests of the State and society, then when there is an intention of both parties – in the event of the fulfillment of an obligation by both parties – to the revenue of the State shall be recovered by decision of a court everything received by them under the obligation, and in the event

of the fulfillment of the obligation by one party, from the other party shall be recovered to the revenue of the State everything received by it, and also everything due from it to the first party in compensation of that received. When there is an intention merely of one party, everything received by it must be returned to the other party, and that received by the last or due to it as compensation for that fulfilled shall be recovered by decision of a court to the revenue of the State.

2. In the event of deeming invalid an obligation on other grounds, each of the parties shall be obliged to return to the other party everything received under the obligation, and when it is impossible to return that received in kind – to compensate the value thereof in money unless other consequences of invalidity of an obligation have been provided for by a law.

Chapter 23
Deeming Subject of Entrepreneurship to be Bankrupt

Article 209. Insolvency of Subject of Entrepreneurship

1. In the event of the inability of a subject of entrepreneurship after the ensuing of the established period to fulfill its monetary obligations to other persons, territorial hromada, or State other than through the restoration of its solvency, this subject (or debtor) shall in accordance with Article 205, paragraph four, of the present Code, be deemed to be insolvent.

2. The inability of a debtor to restore its solvency and satisfy the demands of creditors recognized by a court other than through the application of a liquidation procedure determined by a court shall be considered to be bankrupt.

3. Only a subject of entrepreneurial activity may be a subject of bankruptcy (hereinafter – bankrupt).

4. Additional requirements and guarantees of the right of

ownership of the Ukrainian people shall be provided relative to bankruptcy of State commercial enterprises by a law.

Article 210. Creditors of Insolvent Debtors

1. The subjects specified in Article 209, paragraph one, of the present Code having demands confirmed in accordance with legislation against the debtor with regard to monetary obligations, including creditors whose demands are fully or partially secured by a pledge, shall be creditors of insolvent debtors. Agencies for the recovery of taxes, charges (or obligatory payments) determined by a law also shall enjoy the rights of creditors with respect to insolvent debtors.

2. If two or more creditors have monetary demands simultaneously against one debtor, they shall form a meeting (or committee) of creditors in accordance with the requirements of a law.

Article 211. Measures With Regard to Prevention of Bankruptcy of Subjects of Entrepreneurship

1. The founders (or participants) of a subject of entrepreneurship, owner of property, agencies of State power and agencies of local self-government endowed with economic competence shall within the limits of their powers be obliged to take timely measures with regard to the prevention of bankruptcy thereof.

2. Owners of property of a State (or municipal) or private enterprise, founders (or participants) of a subject of entrepreneurship which has proved to be an insolvent debtor, creditors, and other persons within the limits of measures with regard to the prevention of bankruptcy of the said subject may provide financial assistance to it in the amount sufficient for repayment of its obligations to creditors, including an obligation with regard to the payment of taxes, charges (or obligatory payments), and restoration of solvency of this subject (pre-judicial sanation).

3. The provision of financial assistance to a debtor shall provide

for its duty to assume respective obligations to the persons who have provided the assistance in the procedure established by a law.

4. Pre-judicial sanation of State enterprises shall be effectuated at the expense of budgetary means, the amount of which shall be established by the Law on the State Budget of Ukraine. The conditions of conducting pre-judicial sanation of State enterprises at the expense of other sources of financing shall be agreed with the agency endowed with economic competence with respect to the debtor in the procedure established by the Cabinet of Ministers of Ukraine.

Article 212. Procedures Applicable With Respect to Insolvent Debtor

1. In instances provided for by a law the following procedures shall be applied with respect to an insolvent debtor:
disposition of property of the debtor;
amicable agreement;
sanation (restoration of solvency) of debtor;
liquidation of bankrupt.

2. Sanation of a debtor or liquidation of a bankrupt shall be effectuated in compliance with the requirements of antimonopoly-competition legislation.

3. From the day of rendering a ruling concerning the initiation of a proceeding with regard to a case concerning bankruptcy, the reorganization of a juridical person-debtor by the owner (or agency empowered by it), and also the transfer of property of the debtor to the charter fund, shall be permitted only in the instances and procedure provided for by a law.

Article 213. Property Assets of Insolvent Debtor

1. For the purpose of settling the indebtedness of an insolvent debtor in the procedures specified in Article 212 of the present Code, property assets shall be used that belong to it on the basis of rights to a

thing and rights of obligation, and also rights of intellectual property.

2. Property assets of persons who are liable for obligations of an insolvent debtor in accordance with a law or constitutive documents of the debtor also shall be included within the liquidation mass.

Article 214. State Policy With Regard to Questions of Bankruptcy

1. The agency of State power for questions of bankruptcy shall effectuate State policy with regard to the prevention of bankruptcy, ensuring the conditions of the realization of procedures for the restoration of the solvency of a subject of entrepreneurship or deeming thereof to be bankrupt with respect to State enterprises and enterprises in whose charter fund the participatory share of State ownership exceeds twenty-five per cent, and also subjects of entrepreneurship of other forms of ownership in instances provided for by a law.

2. An agency of State power for questions of bankruptcy shall promote the creation of organizational, economic, and other conditions necessary for the realization of procedures for the restoration of solvency of subjects of entrepreneurship-debtors or deeming them bankrupt. The powers of the agency of State power with regard to questions of bankruptcy shall be determined by a law.

3. Procedures with respect to the insolvency of debtors provided for by the present Code shall not apply to treasury enterprises. The said procedures shall apply to State enterprises which in accordance with a law are not subject to privatization in the part of sanation or liquidation only after their exclusion in the established procedure from the List of objects not subject to privatization.

4. In instances provided for by a law, the procedures of bankruptcy shall not apply with respect to municipal enterprises.

5. With regard to individual categories of subjects of entrepreneurship the peculiarities of the regulation of relations connected

with bankruptcy may be determined by a law.

6. Relations connected with bankruptcy whose participants are foreign creditors shall be regulated by legislation of Ukraine, taking into account the respective provisions of international treaties, consent to whose bindingness has been given by the Supreme Rada of Ukraine.

Article 215. Responsibility for Violation of Legislation on Bankruptcy

1. In instances provided for by a law a subject of entrepreneurship-debtor, founders (or participants) thereof, and owner of property, and also other persons, shall bear legal responsibility for a violation of the requirements of legislation on bankruptcy, in particular, fictitious bankruptcy, concealment of bankruptcy, or intentional bringing into bankruptcy.

2. A fictitious bankruptcy shall be deemed to be the application known to be untrue of a subject of entrepreneurship in a court concerning the inability to fulfill an obligation to creditors and the State. Having established the fact of fictitious bankruptcy, that is, the actual solvency of the debtor, the court shall refuse to satisfy the application of the debtor concerning deeming to be bankrupt and apply the sanctions provided for by a law.

3. Intentional bankruptcy shall be deemed to be a stable inability of a subject of entrepreneurship to pay caused by purposeful actions of the owner of property or official of a subject of entrepreneurship if this caused essential material damage to the interests of the State, society, or interests of creditors which are protected by a law.

4. Concealment of bankruptcy, fictitious bankruptcy, or intentional bringing into bankruptcy, and also unlawful actions in the procedures of insolvency connected with a disposition of property of the debtor that caused essential damage to the interests of creditors and the State shall entail criminal responsibility of the guilty persons in accordance with a law.

Section V
Responsibility for Violation of Law in Sphere of Economic Management

Chapter 24
General Principles of Responsibility of Participants of Economic Relations

Article 216. Economic-Legal Responsibility of Participants of Economic Relations

1. Participants of economic relations shall bear economic-legal responsibility for a violation of law in the sphere of economic management by means of the application with respect to offenders of economic sanctions on the grounds and in the procedure provided for by the present Code, other laws, and a contract.

2. The application of economic sanctions must guarantee the defense of the rights and legal interests of citizens, organizations, and State, including compensation of losses to participants of economic relations caused as a consequence of a violation and ensure legal order in the sphere of economic management.

3. Economic-legal responsibility shall be based on principles according to which:
the victim party shall have the right to compensation of losses irrespective of whether there is a clause concerning this in the contract; responsibility provided for by a law of the producer (or seller) for the poor-quality of a product also shall apply irrespective of whether there is a clause concerning this in the contract or not;
the payment of fine sanctions for a violation of an obligation, an also compensation of losses, shall not relieve an offender without the consent of the other party from the fulfillment of obligations accepted in kind;
clauses in an economic contract shall be inadmissible relating to the exclusion or limitation of responsibility of a producer (or seller) of a product.

Article 217. Economic Sanctions As Legal Means of Responsibility in Sphere of Economic Management

1. Measures of pressure on a violator in the sphere of economic management, as a result of the application of which unfavorable economic and/or legal consequences ensue for it, shall be deemed to be economic sanctions.

2. The following types of economic sanctions shall be applied in the sphere of economic management: fine sanctions; operational-economic sanctions.

3. In addition to the economic sanctions specified in paragraph two of the present Article, administrative-economic sanctions shall apply with respect to subjects of economic management for a violation by them of rules for the effectuation of economic activity.

4. Economic sanctions shall apply in the procedure established by a law at the initiative of participants of economic relations, and administrative-economic sanctions – by empowered agencies of State power or agencies of local self-government.

Article 218. Grounds of Economic-Legal Responsibility

1. A violation of law committed by it in the sphere of economic management shall be grounds for economic-legal responsibility of a participant of economic relations.

2. A participant of economic relations shall be liable for the failure to fulfill or improper fulfillment of an economic obligation or violation of rules for the effectuation of economic activity unless it is proved that all measures within his control were taken by him in order not to permit the economic violation of law. Unless provided otherwise by a law or contract, a subject of economic management shall for a violation of an economic obligation bear economic-legal responsibility unless it is proved that the proper fulfillment of the obligation proved to be impossible as a consequence of the operation of insuperable force, that

is, extraordinary and unavertable circumstances under the said conditions of effectuation of economic activity. A violation of obligations by contracting parties of the violator, absence on the market of goods needed to fulfill the obligation, or the debtor's lack of necessary means shall not, in particular, be considered to be such circumstances.

Article 219. Limits of Economic-Legal Responsibility. Reduction of Amount and Relief from Responsibility

1. For the failure to fulfill or improper fulfillment of economic obligations or a violation of rules for the effectuation of economic activity a violator shall be liable with property belonging to it by right of ownership or consolidated to him by right of economic jurisdiction or operative management, unless provided otherwise by the present Code and other laws.

2. The founders of the subject of economic management shall not be liable for obligations of this subject, except for instances provided for by a law or by constitutive documents concerning the creation of this subject.

3. If unlawful actions (or failure to act) of the other party to the obligation facilitated the violation of law, a court shall have the right to reduce the amount of responsibility or relieved the defendant from responsibility.

4. The parties of an obligation may provide for determined circumstances that in view of the extraordinary character of these circumstances are grounds for relieving them from economic responsibility in the event of a violation of an obligation as a consequence of the said circumstances, and also the procedure for certifying the fact of the arising of such circumstances.

Article 220. Delay of Debtor

1. A debtor who has delayed the fulfillment of an economic obligation shall be liable to the creditor(s) for losses caused by the

delay and for the impossibility of fulfillment which accidentally arose after the delay.

2. If as a consequence of delay of the debtor the fulfillment has lost interest for the creditor, he shall have the right to refuse to accept fulfillment and to demand compensation of losses.

3. A debtor shall not be considered to have delayed the fulfillment of an obligation so long as it can not be fulfilled as a consequence of delay of the creditor.

Article 221. Delay of Creditor

1. A creditor shall be considered to have delayed the fulfillment of an economic obligation if he has refused to accept proper fulfillment proposed by the debtor, or did not fulfill actions provided for by a law, other legal acts, or arising from the content of an obligation until the performance of which the debtor could not fulfill his obligation to the creditor.

2. Delay of a creditor shall give to the debtor the right to compensation of losses caused by the delay unless the creditor proves that the delay was not conditioned by the deliberateness or negligence of he imself or those persons on whom by law or commission of the reditor the acceptance of fulfillment was entrusted. After the end of the delay of the creditor, the debtor shall be liable for fulfillment on general grounds.

3. If a creditor does not fulfill actions specified in paragraph one of the present Article, by agreement of the parties deferral of the fulfillment shall be permitted for the period of delay of the creditor.

Article 222. Pre-Judicial Procedure for Realization of Economic-Legal Responsibility

1. The participants of economic relations who have violated the property rights or legal interests of other subjects shall be obliged to

restore them without waiting for the presentation of claims to them or recourse to a court.

2. When compensation of losses or the application of other sanctions is necessary, the subject of economic management or other juridical person-participant of economic relations whose rights or legal interests have been violated shall have the right for the purpose of direct settlement of the dispute with the violator of these rights or interests to have recourse to a written claim unless established otherwise by a law.

3. There shall be specified in a claim:
the full name and postal requisites of the declarer of the claim and person(s) to whom the claim is presented;
the date of presentation and number of the claim;
the obligations on the basis of which the claim is presented;
the evidence confirming those circumstances;
the demands of the declarer with a reference to normative acts;
the amount of the claim and calculation thereof, if the claim is subject to monetary valuation;
the List of documents appended to the claim.

4. Documents confirming the demand of the declarer shall be appended in originals or duly certified copies. Documents which the other party has may be not appended to the claim.

5. A claim shall be signed by an empowered person of the declarer of the claim or representative thereof and shall be sent to the addressee by recorded or registered letter or handed over to the addressee under signature.

6. A claim shall be subject to consideration within a month from the day of receipt thereof unless another period has been established by the present Code or other legislative acts. Substantiated demands of the declarer the recipient of the claim shall be obliged to satisfy.

7. When considering a claim, the parties must, when necessary, verify the calculations, conduct an expert examination or perform other

actions in order to ensure pre-judicial settlement of the dispute.

8. The declarer must be informed in writing about the results of consideration of the claim. The reply to the claim shall be signed by an empowered person or representative of the recipient of the claim and shall be sent to the declarer by recorded or registered letter or handed over to him under signature.

9. In the event of a violation of the established periods for the consideration of a claim or leaving it without reply, the court when settling an economic dispute shall recover to the revenue of the State from the guilty person a fine in an amount established by a law.

Article 223. Periods for Realization of Economic-Legal Responsibility

1. In the event of the realization in a judicial proceeding of responsibility for a violation of law in the sphere of economic management the general and reduced periods of limitation provided for by the Civil Code of Ukraine shall apply unless other periods have been established by the present Code.

2. Periods for the application of administrative-economic sanctions to subjects of economic management shall be established by the present Code.

Chapter 25
Compensation of Losses in Sphere of Economic Management

Article 224. Compensation of Losses

1. A participant of economic relations who has violated an economic obligation or established requirements for the effectuation of economic activity must compensate to the subject whose rights or legal interests have been violated the losses caused by this.

2. By losses is understood expenses made by an empowered party, loss or damage of the property thereof, and also revenues not received by it, which the empowered party would have received in the event of the proper fulfillment of the obligation or compliance with the rules for the effectuation of economic activity by the other party.

Article 225. Composition and Amount of Compensation of Losses

1. Within the composition of losses which are subject to compensation by the person who has permitted the economic violation shall be included:

the value of the lost, damaged, or destroyed property, determined in accordance with the requirements of legislation;

the additional expenses (fine sanctions paid to other subjects, value of additional work, additionally expended materials, and so on) incurred by the party which incurred losses as a consequence of a violation of an obligation by the other party;

profit not received (lost advantage) on which the party that incurred losses had the right to count on in the event of proper fulfillment of the obligation by the other party;

material contributory compensation of moral harm in instances provided for by a law.

2. Limited responsibility for the failure to fulfill or improper fulfillment of obligations may be established by a law for individual types of economic obligations.

3. When determining the amount of losses, unless provided otherwise by a law or contract, the prices shall be taken into account which existed at the place of fulfillment of the obligation on the day of satisfaction by the debtor voluntarily of the demand of the party which incurred losses, and in the event the demands are not satisfied voluntarily – on the day of filing in court the respective suit concerning the recovery of losses.

4. Proceeding from specific circumstances, the court may satisfy

the demand concerning compensation of losses, taking into account the prices on the day of rendering of the decision of the court.

5. Parties to an economic obligation shall have the right by mutual consent to determine in good time an agreed amount of losses subject to compensation in a lump-sum amount or in the form of percentage rates, depending upon the amount of the obligation not fulfilled or periods for a violation of the obligation by the parties. An agreement between the parties to an obligation with regard to limitation of their responsibility, if the amount of responsibility for a determined type of obligations has been determined by a law, shall not be permitted.

6. Methods for the determination of amounts of compensation of losses in the sphere of economic management may be confirmed by the Cabinet of Ministers of Ukraine.

7. The composition of losses subject to compensation in intra-economy relations shall be determined by the respective subjects of economic management-economic organizations, taking into account the specific nature of their activity.

Article 226. Conditions and Procedure for Compensation of Losses

1. A participant of economic relations who has committed an economic violation shall be obliged to take necessary measures with regard to averting losses in the economic sphere of other participants of economic relations or to reduce the amount thereof, and if losses were caused to other subjects, — obliged to compensate upon the demand of these subjects losses voluntarily in full unless compensation for losses in another amount has been provided for by a law or contract.

2. A party which has violated its obligation or definitely knows that it will violate it when the period of fulfillment ensues must immediately inform the other party thereof. Otherwise this party shall be deprived of the right to refer to the failure of the other party to take measures with regard to averting losses and demand respective reduction

of the amount of losses.

3. A party to an economic obligation shall be deprived of the right to compensation of losses if it was warned in good time by the other party about the possible failure to fulfill its obligation and might avert the arising of losses by its own actions but did not do this, except for instances when a law or contract provides otherwise.

4. Losses caused by a lawful refusal by the obliged party to further fulfill the obligation shall not be subject to compensation.

5. In the event of the failure to fulfill an obligation concerning the transfer of an individually-specified thing to it (or things determined by generic indicia), the empowered party shall have the right to demand this thing(s) be taken away from the obliged party or to demand compensation of losses by the last.

6. In the event of the failure to fulfill an obligation to fulfill determined work (or render a service), the empowered party shall have the right to fulfill this work autonomously or to charge the fulfillment (or rendering of services) to third persons, unless provided otherwise by a law or obligation, and to demand compensation of losses caused by the failure to fulfill the obligation.

7. Compensation of losses caused by the improper fulfillment of the obligation shall not relieve the obliged party from the fulfillment of an obligation in kind, except for instances specified in Article 193, paragraph three, of the present Code.

Article 227. Joint and Several Compensation of Losses

In the event of causing losses simultaneously by several participants of economic relations, each of them shall be obliged to compensate the losses to the subject to which losses were caused in accordance with the requirements of Article 196 of the present Code.

Article 228. Regressive Demands With Regard to Compensation of Losses

A participant of economic relations which has compensated losses shall have the right to recover losses from third persons by way of regression. State (or municipal) enterprises, when there are grounds, shall be obliged to take measures with regard to recovery by way of regression of losses from other subjects of economic management or recover losses from guilty workers of an enterprise in accordance with the requirements of legislation on labor.

Article 229. Compensation of Losses in Event of Violation of Monetary Obligations

1. A participant of economic relations in the event of a violation by it of a monetary obligation shall not be relieved from responsibility in view of the impossibility of fulfillment and shall be obliged to compensate losses caused by the failure to fulfill the obligation, and also to pay fine sanctions in accordance with the requirements established by the present Code and other laws.

2. Calculation of the amount of losses shall be effectuated in the currency in which the settlement of accounts was conducted or should have been conducted between the parties unless established otherwise by a law.

3. In the event of the putting forward of demands with regard to compensation of losses in a foreign currency by the creditor, the monetary equivalent must be specified of the amount of losses in hrivnas at the official exchange rate of the National Bank of Ukraine on the day of putting forward the demands.

Chapter 26
Fine and Operational-Economic Sanctions

Article 230. Fine Sanctions

1. Economic sanctions in the form of a monetary amount (penalty, fine, forfeit) which a participant of economic relations is obliged to pay in the event of a violation of rules by him for the effectuation of economic activity, failure to fulfill, or improper fulfillment of an economic obligation shall be deemed to be fine sanctions in the present Code.

2. Participants of relations in the sphere of economic management specified in Article 2 of the present Code shall be subjects of the right of the application of fine sanctions.

Article 231. Amount of Fine Sanctions

1. The amount of fine sanctions, a change of which by agreement of the parties is not permitted, may be determined by a law with regard to individual types of obligations.

2. If an economic obligation has been violated in which although one party is a subject of economic management relegated to the State sector of the economy or a violation is linked with the fulfillment of a State contract, or fulfillment of an obligation is financed at the expense of the State budget of Ukraine or at the expense of a State credit, fine sanctions shall apply unless provided otherwise by a law or contract in the following amounts:

for a violation of the conditions of an obligation with regard to quality (or completeness) of goods (or work, services) a fine shall be recovered in the amount of twenty percent of the value of the poor-quality (or incomplete) goods (or work, services);

for a violation of the periods for fulfillment of an obligation a forfeit shall be recovered in the amount of 0,1 percent of the value of the goods (or work, services) for which delay was permitted of the fulfillment for each day of delay, and for delay exceeding thirty days a fine shall be recovered additionally in the amount of seven percent of the said value.

3. The amount of fine sanctions also for other violations of individual types of economic obligations specified in paragraph two of the present Article may be determined by a law.

4. If the amount of fine sanctions has not been determined by a law, sanctions shall be applied in the amount provided by the contract. In so doing the amount of sanctions may be established by the contract in a percentage relation to the amount of the unfulfilled part of the obligation or in a certain determined monetary amount, or in a percentage relation to the amount of the obligation irrespective of the degree of fulfillment thereof, or in a multiple of the value of the goods (or work, services).

5. In the event of the failure to reach agreement between the parties concerning the establishment and amount of fine sanctions for a violation of the obligation, the dispute may be settled in a judicial proceeding upon the application of an interested party in accordance with the requirements of the present Code.

6. Fine sanctions for a violation of monetary obligations shall be established as interest, the amount of which shall be determined by the bank rate of the National Bank of Ukraine for the entire time of use of another's means unless another amount of interest has been provided for by a law or contract.

7. The amount of fine sanctions applicable in intra-economy relations for a violation of obligations shall be determined by the respective subject of economic management-economic organization.

Article 232. Procedure for Application of Fine Sanctions

1. If fine sanctions have been established for the failure to fulfill or improper fulfillment of an obligation, losses shall be compensated in the part not covered by these sanctions.

2. Instances may be provided for by a law or contract when:

the recovery only of fine sanctions is permitted;

losses may be recovered in the full amount above the fine sanctions;

at the choice of the creditor either losses or fine sanctions may be recovered.

3. A demand with regard to the payment of fine sanctions for an economic violation may be declared by a participant of economic relations whose rights or legal interests have been violated, and in instances provided for by a law, — the empowered agency endowed with economic competence.

4. Interest for the unlawful use of another's means shall be recovered to the day of payment of the amount of these means to the creditor unless another period has been established for the calculation of interest by a law or contract.

5. A debtor should not pay interest for the time of delay of a creditor with regard to a monetary obligation.

6. The calculation of fine sanctions for delay of the fulfillment of an obligation, unless established otherwise by a law or contract, shall terminate six months from the day when the obligated should have been fulfilled.

7. In instances provided for by a law, fine sanctions for a violation of economic obligations shall be recovered by a court to the revenue of the State.

Article 233. Reduction of Amount of Fine Sanctions

1. If fine sanctions due for payment are excessively high in comparison with the losses of the creditor, a court shall have the right to reduce the amount of sanctions. IN so doing there must be taken into account: the degree of fulfillment of the obligation by the debtor; property state of the parties taking part in the obligation; not only property,

but also other interests of the parties deserving attention.

2. If a violation of an obligation has not caused losses to other participants of economic relations, a court may, taking into account the interests of the debtor, reduce the amount of fine sanctions due for payment.

Article 234. Duty of Debtor Who Paid Fine Sanctions to Fulfill Obligation in Kind

The payment of fine sanctions for the failure to fulfill or improper fulfillment of an economic obligation shall not relieve the debtor from the fulfillment of an obligation in kind, except for instances provided for in Article 193, paragraph three, of the present Code.

Article 235. Operational-Economic Sanctions

1. Operational-economic sanctions – measures of operational impact on an offender for the purpose of terminating or averting a repetition of violations of the obligation which are applied by the parties to the obligation themselves unilaterally may be applied for a violation of economic obligations to subjects of economic management and other participations of economic relations.

2. Only those operational-economic sanctions whose application has been provided for by a contract may be applied to a subject which has violated an economic obligation.

3. Operational-economic sanctions shall be applied irrespective of the fault of the subject which violated the economic obligation.

Article 236. Types of Operational-Economic Sanctions

1. The application of the following types of operational-economic sanctions may be provided for in economic contracts of parties:
(1) unilateral refusal to fulfill its obligation by the empowered party, being relieved from responsibility for this – in the event of a

violation of an obligation by the other party;

refusal to pay with regard to an obligation which has been fulfilled improperly or fulfilled before time by the debtor without the consent of the other party;

deferral of unloading a product or fulfillment of work as a consequence of delay in the presentation of a letter of credit by the payer, termination of the issue of bank loans, and so on);

(2) refusal of an empowered party to an obligation to accept further fulfillment of the obligation violated by the other party, or return unilaterally of that fulfilled by the creditor under the obligation (withdrawal from the account of the debtor in a nonacceptance procedure of means paid for a poor-quality product, and so on);

(3) establishment unilaterally in the future additional guarantees for the proper fulfillment of obligations by the party which has violated the obligation: change of the procedure for payment of the product (or work, service), transfer of the payer to advance payment for the product (or work, service) or to payment after verification of quality, and so on;

(4) refusal to establish in the future economic relations with the party which violates an obligation.

2. The list of operational-economic sanctions established in paragraph one of the present Article is not exhaustive. The parties may provide in the contract also for other operational-economic sanctions.

Article 237. Grounds and Procedure for Application of Operational-Economic Sanctions

1. The fact of a violation of an economic obligation by the other party shall be grounds for the application of operational-economic sanctions. Operational-economic sanctions shall be applied by the party which is the victim of the violation in an extrajudicial proceeding and without prior presentation of the claim to the violator of the obligation.

2. The procedure for the application by the parties of specific operational-economic sanctions shall be determined by a contract. In the event of disagreement with the application of an operational-

economic sanction, the interested party may apply to a court with an application to vacate such sanction and compensation of losses caused by the application thereof.

3. Operational-economic sanctions may be applied simultaneously with compensation of losses and recovery of fine sanctions.

Chapter 27
Administrative-Economic Sanctions

Article 238. Application of Administrative-Economic Sanctions to Subjects of Economic Management

1. Administrative-economic sanctions, that is, measures of an organizational-legal or property character directed towards the termination of a violation by a subject of economic management and liquidation of its consequences, may be applied to subjects of economic management by empowered agencies of State power or agencies of local self-government for a violation of rules established by legislative acts for the effectuation of economic activity.

2. Types of administrative-economic sanctions and the conditions and procedure for their application shall be determined by the present Code and other legislative acts. Administrative-economic sanctions may be established exclusively by laws.

Article 239. Types of Administrative-Economic Sanctions

Agencies of State power and agencies of local self-government may in accordance with their powers and in the procedure established by a law apply to subjects of economic management the following administrative-economic sanctions:
confiscation of profit (or revenue);
administrative-economic fine;
recovery of charges (or obligatory payments);
suspension of operations with regard to accounts of subjects of

economic management;
>application of anti-dumping measures;
>termination of export-import operations;
>application of individual regime of licensing;
>suspension of operation of license (or patent) for effectuation by subject of economic management of determined types of economic activity;
>annulment of license (or patent) for effectuation by subject of economic management of individual types of economic activity;
>limitation or suspension of activity of subject of economic management;
>revocation of State registration and liquidation of subject of economic management;
>other administrative-economic sanctions established by present Code and other laws.

Article 240. Seizure Without Compensation of Profit (or Revenue)

1. Profit (or revenue) received by a subject of economic management as a consequence of a violation of rules established by legislation for the effectuation of economic activity, and also amounts of concealed (or reduced) profit (or revenue) or amount of tax not paid because of a concealed object of taxation, shall be subject to seizure in the procedure determined by a law.

In addition, a fine shall be recovered from a subject of economic management in the instances and in the procedure provided for by a law, but not more than twice the amount seized, and in the event of a second violation within a year after the application of this sanction – thrice the amount seized.

2. A list of violations for which sanctions shall be applied to a subject of economic management provided for by the present Article, and also the procedure for their application, shall be determined by laws.

Article 241. Fine as Administrative-Economic Sanction

1. An administrative-economic fine is a monetary amount to be paid by a subject of economic management to the respective budget in the event of a violation by it of established rules for the effectuation of economic activity.

2. A list of violations for which a fine is recovered from a subject of economic management and the amount and procedure for the recovery thereof shall be determined by laws regulating tax and other relations in which the violation was permitted.

3. An administrative-economic fine may be applied in the instances determined by law simultaneously with other administrative-economic sanctions provided for by Article 239 of the present Law.

Article 242. Recovery of Charges (or Obligatory Payments)

In the event of a violation by a subject of economic management of the established rules for records or reporting with regard to the payment of charges (or obligatory payments) or the failure to pay them or incomplete payment, the amount subject to payment shall be recovered to the respective budget. In addition, a fine may be recovered from a subject of economic management in instances determined by a law in an amount of up to fifty percent of the amount of charge (or obligatory payment) due for payment.

Article 243. Suspension of Operations With Regard to Accounts of Subjects of Economic Management

1. In the event of a refusal of management organs or officials of a subject of economic management to conduct a documentary verification or to admit workers of tax agencies for an investigation of premises used for the effectuation of economic activity, or the failure to submit to tax and other agencies or officials thereof the reports, accounts, declarations, or other documents connected with the calculation and payment of taxes and charges (or obligatory payments)

established by a law, the operations of this subject with regard to its accounts in branches of a bank shall be suspended.

2. The procedure and periods for suspension of the operations of subjects of economic management with regard to the accounts thereof shall be determined by a law.

Article 244. Application of Anti-Dumping Measures

1. In the event of the effectuation by individual participants of economic relations of foreign economic activity connected with the receipt of an illegal preference on the market of Ukraine (effectuation of dumping import, subsidizing of import, and also other actions which are determined by a law as unfair competition) that has caused damage to the economy of Ukraine or entailed a threat of the arising of such damage, anti-dumping, contributory compensatory, or special measures in accordance with a law may be applied to these participants of relations.

2. The procedure for determining the amount of damage (or threat of damage) to the economy of Ukraine and application of measures specified in the present Article shall be established by the Cabinet of Ministers of Ukraine in accordance with a law.

Article 245. Termination of Export-Import Operations. Application of Individual Regime of Licensing

1. In the event of unfair competition, placement of hard currency valuables in violation of the procedure established by legislation in accounts and deposits beyond the limits of Ukraine, and also in other instances if the actions of participants of foreign economic activity cause damage to the economy of Ukraine, export-import operations of such subjects of economic management shall be terminated on the grounds and in the procedure provided for by a law.

2. For a violation by subjects of economic management of rules for the effectuation of foreign economic activity relative to antimonopoly measures, prohibition against unfair competition, and other rules specified

in paragraph one of the present Article by which determined limitations or prohibitions are established in the effectuation of foreign economic activity, to such subjects may be applies an individual regime of licensing. The procedure and periods for the individual regime of licensing shall be established by a law.

Article 246. Limitation and Suspension of Activity of Subject of Economic Management

1. The effectuation of any economic activity whatsoever which threatens human life and health or represented a increased danger for the environment shall be prohibited.

2. In the event of the effectuation of economic activity in violation of ecological requirements the activity of a subject of economic management may be limited or suspended by the Cabinet of Ministers of Ukraine, Council of Ministers of the Autonomous Republic Crimea, and also other empowered agencies in the procedure established by a law.

3. Administrative-economic sanctions, including seizure of poor-quality goods and suspension of the activity of the said subjects in the procedure established by a law, may be applied to enterprises of trade, public dining, and sphere of services which repeatedly have permitted the realization of poor-quality goods or systematically violate the rules established by legislation of trade and rendering services or conditions for the keeping and transporting of goods, in addition to the economic and administrative-economic sanctions provided for by the present Code.

4. Agencies of State power with regard to questions of the defense of rights of consumers shall have the right in the instances and procedure provided for by a law to adopt obligatory decisions concerning the termination by a subject of economic management of the production of a product (or fulfillment of work, service), shipment and realization of goods not meeting the requirements of normative acts.

Article 247. Revocation of State Registration of Subject of Economic Management for Violation of Law

1. In the event of the effectuation by a subject of economic management of activity which is contrary to a law or constitutive documents, an administrative-economic sanction in the form of revocation of State registration of this subject and the liquidation thereof may be applied to it.

2. The State registration of a subject of economic management shall be revoked by decision of a court, which shall be grounds for the liquidation of the particular subject of economic management in accordance with Article 59 of the present Code.

Article 248. Procedure for Liquidation of Subject of Economic Management for Violation of Law

The liquidation of a subject of economic management in connection with the revocation of its State registration for a violation of a law shall be effectuated in the procedure established by Articles 60 and 61 of the present Code.

Article 249. Guarantees of Rights of Subjects of Economic Management in Event of Unlawful Application Thereto of Administrative-Economic Sanctions

1. A subject of economic management shall have the right to appeal to a court the decision of any agency of State power or agency of local self-government concerning the application to it of administrative-economic sanctions.

2. In the event of the adoption by an agency of State power or agency of local self-government of an act not corresponding to legislation and violating the right or legal interests of a subject of economic management, the last in accordance with Article 20 of the present Code shall have the right to apply to a court with an application to deem such act to be invalid.

3. Losses caused to the subject of economic management in connection with the unlawful application of administrative-economic sanctions to it shall be subject to compensation in the procedure established by the present Code and other laws.

Article 250. Periods for Application of Administrative-Economic Sanctions

Administrative-economic sanctions may be applied to a subject of economic management within six months from the day of eliciting the violation, but not later than one year from the day of the violation by this subject of the rules established by legislative acts for the effectuation of economic activity, except for instances provided for by a law.

Chapter 28
Responsibility of Subjects of Economic Management for Violation of Antimonopoly-Competition Legislation

Article 251. Imposition of Fines for Violation of Antimonopoly-Competition Legislation

1. The Antimonopoly Committee of Ukraine shall impose fines on subjects of economic management-juridical persons for:

the commission of actions provided for by Articles 29, 30, and 32 of the present Code, evasion of the fulfillment or untimely fulfillment of decisions of the Antimonopoly Committee of Ukraine or its territorial divisions concerning the termination of violations of antimonopoly-competition legislation, restoration of the initial position, or change of transactions which are contrary to antimonopoly-competition legislation;

the creation, reorganization (or merger, accession), and liquidation of subjects of economic management, entry of one or several subjects of economic management into an association, acquisition, or receipt by any other means in ownership, receipt in management (or use) of participatory shares (or stocks, shares) and assets (or property) in the form of integral property complexes of enterprises or structural subdivisions thereof, and also on lease integral property complexes of enterprises or structural subdivisions thereof without the consent for this of the Antimonopoly Committee of Ukraine or its agencies in instances when the necessity for receiving such consent is provided for by a law;

the failure to submit or untimely submission of information provided for by a law, or the submission of information known to be unreliable, to the Antimonopoly Committee of Ukraine and its territorial divisions.

2. The commission of actions defined by the present Code as unfair competition by juridical persons which are not subjects of economic management shall entail the imposition on them by the Antimonopoly Committee of Ukraine or its territorial divisions of a fine in the amount provided for by a law.

Article 252. Administrative Responsibility of Citizens-Entrepreneurs and Officials

1. Officials of agencies of State power and agencies of local self-government, enterprises, institutions, organizations, and also citizens registered as entrepreneurs shall bear administrative responsibility according to a law for:

the commission of actions provided for by Articles 29-32 of the present Code;

the failure to submit or untimely submission of information provided for by a law, or the submission of information known to be unreliable to the Antimonopoly Committee of Ukraine and its territorial divisions;

the evasion of fulfillment or untimely fulfillment of decisions of the Antimonopoly Committee of Ukraine and its territorial divisions.

2. The commission of actions defined by the present Code as unfair competition by citizens-entrepreneurs, and also the commission in the interests of third persons of the said actions by citizens who are not entrepreneurs, shall entail administrative responsibility provided for by a law.

3. Fines for a violation of antimonopoly-competition legislation shall be recovered in a judicial proceeding.

Article 253. Seizure of Illegally Received Profit (or Revenue)

The profit (or revenue) illegally received by subjects of entrepreneurial activity as a result of a violation of Articles 29, 30, and 32 of the present Code shall be recovered by decision of a court to the State budget of Ukraine.

Article 254. Seizure of Goods with Unlawfully Used Designations and Copes of Manufactures of Another Subject of Economic Management

1. In the event of establishing the fact of unlawful use of another's designations, advertising materials, packaging, or fact of copying manufactures provided for by Article 33 of the present Code, the interested persons may apply to the Antimonopoly Committee of Ukraine and its territorial divisions with an application concerning the seizure in a judicial proceeding of goods with the unlawfully used designation or copies of manufactures of another subject of economic management both from the producer and from the seller.

2. The seizure of goods with an unlawfully used designation and copies of manufactures of another subject of economic management shall apply if the possibility of confusion with the activity of another subject of economic activity can not be eliminated by other means.

3. The procedure for the use of seized goods shall be determined by the Cabinet of Ministers of Ukraine.

Article 255. Compensation of Losses

Losses caused by an abuse of monopoly position, anticompetitive concordant actions, and discrimination against subjects of economic management by agencies of State power and agencies of local self-government, and also losses caused as a consequence of the performance of actions defined by the present Code as unfair competition, shall be subject to compensation under suits of interested persons in the procedure established by a law.

Article 256. Refutation of Unjust, Inaccurate, or Incomplete Information

In the event of the establishment of the fact of discrediting a subject of economic management the Antimonopoly Committee of Ukraine and its territorial divisions shall have the right to adopt a decision concerning the refutation at the expense of the offender of unjust, inaccurate, or incomplete information disseminated by him within the period and by the means determined by legislation or by this decision.

Article 257. Procedural Foundations for Consideration by Antimonopoly Committee of Ukraine and Territorial Divisions Thereof of Cases Concerning Unfair Competition

Cases concerning a violation of antimonopoly-competition legislation shall be considered by the Antimonopoly Committee of Ukraine and its territorial divisions in the procedure established by a law.

Section VI
Peculiarities of Legal Regulation in Individual
Branches of Economic Management

Chapter 29
Branches and Types of Economic Activity

Article 258. General Conditions Determining Peculiarities of Regulation of Economic Relations

1. The peculiarities of the legal regulation of economic relations shall be determined depending upon the sphere of social production in which these relations are formed, peculiarities of the branch of economic management, type of economic activity, economic form of the result of

economic activity, space in which economic relations are formed (internal or external market), and peculiarities of subjects between which economic relations arise.

2. Legal regulation of economic relations shall be effectuated by taking into account the social division of labor which has formed and objectively existing branches of the national economy.

3. The peculiarities of legal regulation of foreign economic relations shall be determined by Section VII of the present Code.

Article 259. Types of Economic Activity and Classification Thereof

1. A type of economic activity shall happen in the event of the combining of resources (or equipment, technological means, raw material, and materials, work force) for the creation of the production of a determined product or rendering of services. An individual type of activity may consist of a unified simple process or encompass a number of processes, each of which is within a respective category of classification.

2. The peculiarities of the effectuation by subjects of economic management of individual types of this activity shall be taken into account in the legal regulation of economic activity and in the effectuation of State administration of the national economy.

3. The basic, secondary, and auxiliary types of economic activity shall be determined in order to relegate a subject of economic management to the respective category of recording.

4. For the purposes of providing the system of State administration of the national economy with records-statistical information satisfying the requirements of participants of economic relations for objective data concerning the state and trends of socio-economic development, economic and financial interconnections at the inter-State, State, regional, and branch levels, and also the introduction of international standards in the domain of records and reports and the

transition to the international system of records and statistics, the Cabinet of Ministers of Ukraine shall confirm measures relating to the development of national statistics of Ukraine and the State system of classification of technical-economic and social information.

5. The classification of types of economic activity (KVED) shall be an integral part of the State system of classification and coding of technical-economic and social information, which shall be confirmed by the central agency of executive power for questions of standardization and have the status of a State standard.

6. All types of economic activity of subjects shall be objects of classification in the KVED.

Article 260. Branches of National Economy and Classification Thereof

1. The aggregate of all production entities effectuating primarily identical or similar types of production activity shall constitute a branch.

2. The general classification of branches of the national economy shall be an integral part of a unified system of classification and coding of technical-economic and statistical information which shall be used by subjects of economic management and other participants of economic relations, and also by agencies of State power and agencies of local self-government in the process of managing economic activity.

3. The requirements for the classifications of branches of the national economy shall be established by a law.

Article 261. Branches of Sphere of Material Production

1. To the sphere of material production shall be relegated branches determined by types of activity which create, restore, or find material benefits (products, electric power, natural resources), and also continue production in the sphere of turnover (or realization) by means of the movement, keeping, sorting, and packaging of products or any types of activity.

2. All other types of activity in aggregate shall comprise the sphere of nonmaterial production (or nonproduction sphere).

Article 262. Product of Production-Technical Designation and Consumer Manufacture

1. The production of material benefits intended either for use in the sphere of production as means of production (product of production-technical designation) or for use in the sphere of personal consumption (consumer manufacture).

2. If products of production can be used both in production and for personal consumption, the economic form of such products shall be determined depending upon the special-purpose designation of the determined product of production.

3. The turnover of products of production-technical designation and turnover of consumer manufactures in the sphere of economic management shall be regulated by the present Code and other normative-legal acts adopted in accordance therewith and in the part not regulated by these acts, the respective provisions of the Civil Code of Ukraine shall apply.

4. The peculiarities of legal regulation of economic activity connected with the realization of products of production-technical designation and consumer manufactures shall be established by the present Code and other normative-legal acts not contrary to it.

Chapter 30
Peculiarities of Legal Regulation of Economic-Trade Activity

Article 263. Economic-Trade Activity

1. Activity which is effectuated by subjects of economic management in the sphere of trade turnover directed towards the

realization of a product of production-technical designation and consumer manufactures, and also auxiliary activity ensuring the realization thereof by means of rendering respective services, shall be economic trade [activity].

2. Depending upon the market (internal or foreign) within those limits the goods turnover is effectuated, economic-trade activity shall be either internal trade or foreign trade.

3. Economic-trade activity may be effectuated by subjects of economic management in the following forms: material-technical supply and sale; electric power supply; procurement; wholesale trade; retail trade and public dining; sale and transfer on lease of means of production; commercial intermediation in the effectuation of trade activity and other auxiliary activity with regard to ensuring the realization of goods (or services) in the sphere of circulation.

4. Economic-trade activity shall be mediated by economic contracts of delivery, procurement of agricultural products, electric power supply, purchase-sale, lease, barter, finance lease, and other contracts.

§1. Delivery

Article 264. Material-Technical Supply and Sale

1. Material-technical supply and sale of products of production-technical designation and consumer manufactures both of own production an acquired from other subjects of economic management shall be effectuated by subjects of economic management by means of delivery, and in instances provided for by the present Code, also on the basis of contracts of purchase-sale.

2. Peculiarities of the deliver of individual types of products of production-technical designation or consumer manufactures, and also a special procedure for the effectuation of deliveries of products for

State needs, may be provided for by legislation.

3. The basic requirements for the conclusion and fulfillment of contracts of delivery shall be established by the present Code and other legislative acts.

Article 265. Contract of Delivery

1. Under a contract of delivery one party-supplier shall be obliged to transfer (or to deliver) within the stipulated period(s) to the other party-purchaser a good(s), and the purchaser shall be obliged to accept the said good(s) and to pay for it the determined monetary amount.

2. A contract of delivery shall be concluded at the discretion of th eparties or in accordance with a State order.

3. Subjects of economic management specified in Article 55, paragraph two, points (1) and (2), of the present Code may be parties to the contract.

4. The conditions of a contract of delivery must be set out by the parties in accordance with the requirements of the International Rules for the Interpretation of Terms "Incoterms".

5. Delivery of goods without the conclusion of a contract of delivery may be effectuated only in the instances and in the procedure provided for by a law.

6. The realization by subjects of economic management of goods by noneconomic subjects shall be effectuated according to the rules on contracts of purchase-sale. The respective provisions of the Civil Code of Ukraine on the contract of purchase-sale shall apply to relations of delivery not regulated by the present Code.

Article 266. Subject, Quantity, and Assortment of Delivery

1. The subject of delivery shall be a product determined by

generic indicia, manufactures with the name specified in standards, technical conditions, documentation for models (etalons), pricelists, or goods manuals. A subject of delivery also may be a product or manufacture determined by individual indicia.

2. The total quantity of goods subject to delivery, the participatory share correlation thereof (assortment, gauge, nomenclature) by grade, groups, subgroups, types, marks, forms, and dimensions shall be determined by the specification by agreement of the parties unless provided otherwise by a law.

Article 267. Periods and Procedure of Delivery

1. A contract of delivery may be concluded for one year, for a period of more than one year (long-term contract) or for another period determined by agreement of the parties. If the period of its operation is not determined within the contract, it shall be considered to be concluded for one year.

2. The periods of delivery shall be established by the parties in the contract, taking into account the need for rhythmic and uninterrupted deliveries of goods to consumers, unless provided otherwise by legislation.

3. If in a long-term contract the quantity of deliveries has been determined only for a year or lesser period, the procedure for the parties to agree the periods of delivery for subsequent periods before the expiry of the period of operation of the contract must be provided for in the contract. If such period is not provided for, the contract shall be considered to be concluded for one year.

4. If delivery of goods by individual lots has been provided for by the parties, the period for delivery of a product of production-technical designation shall be, as a rule, the quarter, and consumer manufactures, — a month. The parties also may agree a schedule of delivery (month, ten days, twenty-four hours, and so on) in the contract.

5. The procedure for unloading goods by any type of transport, and also the removal of goods by the purchaser, may be provided for by agreement of the parties in a contract of delivery.

6. The procedure for unloading goods by the goods-consignor (or manufacturer) who is not the deliverer may be provided for by the contract, and the receipt of goods by the goods-recipient who is not the purchaser, and also the payment for goods by a payer who is not the purchaser.

7. The procedure for delivery of the quantity of goods not received by the purchaser within the established period may be provided for by the contract.

Article 268. Quality of Goods to be Delivered

1. The quality of goods to be delivered must correspond to the standards, technical conditions, and other technical documentation which establishes the requirements for their quality, or models (etalons) if the parties do not determine in the contract higher requirements for the quality of goods.

2. The number and indexes of standards, technical conditions, or other documentation concerning the quality of goods shall be specified in the contract. If the said documentation is not published in generally-accessible publications, copies thereof must be appended by the supplier to the example of the contract of the purchase at this request.

3. In the absence in the contract of conditions concerning the quality of goods, the last shall be determined in accordance with the purpose of the contract or the usual level of quality for the subject of the contract or general criteria of quality.

4. The supplier must certify the quality of goods being delivered by a proper goods-accompanying document, which shall be sent together with the good unless provided otherwise in the contract.

5. In the vent of the delivery of goods of lower quality than is required by the standard, technical conditions, or model (etalon), the purchaser shall have the right to refuse to accept and to pay for the goods, and if the goods already have been paid for by the purchaser, — to demand the return of the amount paid.

6. If the defects of the goods delivered can be eliminated without return thereof to the supplier, the purchaser shall have the right to demand from the supplier the elimination of defects at the location of the goods or to eliminate them by his own means at the expense of the supplier.

7. If the goods delivered correspond to standards or technical conditions but prove to be of a lower grade than was stipulated, the purchase shall have the right to accept the goods with payment at the price established for goods of the respective grade or to refuse to accept and to pay for the goods delivered.

8. If the purchaser (or recipient) refused to accept the goods which do not correspond in quality to the standards, technical conditions, models (or etalons) or conditions of the contract, the supplier (or producer) shall be obliged to dispose of the goods within a ten-day period, and with regard to perishable goods – within 24 hours from the moment of receiving notification of the purchaser (or recipient) about the refusal of the goods. If the supplier (or producer) within the said period has not disposed of the goods, the purchaser (or recipient) shall have the right to realize them on the spot or to return them to the producer. Perishable goods shall be subject in all instances to realization on the spot.

Article 269. Guarantees of Quality of Goods. Claims in Connection with Defects of Goods Delivered

1. The periods and procedure for the establishment by the purchaser of defects in goods delivered to him which could not be discovered during the ordinary acceptance thereof and the presentation to the supplier of claims in connection with defects of goods delivered shall be determined by legislation in accordance with the present Code.

2. Longer periods for the establishment by the purchaser in a proper procedure of the said defects (guarantee periods) may be provided for by standards, technical conditions, or the contract on the goods intended for prolonged use or keeping. The parties may agree guarantee periods in the contract longer in comparison with those provided for by standards or technical conditions.

3. The guarantee period of operation shall be calculated from the day of introduction of the manufacture into operation, but not later than one year from the day of receipt of the manufacture by the purchaser (or consumer), and with regard to consumer manufactures which are realized through retail trade, — from the day of retail sale of the thing unless provided otherwise by standards, technical conditions, or the contract.

4. The guarantee period of fitness and keeping of goods shall be calculated from the day of manufacture of the good.

5. A supplier (or producer) shall guarantee the quality of goods as a whole. A guarantee period for sets of manufactures and component parts shall be considered to be equal to the guarantee period for the basic manufacture unless provided otherwise by the contract or standards (or technical conditions) for the basic manufacture.

6. A supplier (or producer) shall be obliged at his own expense to eliminate the defects of the manufacture elicited during the guarantee period, or replace the good unless it is proved that the defects arose as a consequence of a violation by the purchaser (or consumer) of the rules for the operation or keeping of the manufacture. In the event of the elimination of defects in a manufacture for which a guarantee period of operation has been established, this period shall be extended for the time during which it was not used because of the defect, and in the event of replace of a manufacture, the guarantee period shall be calculated anew from the day of replacement.

7. In the event of the delivery of goods of improper quality, the purchaser (or recipient) shall have the right to recover from the

manufacturer (or supplier) a fine in the amount provided for by Article 231 of the present Code unless another amoung has been provided for by a law or contract.

8. Suits arising from the delivery of goods of improper quality may be presented within six months from the day of establishment by the purchaser in a proper procedure of the defects of goods delivered to him.

Article 270. Completeness of Goods Delivered

1. Goods must be delivered complete in accordance with the requirements of standards, technical conditions, or pricelists. A delivery with additional manufactures (or parts) to the set or without separate manufactures (or parts) within a set which are not needed by the purchaser may be provided for by the contract.

2. If completeness has not been determined by standards, technical conditions, or pricelists, it may be determined by the contract in necessary instances.

3. In the event of the delivery of incomplete manufactures the supplier (or producer) shall be obliged upon the demand of the purchaser (or recipient) to make them complete within a twenty-day period after receipt of the demand or to replace with complete manufactures within the same period unless the parties have agreed another period. Thereafter until the manufacture is made complete or the replacement thereof the purchaser (or recipient) shall have the right to pay for it, and if the good already has been paid for, to demand in the established procedure the return of the amounts paid. If the supplier (or producer) within the established period does not make the manufacture complete or replace it with a complete one, the purchaser shall have the right to refuse the good.

4. The acceptance of a purchaser of incomplete manufactures shall not relieve the supplier (or producer) from responsibility.

Article 271. Statute on Deliveries and Special Conditions of Deliveries

The Cabinet of Ministers of Ukraine in accordance with the requirements of the present Code and other laws shall confirm the Statute on Deliveries of Products of Production-Technical Designation and Deliveries of Consumer Manufactures, and also the Special Conditions of Delivery of types of goods.

§2. Contract of Agricultural Procurement of Agricultural Product

Article 272. Contract of Agricultural Procurement of Agricultural Product

1. The State procurement of an agricultural product shall be effectuated under contracts of agricultural procurement which shall be concluded on the basis of State orders for delivery of the agricultural product to the State.

2. Under a contract of agricultural procurement the producer of the agricultural product (hereinafter – producer) shall be obliged to transfer to the procurer (or purchaser) or processing enterprise or organization (hereinafter – contractor) the product produced by him within the periods, in the quantity, and in the assortment provided for by the contract, and the contractor shall be obliged to assist the producer in the production of the said product and to accept to pay for it.

3. There must be provided in contracts of agricultural procurement:
the types of product (or assortment), number of State standard or technical conditions, maximum admissible content of harmful substances in the product;
the quantity of the product which the contractor accepts directly from the producer;
the price per unit, total amount of the contract, procedure and

conditions of delivery, and periods for handing over-acceptance of the product;

the duties of the contractor with regard to rendering assistance to the organization of production of the agricultural product and transporting thereof to acceptance centers and enterprises;

the mutual property responsibility of the parties in the event of the failure to fulfill the conditions of the contract by them;

the other conditions provided for by the Standard Contract of Agricultural Procurement of Agricultural Product, confirmed in the procedure established by the Cabinet of Ministers of Ukraine.

Article 273. Peculiarities of Fulfillment of Contracts of Agricultural Procurement

1. A producer must not later than fifteen days from the commencement of procurement of a product inform the contractor about the quantity and periods of handing over the agricultural product proposed for sale and agree the calendar schedule for the handing over thereof.

2. A contractor shall be obliged to accept from the producer all the product presented by him on the conditions provided for in the contract. Nonstandard perishable products fit for use in fresh or processed form and standard perishable products which is handed over in excess of the amounts provided for by the contract the contractor shall accept at the prices and on the conditions agreed by the parties.

3. Amounts of agricultural products, the acceptance of which the contractor shall effectuate directly from the producer and produces delivered directly by the producer to trade enterprises may be provided for in a contract of agricultural procurement. The remaining product shall be accepted by the contractor at the acceptance centers determined by the contract which are located within the limits of the administrative district at the location of the producer.

4. Provision of wrapping by the producers and necessary materials for packaging the product shall be effectuated in the quantity, procedure, and periods provided for by the contract.

5. Other peculiarities of the fulfillment of contracts of agricultural procurement shall be established by the Statute on Agricultural Procurement of Agricultural Product, which shall be confirmed by the Cabinet of Ministers of Ukraine.

Article 274. Responsibility Under Contract of Agricultural Procurement

1. For the failure to hand over an agricultural product within the periods provided for by the contract of agricultural procurement the producer shall pay a penalty to the contractor in the amount established by the contract unless another amount has been provided by a law.

2. For the failure to fulfill an obligation with regard to the acceptance of an agricultural product directly from the producer, and also in the event of a refusal to accept a product presented by the producer within the periods and in the procedure agreed by the parties, the contractor shall pay a fine to the producer in the amount of five percent of the product not accepted, taking into account increments and discounts, and also compensate the losses caused to the producer, and with regard to a perishable product – the full value thereof.

3. If a product was not prepared in a timely way for handing over-acceptance and the contractor was not warned thereof, the producer shall compensate the contractor for losses caused by this.

4. Other sanctions for the failure to fulfill or improper fulfillment of obligations in accordance with the requirements of the present Code also may be provided for in a contract of agricultural procurement.

§3. Electric Power Supply

Article 275. Contract of Electric Power Supply

1. Under a contract of electric power supply, the electric supply enterprise (or electric power supplier) shall sell electricity power, steam,

hot or warmed water (hereinafter – electric power) to the consumer (or subscriber), who is obliged to pay for the electric power accepted and to comply with the regime for use thereof provided by the contract, and also to ensure the safe operation of electric power equipment used by him.

2. The sale of electric power without the formalization of a contract of electric power supply shall not be permitted.

3. Individual types of electric power with a name provided for in State standards or technical conditions shall be the subject of a contract of electric power supply.

4. Producers and suppliers of electric power occupying a monopoly position, in particular, subjects of natural monopolies, shall be obliged to conclude a contract of electric power supply upon the demand of consumers having the technical means t receive electric power. Disagreements arising when concluding such a contract shall be regulated in accordance with the requirements of the present Code.

5. Electric power supply enterprises of other, besides State and municipal, forms of ownership may take part in the provision of electric power of any consumers, including through the State (or municipal) electric power network on the conditions determined by respective contracts.

Article 276. Quantity and Quality of Electric Power. Periods, Prices, and Procedure for Settlements Under Contract of Electric Power Supply

1. The total quantity of electric power to be sold shall be determined by agreement of the parties. If electric power is allocated at the expense of an order for State needs (or ceiling), the electric power supplier shall not have the right to lower this ceiling for the subscriber without his consent.

2. Proposals of a subscriber concerning the quantity and types

of electric power and periods for the sale thereof, shall be priority when the electric power supplier has production possibilities.

3. Indicia of the quality of electric power shall be agreed by the parties on the basis of State standards or technical conditions by means of agreeing a list (or amount) of indicia, the maintenance of which is a duty for the parties of the contract.

4. The periods of delivery of electric power shall be established by the parties in the contract by proceeding, as a rule, from the need to ensure the rhythmic and uninterrupted receipt thereof by the subscriber. The basic recording period for electric power supply shall be ten days, with adjustment for amounts during twenty-four hour periods. The parties may agree the delivery of electric power within twenty-four hour periods by hours, and also the time and duration of maximum and minimum loads.

5. The quantity of electric power not received in preceding periods through the fault of the electric power supplier shall be subject to augmentation at the demand of the subscriber. If electric power was not chosen by the subscriber or not received by him for heating in connection with favorable weather conditions, the augmentation of the electric power not received shall be effectuated by agreement of the parties.

6. Settlements of accounts under contracts of electric power supply shall be effectuated on the basis of prices (or tariffs) established in accordance with the requirements of a law.

7. Payment for electric power sold shall be effectuated, as a rule, in the form of advance payment. By agreement of the parties, planned payments may be applied with subsequent recalculation or payment, which shall be made for electric power actually sold.

8. If a subscriber has an own electric power source and sells electric power to the network of the electric power supplier, settlements of accounts shall be permitted by balancing the mutual received electric power.

Article 277. Rules for Use of Electric Power

1. Subscribers shall use electric power in compliance with the rules for the use of electric power of the respective types, which shall be confirmed by the Cabinet of Ministers of Ukraine.

2. Standard contracts of delivery of different types of electric power may be provided for by the rules.

3. A subscriber shall have the right to sell electric power to networks acceding thereto as secondary consumers (sub-subscribers). In this event the sub-subscribers shall conclude a contract of electric power supply with the subscriber and have the rights and bear the duties of a subscriber, and the subscriber shall have the right and bear the duties of an electric power supplier.

4. A subscriber shall be obliged to communicate the list of sub-subscribers to the electric power supplier having the right of control of the electric power network and instruments of the sub-subscribers and the right of control over compliance by sub-subscribers with the rules for the use of electric power.

5. Responsibility for a violation of the rules for use of electric power shall be established by a law.

§4. Exchange Trade

Article 278. Trade-Exchange Activity

1. The effectuation of trade-exchange activity shall have the purpose of the organization and regulation of trade by means of rendering services to subjects of economic management in the effectuation by them of trade operations of a specially-formed economic organization – a trade exchange.

2. The legal conditions for the creation and activity of trade

exchanges, and also the basic rules for the effectuation of trade-exchange activity, shall be determined by the present Code and by laws and other normative-legal acts adopted in accordance with it.

Article 279. Trade Exchange

1. A trade exchange shall be a special subject of economic management which renders services in the conclusion of exchange transactions, eliciting supply and demand for goods and goods prices, studies and regulates goods-turnover, and promotes trade operations connected therewith.

2. A goods exchange shall be a juridical person, operate on the principles of self-government and economic autonomy, have solitary property and an autonomous balance sheet, accounts in branches of a bank, and a seal with its own name.

3. A goods exchange shall be created on the basis of the voluntary association of interested subjects of economic management. Agencies of State power and agencies of local self-government, and also State and municipal enterprises, institutions, and organizations which are fully or partially maintained at the expense of the State budget of Ukraine or local budgets may not be founders or members of a goods exchange.

4. The founding of a goods exchange shall be effectuated by means of the conclusion by the founders of an agreement determining the procedure of its creation, composition of the founders, the duties thereof, the amount and periods for payment of share, entry, and periodic dues. The founders shall pay a share contribution.

5. A goods exchange shall operate on the basis of a charter, which shall be confirmed by the founders of the exchange.

6. State registration of a goods exchange shall be conducted in accordance with the requirements of Article 58 of the present Code.

7. A goods exchange shall not engage in commercial

intermediation nor have the purpose of receiving a profit.

8. A goods exchange shall effectuate its activity on the principles of equality of participants of exchange public sales, public conducting of exchange public sales, and application of free (or market) prices.

Article 280. Rights and Duties of Goods Exchange

1. A goods exchange shall have the right to:
establish own rules for exchange public sales and exchange arbitration in accordance with legislation which are binding upon all participants of public sales;
establish entry and periodic dues for members of the exchange and the amount of payment for services rendered by the exchange;
establish and recover in accordance with the charter of the exchange payment for the registration of transactions on the exchange, and also sanctions for a violation of the charter of the exchange and exchange rules;
create subdivisions of the exchange and confirm statutes on them;
found arbitration commissions for the settlement of disputes in trade transactions;
work out, taking into account State standards, own standards and standard contracts;
conclude transactions with other exchanges, have its own representatives on exchanges, including those located beyond the limits of Ukraine;
publish exchange bulletins, manuals, and other informational and advertising publications;
decide other questions provided for by a law.

2. A goods exchange shall be obliged to:
create conditions for conducting exchange trade;
regulate exchange operations;
regulate prices for goods permitted for turnover on the exchange;
render to members and visitors of the exchange organizational, informational, and other services;
ensure the collecting, processing, and dissemination of

information concerning the market on the exchange.

Article 281. Rules of Exchange Trade. Exchange Public Sales

1. The rules of exchange trade shall be worked out in accordance with legislation and shall be the basic document regulating the procedure for the effectuation of exchange operations, conducting exchange trade, and the settlement of disputes with regard to these questions.

2. The rules of exchange trade shall be confirmed by the general meeting of members of the goods exchange or organ empowered by it.

3. Public sales which are publicly and openly conducted in trading halls of the exchange with the participation of members of the exchange for goods admitted for realization on the exchange in the procedure established by the rules of exchange trade shall be exchange public sales.

4. Only members of the exchange or brokers-citizens registered on the exchange in accordance with its charter shall be authorized to effectuate exchange operations for the fulfillment of commissions of members of the exchange which they submit with regard to the effectuation of exchange operations.

Article 282. Termination of Goods Exchange

The termination of a good exchange shall occur by decision of the general meeting of members of the exchange, and also by decision of a court in the instances provided for by a law.

§5. Lease of Property and Finance Lease

Article 283. Lease of Property in Sphere of Economic Management

1. Under a contract of lease one party (lessor) transfers to the

other party (lessee) for payment for a determined period in use property for the effectuation of economic activity.

2. Individually-determined property of production-technical designation (or integral property complex) which does not lose in the process of use its consumer quality (or nonconsumer thing) shall be transferred for use under a contract of lease.

3. An object of lease may be:
State and municipal enterprises or structural subdivisions thereof as integral property complexes, that is, economic objects with a completed cycle for the production of products (or work, services), solitary land plot on which the object is sited, autonomous engineering communications and system of electric power supply;
immoveable property (buildings, installations, premises);
other separate individually-determined property of production-technical designation belonging to subjects of economic management.

4. The lease of structural subdivisions of State and municipal enterprises must not disturb the production-economic integrity and technological unity of the particular enterprise.

5. A list of State and municipal enterprises whose integral property complexes may not be the object of lease may be established by a law.

6. Respective provisions of the Civil Code of Ukraine, taking into account the peculiarities provided for by the present Code, shall apply to relations of lease.

Article 284. Conditions of Contract of Lease

1. The material conditions of a contract of lease shall be: object of lease (composition and value of property, taking into account the indexation thereof); period for which a contract of lease is concluded; lease payment, taking into account the indexation thereof; procedure for use of amortization deductions; restoration of leased property and conditions of the return or purchase thereof.

2. The valuation of the object of lease shall be effectuated at the restored value. The conditions of a contract of lease shall retain their force for the entire period of operation of the contract, and also if after the conclusion thereof rules worsening the position of the lessee have been established by legislation.

3. Reorganization of the lessor shall not be grounds for a change of the conditions or dissolution of the contract of lease.

4. The period of a contract of lease shall be determined by agreement of the parties. In the absence of the declaration of one of the parties concerning the termination or change of conditions of the contract of lease within one month after the expiry of the period of operation of the contract, it shall be considered to be extended for the same period and on the same conditions which were provided for by the contract.

Article 285. Basic Rights and Duties of Lessee

1. A lessee shall have a preferential right ahead of other subjects of economic management to extend the period of operation of a contract of lease.

2. A lessee may be obliged to use the object of lease for a special-purpose designation in accordance with the profile of production activity of the enterprise whose property is transferred on lease.

3. A lessee shall be obliged to care for lease property in accordance with the conditions of the contract, preventing the spoilage thereof or damage and to pay in a timely way and in full the lease payment.

4. A lessee shall compensate the lessor for the value of leased property in the event of the alienation of this property or destruction thereof or spoilage through the fault of the lessee.

Article 286. Lease Payment

1. Lease payment is a fixed payment which the lessee pays to

the lessor irrespective of the results of its economic activity. The amount of lease payment may be changed by agreement of the parties, and also in other instances provided for by legislation.

2. A lessee shall have the right to demand a reduction of the amount of lease payment if for circumstances for which he is not liable the conditions of economic management provided for by the contract have changed or the state of object of lease has materially worsened.

3. Lease payment shall be established in monetary form. Depending upon the specific nature of production activity of the lessee, lease payment may b agreement of the parties be established in kind or in monetary-in kind form.

4. The periods for making lease payment shall be determined in the contract.

Article 287. Lease of State and Municipal Property

1. The lessors with respect to State and municipal property shall be:

(1) the State Property Fund of Ukraine and its regional divisions – with regard to integral property complexes of enterprises, structural subdivisions thereof, and immoveable property which is State ownership, and also other property in the instances provided for by a law;

(2) agencies empowered by the Supreme Rada of the Autonomous Republic Crimea or local soviets to manage property – respectively with regard to property which belongs to the Autonomous Republic Crimea or is in municipal ownership;

(3) State (or municipal) enterprises – with regard to individually-determined property, and with the authorization of the lessors specified in point 2 of the present Article, — also with regard to integral property complexes, structural subdivisions thereof, and immoveable property.

2. Organizational and property relations connected with the transfer on lease of integral property complexes of the State sector of

the economy, and also integral property complexes which are municipal ownership, shall be regulated by legislation in accordance with the present Code.

3. The formation of a lease enterprise shall be effectuated in accordance with Article 115 of the present Code. The charter of a subject of economic management formed on the base of leased property may not be contrary to the conditions of a contract of lease.

Article 288. Sublease of State and Municipal Property

1. A lessee shall have the right to transfer individual objects of lease on sublease unless provided otherwise by a law of the contract of lease.

2. The transfer of integral property complexes on sublease shall not be permitted.

Article 289. Purchase (or Privatization) of Object of Lease

1. A lessee shall have the right to purchase the object of lease if such right has been provided for by the contract of lease.

2. The conditions of purchase of leased State (or municipal) property (or integral property complex) shall be determined in accordance with a law.

3. A lessee shall have the right at any time to refuse to effectuate the right provided for in a contract to purchase the object of lease.

4. The privatization of integral property complexes lease out shall be effectuated in the instances and procedure provided by a law.

Article 290. Lease of Land in Sphere of Economic Management

1. Relations connected with the lease of land as a means of

production shall be regulated by the Land Code of Ukraine and other laws.

2. Lease of a land plot without a contract concluded in written form, certified notarially, and registered in the procedure established by a law shall not be permitted.

3. The amount of payment for the use of a land plot which is State or municipal ownership may not be lower than established in accordance with a law. Instances of relieving from payment for use of a land plot or reduction of the amount of payment shall be determined by a law.

Article 291. Termination of Contract of Lease

1. A unilateral renunciation of a contract of lease shall not be permitted.

2. A contract of lease shall be terminated in the event of:
expiry of the period for which it was concluded;
purchase (or privatization) of the object of lease;
liquidation of the subject of economic management-lessee;
perishing (or destruction) of the object of lease.

3. A contract of lease may be dissolved by agreement of the parties. Upon the demand of one of the parties a contract of lease may be dissolved before time on the grounds provided for the Civil Code of Ukraine for dissolution of a contract of hire in the procedure established by Article 188 of the present Code.

4. The legal consequences of the termination of a contract of lease shall be determined in accordance with the conditions of the regulation of a contract of hire of the Civil Code of Ukraine.

Article 292. Finance Leasing in Sphere of Economic Management

1. Finance leasing is economic activity directed towards the investing of own or attracted financial means and consisting in the granting under a contract of finance leasing by one party (finance lessor) to the exclusive use of the other party (finance lessee) for a determined period property belonging to the finance lessor or acquired by him in ownership (or economic jurisdiction) on behalf of or by agreement with the finance lessee from a respective supplier (or seller) of property on condition of the payment by the finance lessee of periodic finance leasing payments.

2. Depending on the peculiarities of the effectuation of finance leasing operations, finance leasing may be of two types – financial or operational. According to the form of effectuation, finance leasing may be lease-back, share, international, and so on.

3. Immoveable and moveable property intended for use as basic funds, not prohibited in free turnover by a law on the market and with regard to which there are no limitations concerning the transfer thereof on finance leasing may be an object of finance leasing.

4. Property specified in paragraph one of the present Article which is State (or municipal ownership) may be the object of finance lease only by agreement with the agency effectuating the administration of that property in accordance with a law.

5. Land plots, other natural objects, and also integral property complexes of State (or municipal) enterprises and structural subdivisions thereof, may not be objects of finance leasing.

6. The transfer of the right of ownership to an object of finance leasing to another person shall not be grounds for dissolution of the contract of finance leasing.

7. Legal regulation of finance leasing shall be effectuated in

accordance with the present Code and other laws.

§6. Other Types of Economic-Trade Activity

Article 293. Barter in Sphere of Economic Management

1. Under a contract of barter, each of the parties shall be obliged to transfer to the other party in ownership, full economic jurisdiction, or operative management a determined good in exchange for another good.

2. The party to a contract shall be considered the seller of this good which it transferred in exchange and the purchaser of the good which it received instead.

3. By agreement of the parties, monetary supplemental payment for a good of greater value which is exchange for a good of lesser value shall be possible if this is not contrary to legislation.

4. Property relegated by legislation to basic funds relegated to State or municipal ownership, if the other party to a contract of barter is not respectively a State or municipal enterprise, may not be an object of barter. Other peculiarities of the effectuation of barter (or goods-exchange) operations connected with the acquisition and use of individual types of property, and also the effectuation of such operations in individual branches of economic management, also may be established by legislation.

5. The rules regulating contracts of purchase-sale, delivery, agricultural procurement, elements of which are contained in the contract of barter, if this is not contrary to legislation and corresponds to the essence of relations of the parties, may apply to a contract of barter.

Article 294. Keeping of Goods Warehouse

1. An organization effectuating the keeping of goods and rendering services connected with keeping on the principles of entrepreneurial activity shall be deemed to be a goods warehouse.

2. A goods warehouse shall be a warehouse of general use if it arises from a law, other legal acts, or authorization (or license) issued to the subject of economic management that it is obliged to accept for keeping goods from any goods-possessor.

3. Keeping in a goods warehouse shall be effectuated under a contract of warehouse keeping.

4. Respective provisions of the Civil Code of Ukraine shall apply to the regulation of relations arising from the keeping of goods under a contract of warehouse keeping.

Chapter 31
Commercial Intermediation (Agency Relations) in the Sphere of Economic Management

Article 295. Agency Activity

1. Commercial intermediation (or agency activity) shall be entrepreneurial activity consisting in the rendering by a commercial agent of services to subjects of economic management in the event of their effectuating economic activity by means of intermediation in the name of, in the interests of, under the control of, and at the expense of the subject that he represents.

2. A subject of economic management (citizen or juridical person) which according to the powers based on the agency contract effectuated commercial intermediation may be a commercial agent.

3. Entrepreneurs acting although in another's interests but in

own name shall not be commercial agents.

4. A commercial agent may not conclude transactions in the name of that whom he represents with respect to himself personally.

5. Limitations or a prohibition against the effectuation of commercial intermediation in individual branches of economic management may be established by a law.

Article 296. Grounds for Arising of Agency Relations

Agency relations shall arise in the event of:
the granting of powers by a subject of economic management on the basis of a contract to a commercial agency for the performance of respective actions;
the approval by a subject of economic management which the commercial agent represents of a transaction concluded in the interests of this subject by the agent without powers for the conclusion thereof or in excess of the powers granted to him.

Article 297. Subject of Agency Contract

1. Under an agency contract one party (commercial agent) shall be obliged to render services to the other party (subject whom the commercial agent represents) in the conclusion of transactions or promote the conclusion thereof (or rendering of actual services) in the name of this subject and at his expense.

2. An agency contract must determined the sphere, character, and procedure for the fulfillment by a commercial agent of intermediation services, rights and duties of the parties, conditions and amount of remuneration to the commercial agent, period of operation of the contract, sanctions in the event of a violation by the parties of the conditions of the contract, other necessary conditions determined by the parties.

3. A condition concerning the territory within whose limits the

commercial agent effectuates activity determined by agreement the parties must be provided by the contract. If the territory of operation of the agent has not been determined in the contract, it shall be considered that the agent operates within the limits of the territory of Ukraine.

4. An agency contract shall be concluded in written form. The form of confirmation of powers (or representation) of a commercial agent must be determined in the contract.

Article 298. Approval of Transaction Concluded by Commercial Agent Without Powers for Conclusion Thereof or In Excess of Powers

1. A commercial agent shall inform the subject whom he represents about each instance of his intermediation in the conclusion of transactions and each transaction concluded by him in the interests of this subject.

2. A transaction concluded in the name of the subject whom the commercial represents without powers for the conclusion thereof or in excess of the powers granted to him shall be considered to be approved by this subject on condition that he does not reject before a third person the action of the commercial agent. Subsequent approval of a transaction by a subject whom the agent represents shall make the transaction valid from the day of conclusion thereof.

Article 299. Nonmonopoly and Monopoly Agency Relations

1. A subject whom a commercial agent represents shall have the right to entrust commercial intermediation also to other subjects, having notified the agent thereof, and the agent shall have the right to effectuate commercial intermediation also for other subjects of economic management if the interests of the subjects whom the commercial agent represents are not contrary in the questions for the resolving of which this agent has been invited.

2. In the event of monopoly agency relations the commercial

agent which represents the subject of economic management shall not have the right to effectuate commercial intermediation for other subjects within the limits provided by the agency contract.

Article 300. Transfer of Rights of Commercial Agent

1. A commercial agent must personally fulfill actions for which he is empowered by the subject whom he represents.

2. Unless provided otherwise by the agency contract, a commercial agent may not transfer the rights which he possesses in the interests of he whom he represents to other persons at his discretion.

Article 301. Mutual Settlements in Agency Relations

1. In accordance with an agency contract the commercial agent shall receive agency remuneration for intermediation operations effectuated by him in the interests of the subject whom he represents in the amount provided for by the contract.

2. Agency remuneration shall be paid to a commercial agent after the paying up by the third person under the transaction concluded with his intermediation unless provided otherwise by the contract of the parties.

3. The parties may provide in the contract that additional remuneration shall be paid to a commercial agent if he assumes an obligation to guarantee the fulfillment of the transaction concluded by him in the interests of the subject whom he represents.

4. A subject who a commercial agent represents shall settle the remuneration to which the commercial agent has a right in accordance with the amounts and periods provided for by the contract of the parties.

5. A commercial agent shall have the right to demand a bookkeeping extract for settlement concerning all transactions for which agent remuneration is due to him.

6. The conditions of payment of remuneration to a commercial agent for transactions concluded after the end of contractual relations, and also other conditions affecting settlements of the parties, shall be determined by a contract.

Article 302. Duties With Regard to Nondivulgence of Confidential Information in Agency Relations

1. A commercial agent shall not have the right to transfer confidential information received from the subject whom he represents without the consent of this subject, use it in own interests, or in the interests of other persons contrary to the interests of the subject whom he represents, either in the event of the effectuation by the commercial agent of his activity in the interests of the said subject or after the termination of agency relations with him.

2. The parties to an agency contract may conclude a separate agreement concerning the defense of confidential information of the subject whom the commercial agent represents (contract on nondisclosure).

3. A commercial agent shall bear responsibility for the divulgence of confidential information in accordance with a law and the contract.

Article 303. Responsibility for Violation of Agency Contract

1. A commercial agent shall bear responsibility in full for damage caused to the subject whom he represents as a consequence of the failure to fulfill or improper fulfillment of his duties, unless provided otherwise by the agency contract.

2. Unless provided otherwise by a contract, a commercial agent shall not guarantee to the subject whom he represents the fulfillment by third persons of obligations with regard to transactions concluded with his intermediation.

3. In the event of a violation of an agency contract by the subject

whom the commercial agent represents, the last shall have the right to receive remuneration in amounts provided for by the agency contract, and also compensation of losses incurred by him as a consequence of the failure to fulfill or improper fulfillment of the contract by the other party.

Article 304. Termination of Agency Contract

1. An agency contract shall terminate by agreement of the parties, and also in the event of: revocation of the powers of the commercial agent by the subject whom he represents, or renunciation by the commercial agent of further effectuation of commercial intermediation with regard to the contract concluded by the parties without the determination of the period of its operation; withdrawal by one of the parties from the contract as a consequence of the termination or death thereof; arising of other circumstances terminating the powers of the commercial agent or subject whom he represents.

2. In the event of the revocation of powers of a commercial agent the subject whom the commercial agent represents must inform him about the termination of the contract not less than one month in advance unless a longer period had been provided by the contract.

3. In the event of the elimination (or ending) of the circumstances which entailed the termination of powers of the commercial agent, these powers by agreement of the parties may be renewed.

Article 305. Legislation on Commercial Intermediation in Sphere of Economic Management

1. Relations arising when effectuating commercial intermediation (agency activity) in the sphere of economic management shall be regulated by the present Code and other normative legal acts adopted in accordance therewith, which determined the peculiarities of commercial intermediation in individual branches of economic management.

2. In the part not regulated by normative-legal acts specified in

the present Article the respective provisions of the Civil Code of Ukraine by which relations of commission are regulated may apply to agency relations.

Chapter 32
Legal Regulation of Carriage of Goods

Article 306. Carriage of Goods as Type of Economic Activity

1. The carriage of goods in the present Code shall be deemed to be economic activity connected with the movement of products of production-technical designation and consumer manufactures by railway, motor vehicle, water and air, and also the transporting of products by pipelines.

2. Carriers, goods consignors, and goods recipients shall be the subjects of relations of the carriage of goods.

3. Railway freight transport, motor vehicle freight transport, maritime cargo transport and internal cargo fleet, aviation cargo transport, pipeline transport, space transport, and other types of transport shall effectuate the carriage of goods.

4. Transport expediting shall be an auxiliary type of activity connected with the carriage of goods.

5. General conditions for the carriage of goods, and also special conditions for the carriage of individual types of goods (explosive substances, weapons, poisonous, inflammable, radioactive, and other dangerous substances, and so on) shall be determined by the present Code, transport statutes, and other normative-legal acts.

6. Relations connected with the carriage of passengers and baggage shall be regulated by the Civil Code of Ukraine and other normative-legal acts.

Article 307. Contract of Carriage of Goods

1. Under a contract of carriage of goods, one party (carrier) shall be obliged to deliver cargo entrusted to it by the other party (goods consignor) to the point of destination within the period established by legislation or contract and to issue to the person empowered to receive the cargo (goods recipient), and the goods consignor shall be obliged to pay the established payment for the carriage of goods.

2. A contract for the carriage of goods shall be concluded in written form. The conclusion of a contract for carriage of goods shall be confirmed by drawing up a carriage document (transport waybill, bill of lading, and so on) in accordance with the requirements of legislation. The carriers shall be obliged to provide goods consignors with blank forms of carriage documents according to the rules for the effectuation of the respective carriages.

3. A goods consignor and the carrier may, when necessary to effectuate systematic carriages of goods during a determined period, conclude a long-term contract under which the carrier is obliged within established periods to accept, and the goods consignor – to give over for carriage, goods in an amount agreed by the parties.

4. Depending upon the type of transport by which the systematic carriage of goods is provided, the following long-term contracts shall be concluded: long-term – for rail and maritime transport; navigational – on river transport (internal fleet); special – on air transport; yearly – on motor vehicle transport. The procedure for the conclusion of long-term contracts shall be established by respective transport codes, transport statutes, or rules of carriage.

5. The conditions for the carriage of goods by individual types of transport, and also the responsibility of subjects of economic management for these carriages, shall be determined by transport codes, transport statutes, and other normative-legal acts. The parties may provide in the contract also conditions of carriage not contrary to legislation and additional responsibility for improper fulfillment of

contractual obligations.

Article 308. Acceptance of Goods for Carriage

1. Goods for carriage shall be accepted by carriers depending upon the type of transport and goods at places of general or not general use.

2. Responsibility of the carrier for the preservation of goods shall arise from the moment of acceptance of the goods for carriage.

3. A goods consignor shall be obliged to prepare the goods for carriage by taking into account the necessity of ensuring transportability and preservation thereof in the process of carriage and has the right to insure goods in the procedure established by legislation.

4. If special documents (or certificates) confirming the quality and other properties of goods being carried have been provided for the effectuation of carriage of goods by legislation or by contract, the goods consignor shall be obliged to transfer such documents to the carrier together with the goods.

5. A carrier shall issue a document to the goods consignor at the point of consignment duly formalized concerning acceptance of the goods for carriage.

Article 309. Change of Conditions of Carriage

1. A goods consignor shall have the right in the procedure established by transport codes or statutes to receive back goods handed over for carriage before the sending thereof, replace the recipient of the goods specified in the carriage document (before the issuance thereof to the addressee), dispose of the cargo in the event of the failure of the recipient to accept them or impossibility of the issuance of the goods to the recipient.

2. In the event of the interruption or termination of the carriage

of goods for circumstances beyond the carrier's control the carrier shall be obliged to notify the goods consignor and receive from his respective instructions relative to the goods.

Article 310. Receipt of Goods at Point of Destination

1. A carrier shall be obliged to inform the recipient about the arrival of the goods at his address.

2. The recipient shall be obliged to accept the goods which arrived at his address. He shall have the right to refuse to accept damaged or spoiled goods if it is established that as a consequence of the change of quality the possibility of full or partial use thereof for the original designation is excluded.

3. Responsibility of the carrier for the preservation of goods shall terminate from the moment of issuance thereof to the recipient at the point of destination. If the recipient has not demanded the goods which have arrived within the established period or refused to accept them, the carrier shall have the right to leave the goods with himself for keeping at the expense and risk of the goods consignor, having informed him in writing thereof.

4. Goods not received within a month after the recipient being informed by the carrier, it shall be considered to be unclaimed and shall be realized in the procedure established by legislation.

Article 311. Payment for Carriage of Goods

Payment for the carriage of goods and fulfillment of other work connected with carriage shall be determined at prices established in accordance with legislation.

Article 312. Contract for Carriage of Goods in Direct Mixed Transport

1. Under a contract for the carriage of goods in direct mixed

transport, the carriage shall be effectuated from the goods consignor to the goods recipient by two or more carriers of different types of transport under a single carriage document.

2. The rules of Article 307 of the present Code, unless provided otherwise by transport codes or charters, shall apply to contracts for the carriage of goods in direct mixed transport.

3. Relations of carriers in the event of the carriage of goods indirect mixed transport and conditions of work of reloading points shall be regulated by junction agreements. The procedure for the conclusion of junction agreements shall be established by transport codes and charters.

Article 313. Responsibility of Carrier for Delay of Delivery of Goods

1. A carrier shall be obliged to deliver goods to the point of destination within the period provided for by transport codes, charters, or rules. If the period of delivery of goods within the said procedure is not established, the parties shall have the right to establish this period in the contract.

2. A carrier shall be relieved from responsibility for delay in the delivery of goods if the delay occurred not through his fault.

3. The amount of fines to be recovered from carriers for delay in the delivery of goods shall be determined in accordance with a law.

4. The payment of a fine for the delivery of goods with delay shall not relieve the carrier from responsibility for loss, shortage, or damaging of goods which occurred as a consequence of delay.

Article 314. Responsibility of Carrier for Loss, Short Delivery, and Damage of Goods

1. A carrier shall bear responsibility for loss, shortage, and damage

of goods accepted for carriage unless it is proved that the loss, shortage, or damage occurred through his fault.

2. Instances may be provided in transport codes or charters when evidence of the fault of the carrier in loss, shortage, or damage is placed on the recipient or consignor.

3. For damage caused during the carriage of goods the carrier shall be liable in the event of:
loss or shortage of goods – in the amount of the value of the goods which were lost or which do not suffice;
damage of goods – in the amount by which the value thereof has been reduced;
loss of goods handed over for carriage with a declaration of the value thereof, — in the amount of the declared value unless it is proved that it is lower than the actual value of the goods.

4. If as a consequence of the damage to goods the quality thereof has been so changed that it can not be used for direct designation, the recipient of the goods shall have the right to refuse it and to demand compensation for the loss thereof.

5. If goods for those loss or shortage the carrier has paid respective compensation are found in the course of time, the recipient (or consignor) shall have the right to demand the issuance of this good to him, having returned the compensation received for the loss or shortage thereof.

Article 315. Procedure for Settlement of Disputes Concerning Carriages

1. Before the presentation of a suit against a carrier arising from a contract for the carriage of goods, the presentation of a claim to him shall be obligatory.

2. Claims may be presented within six months, and claims with regard to the payment of fines and bonuses – within forty-five days.

3. A carrier shall be obliged to consider a declared claim and to inform the applicant about satisfaction or rejection thereof within three months, and with regard to a claim for carriage in direct mixed transport – within six months. Claims with regard to payment of a fine or bonus must be considered within forty-five days.

4. If a claim has been rejected or reply thereto not received within the period specified in paragraph three of the present Article, the applicant shall have the right to apply to a court within six months from the day of receipt of the reply or expiry of the period established for reply.

5. A six-month period shall be established for the presentation by the carrier of suits arising from carriage against the goods consignor and goods recipient.

6. With regard to disputes connected with inter-State carriages of goods, the procedure for the presentation of suits and the periods of limitation shall be established by transport codes or charters or by international treaties, consent to the bindingness of which has been given by the Supreme Rada of Ukraine.

Article 316. Contract of Transport Expediting

1. Under a contract of transport expediting one party (expeditor) shall be obliged for payment and at the expense of the other party (client) to fulfill or to organize the fulfillment of services determined by the contract which are connected with the carriage of goods.

The duty of the expeditor to organize the carriage of goods by transport and according to a route selected by the expeditor or client, conclude in his name or in the name of the client a contract for the carriage of goods, ensure the dispatch and receipt of the goods, and also the fulfillment of other obligations connected with the carriage, may be established by a contract of transport expediting.

The rendering of additional services necessary for the delivery of goods (verification of quantity and state of the goods, loading and unloading thereof, payment of customs duty, charges, and expenses placed on the client, keeping of the goods until the receipt thereof at the point of destination, receive documents necessary for export and import, fulfillment of customs formalities, and so on) may be provided for by the contract of transport expediting.

2. Payment with regard to a contract of transport expediting shall be effectuated at prices which are determined in accordance with Chapter 21 of the present Code.

Chapter 33
Capital Construction

Article 317. Independent-Work Relations in Capital Construction

1. The construction of objects of production and other designation, preparation of construction plots, work with regard to the equipping of buildings, work relating to the completion of construction, applied and experimental research, developments, and so on which are fulfilled by subjects of economic management for other subjects or upon their order shall be effectuated on conditions of independent-work.

2. In order to effectuate work specified in paragraph one of the present Article contracts of independent-work may be concluded for: capital construction (including subindependent-work); the fulfillment of design and survey work; the fulfillment of geological, geodesic, and other work necessary for capital construction; other contracts. The general conditions of contracts of independent-work shall be determined in accordance with the provisions of the Civil Code of Ukraine on the independent-work contract, unless provided otherwise by the present Code.

3. Economic relations in the sphere of material-technical provision of capital construction shall be regulated by the respective independent-work contracts unless provided otherwise by legislation or contract of

the parties. By agreement of the parties construction deliveries may be effectuated on the basis of contracts of delivery.

Article 318. Contract of Independent-Work in Capital Construction

1. Under a contract of independent-work for capital construction one party (independent-work contractor) shall be obliged with its forces and means upon the order of the other party (customer) to build and hand over to the customer within the established period an object determined by the contract in accordance with the design-estimate documentation or to fulfill construction and other work stipulated by the contract, and the customer shall be obliged to transfer to the independent-work contractor confirmed project-estimate documentation, provide him a construction space, accept the completed construction, and pay for it.

2. A contract of independent-work shall in accordance with the present Article be concluded for the construction, expansion, conversion, and re-profiling of objects; construction of objects with the placement wholly or partially on the independent-work contractor the fulfillment of work with regard to the design and delivery of equipment, launching and other work; fulfillment of individual complexes of construction, assembly, special, design-construction design, and other work connected with the construction of objects.

3. Provision of the construction with materials, technological, electric power, electrical engineering, and other equipment shall be placed on the independent-work contractor unless provided otherwise by legislation or the contract.

4. The content of a contract of independent-work for capital construction which is concluded on the basis of a State order must correspond to this order.

5. A contract of independent-work for capital construction must provide for: the name of the parties, place and date of conclusion,

subject of the contract (or name of the object, amounts and types of work provided for by the design); periods for commencement and completion of construction or fulfillment of work; rights and duties of the parties; cost and procedure for financing the construction of the object (or work); procedure for material-technical, design, and other provision of the construction; regime for control of quality of the work and materials by the customer; procedure for acceptance of the object (or work), procedure for the settlement of accounts for work fulfilled, conditions concerning defects and guarantee periods; insurance of risks, financial guarantees; responsibility of the parties (compensation of losses); settlement of disputes, grounds and conditions for change and dissolution of the contract.

Article 319. General Independent-Work Contractor and Subindependent-Work Contractor

1. A customer may conclude a contract of independent-work for capital construction with one independent-work contractor or with two or more independent-work contractors.

2. An independent-work contractor shall have the right by agreement with the customer to enlist for the fulfillment of the contract as third persons subindependent-work contractors on conditions of subindependent-work contracts concluded with them, being liable to the customer for the results of their work. In this event the independent-work contractor shall act to the customer as a general independent-work contractor, and to the subindependent-work contractors – as the customer.

3. A contract of independent-work for the fulfillment of work with regard to the assembly of equipment the customer may conclude with the general independent-work contractor or with the supplier of the equipment. With the consent of the general independent-work contractor contracts for the fulfillment of assembly and other special work may be concluded by the customer with the respective specialized enterprises.

Article 320. Rights of Customer

1. A customer shall have the right, without interfering in the economic activity of the independent-work contractor, to effectuate control and technical supervision over the conformity of the amount, cost, and quality of work fulfilled to the designs and estimates. He shall have the right to verify the course and quality of construction and assembly work, and also the quality of materials being used.

2. If an independent-work contractor does not apply himself in good time for the fulfillment of the contract or fulfills the work so slowly that the end thereof within the period becomes clearly impossible, the customer shall have the right to demand dissolution of the contract and compensation of losses.

3. An independent-work contractor shall have the right to not apply himself to the work, and to suspend work commenced, in the event of a violation by the customer of his obligations under the contract, as a consequence of which the commencement or continuation of the work by the independent-work contractor is impossible or significantly complicated.

4. Defects in the fulfillment of work or materials to be used for the work which are permitted through the fault of the independent-work contractor or subindependent-work contractor must be eliminated by the independent-work contractor at his own expense.

Article 321. Settlements Under Contract of Independent-Work for Capital Construction

1. In a contract of independent-work for capital construction the parties shall determine the value of work (or price of the contract) or means of determination thereof.

2. The value of work under a contract of independent-work (or contributory compensation of expenses of the independent-work contractor and remuneration due thereto) may be determined by drawing

up an approximate or firm estimate. The estimate shall be considered firm unless provided otherwise by the contract. Changes in the firm estimate may be made only by agreement of the parties.

3. In the event the need arises to significantly exceed an approximate estimate, the independent-work contractor shall be obliged to warn the customer thereof in a timely way. If the independent-work contractor has not warned the customer about exceeding the estimate, he shall be obliged to fulfill the work without demanding compensation for additional expenses incurred.

4. An independent-work contractor shall not have the right to demand an increase of the firm estimate, and the customer – a reduction thereof. In the event of the material growth after conclusion of the contract of the cost of materials and equipment which should have been provided by the independent-work contractor, and also services which were rendered to him by third persons, an independent-work contractor shall have the right to demand an increase of the established cost of the work, and in the event of the refusal of the customer – dissolution of the contract in the established procedure.

5. Unless advance payment has been provided for by the contract for work fulfilled or individual stages thereof, the customer shall be obliged to pay the independent-work contractor the price stipulated by the contract after the final handing over of the object of construction, on condition that the work was properly fulfilled and within the agreed period or, by agreement with the customer – before time.

6. An independent-work contractor shall have the right to demand payment of an advance to him if such payment and the amount of the advance have been provided for by the contract.

7. When the shutting down of construction is necessary for circumstances beyond the control of the parties, the customer shall be obliged to pay the independent-work contractor for work fulfilled before the shutting down and compensate him for expenses connected with the shutting down.

Article 322. Responsibility for Violation of Contract of Independent-Work for Capital Construction

1. For the failure to fulfill or improper fulfillment of obligations under a contract of independent-work for capital construction the guilty party shall pay fine sanctions, and also compensate the other party for losses (expenses made by the other party, loss or damage of its property, revenues not received) in the amount not covered by fine sanctions unless another procedure has been established by a law.

2. Defects discovered when accepting work (or object) the independent-work contractor shall be obliged to eliminate at his own expense within the periods agreed with the customer. In the event of a violation of periods for the elimination of defects the independent-work contractor shall bear responsibility provided for by the contract.

3. The period of limitations for demands arising from improper quality of work under a contract of independent-work for capital construction shall be determined from the day of acceptance of work by the customer and shall comprise:
one year – with regard to defects of noncapital construction designs, and in the event defects could not be discovered by ordinary means of accepting work, — two years;
three years – with regard to defects of capital construction designs, and in the event defects could not be discovered by ordinary means of accepting work, — ten years;
thirty years – with regard to compensation of losses caused to a customer by unlawful actions of the independent-work contractor which entailed destruction or accident.

4. If by a contract of independent-work or by legislation the granting of guarantees has been provided for the quality of work and defects have been discovered within the limits of the guarantee period, the running of the period of limitations shall commence from the day of discovery of the defects.

Article 323. Conditions of Conclusion and Fulfillment of Contracts of Independent-Work in Capital Construction

1. Contracts of independent-work (or subindependent-work) for capital construction shall be concluded and fulfilled on the general conditions for the conclusion and fulfillment of contracts of independent-work in capital construction confirmed by the Cabinet of Ministers of Ukraine in accordance with a law.

2. Contracts of independent-work for capital construction with the participation of foreign subjects of economic management shall be concluded and fulfilled in the procedure provided for by the present Code, inter-State agreements, and also special conditions for the conclusion and fulfillment of contracts of independent-work in capital construction confirmed in the procedure established by the Cabinet of Ministers of Ukraine.

Article 324. Contract of Independent-Work for Conducting Design and Survey Work

1. Under a contract for conducting design and survey work the independent-work contractor shall be obliged to work out according to the planning task of the customer design documentation or to fulfill design work stipulated by the contract, and also to fulfill survey work, and the customer shall be obliged to accept and to pay for it.

2. The provisions of Article 318 of the present Code may apply to relations arising in the process of the fulfillment of design and survey work.

3. An independent-work contractor shall bear responsibility for defects of the design, including discovered in the process of its realization and operation of the object built according to the particular design.

4. In the event of the discovery of defects of a design the independent-work contractor shall be obliged to redo the design without compensation, and also to compensate the customer for losses caused

by the defects of the design.

5. A suit concerning compensation to a customer of losses caused by defects of a design may be declared within ten years, and if losses to the customer were caused by lawful actions by the independent-work contractor which entailed destruction, accidents, collapse, — within thirty years from the day of acceptance of the built object.

Chapter 34
Legal Regulation of Innovation Activity

Article 325. Innovation Activity

Activity of participants of economic relations which is effectuated on the basis of the realization of investments for the purpose of the fulfillment of long-term scientific-technical programs with lengthy period of nonsubsidy of expenses and the introduction of new scientific-technical achievements in production and other spheres of social life shall be innovation activity in the sphere of economic management.

Article 326. Investing in Innovation Activity

1. Long-term investments of various types of property, intellectual valuables, and property rights in objects of economic activity for the purpose of receiving revenue (or profit) or achieving another social effect shall be deemed to be investments in the sphere of economic management.

2. The forms of investing in innovation activity shall be:
State (or municipal) investing, which shall be effectuated by agencies of State power or agencies of local self-government at the expense of budgetary means and other means in accordance with a law;
commercial investing, which shall be effectuated by subjects of economic management at the expense of own or borrowed means for the purpose of the development of the base of entrepreneurship;

social investing, which shall be effectuated in objects of the social sphere and other nonproduction spheres;

foreign investing, which shall be effectuated by foreign juridical persons or foreigners, and also by other States;

joint investing, which shall be effectuated by subjects of Ukraine jointly with foreign juridical persons or foreigners.

3. The general conditions for the realization of investments in Ukraine shall be determined by a law.

Article 327. Types of Innovation Activity

1. Innovation activity provides for the investing in scientific research and development directed towards the effectuation of qualitative changes in the state of productive forces and progressive inter-branch structural advances, and the working out and introduction of new types of products and technologies.

2. Innovation activity shall be effectuated according to the following orientations:

conducting of scientific research and developments directed towards the creation of objects of intellectual property and scientific-technical products;

working out, exploitation, issue, and dissemination of types of technology and technologies new in principle;

working out and introduction of new resource-saving technologies intended to improve the social and ecological state;

technical re-equipping, conversion, expansion, and construction of new enterprises which are effectuated for the first time as the industrial exploitation of production of a new product or introduction of a new technology.

3. Investing in the regeneration of basic funds and increment of material-production reserves shall be effectuated as capital investments.

Article 328. State Regulation of Innovation Activity

1. The State shall regulate innovation activity by means of:
determination of innovation activity as a necessary integrated investment and structural-branch policy; forming and ensuring the realization of innovation programs and special-purpose projects;
creation of economic, legal, and organizational conditions in order to ensure the State regulation of innovation activity;
creation and promotion of the development of the infrastructure of innovation activity.

2. The State shall effectuate control over innovation activity of subjects of economic management and other participants of economic relations, the conformity thereof to the requirements of legislation and State innovation programs. Branches and objects of innovation activity in which the use of foreign investments is limited or prohibited may be provided for by a law.

Article 329. State Guarantees of Innovation Activity

The State shall guarantee to subjects of innovation activity:
support for innovation programs and projects directed towards the realization of economic and social policies of the State;
support for the creation and development of subjects of the infrastructure of innovation activity;
protection and defense of the rights of intellectual property, defense against unfair competition in the sphere of innovation activity;
free access to information concerning the priorities of State economic and social policies, innovation requirements, and the results of scientific-technical activity, except for instances provided for by a law;
support for the training, retraining, and increasing the qualifications of cadres in the sphere of the effectuation of innovation activity.

Article 330. State Expert Examination of Innovation Projects

1. Innovation projects which are invested in at the expense of the State budget of Ukraine or local budgets, and also projects whose customers are agencies of State power or agencies of local self-government, shall be subject to obligatory State expert examination in accordance with legislation. Innovation projects which are invested in at the expense of other sources shall be subject to obligatory State expert examination with regard to questions of compliance with ecological, urban construction, and sanitary-hygienic requirements.

2. When necessary, the expert examination of individual innovation projects having important national economic significance may be effectuated by decision of the Cabinet of Ministers of Ukraine.

Article 331. Contract on Creation and Transfer of Scientific-Technical Product

1. Under a contract for the creation and transfer of a scientific-technical product, one party (executor) shall be obliged to fulfill scientific-research or experimental-construction design work (hereinafter: NIOKP) stipulated by a planning task of the other party (customer), and the customer shall be obliged to accept the work fulfilled (or product) and to pay for it.

2. A modified scientific-technical product may be the subject of a contract for the transfer of a scientific-technical product.

3. A finished scientific-research, design, construction design, technological work and services, the creation of experimental models or lots of manufactures necessary in order to conduct a NIOKP according to requirements agreed with the customer, which shall be fulfilled or rendered by subjects of economic management (scientific-research, construction design, design-construction design, and technological institutions, organizations, and also scientific-research and construction design subdivisions of enterprises, institutions, and organizations, and so on) shall be a scientific-technical product.

4. A contract may be concluded for the fulfillment of the entire complex of work from research to introduction into production of a scientific-technical product, and also for the further technical accompaniment (or servicing) thereof.

5. If a scientific-technical product is the result of initiative work, the contract shall be concluded for the transfer thereof, including the rendering of services for the introduction and mastery thereof.

6. Contracts for the creation and transfer of a scientific-technical product for State needs and with the participation of foreign subjects of economic management shall be concluded and fulfilled in the procedure established by the Cabinet of Ministers of Ukraine in accordance with a law.

Article 332. Legislation on Innovation Activity

Relations arising in the process of the effectuation of innovation activity shall be regulated by the present Code and by other legislative acts. The respective provisions of the Civil Code of Ukraine shall apply to the said relations in the part not regulated by the present Code.

Chapter 35
Peculiarities of Legal Regulation of Financial Activity

§1. Finances and Banking Activity

Article 333. Financial Activity of Subjects of Economic Management

1. Finances of subjects of economic management shall be an autonomous link of the national financial-credit system with individual turnover of means ensuring the covering of expenses of the production of products (or work, services) and receipt of profit.

2. Financial activity of subjects of economic management shall

include monetary and other financial intermediation, insurance, and also auxiliary activity in the sphere of finances and insurance.

3. Activity connected with the receipt and redistribution of financial means, except for instances provided for by legislation, shall be financial intermediation. Financial intermediation shall be effectuated by branches of banks and by other financial-credit organizations.

4. Activity directed towards covering long-term and short-term risks of subjects of economic management with or without the use of savings through a credit-financial system shall be insurance in the sphere of economic management.

5. Non-State management of the financial markets stock exchange operations with stock exchange valuables, other types of activity (intermediation in granting credits, financial consultations, activity connected with foreign currency, insurance of cargoes, assessment of insured risk and losses, and other types of auxiliary activity) shall be auxiliary activity in the sphere of finances and insurance.

Article 334. Legal Status of Banks

1. The banking system of Ukraine shall consist of the National Bank of Ukraine and other banks (State and non-State) created and operating on the territory of Ukraine in accordance with a law.

2. Banks are financial institutions whose functions are the attraction of contributions of monetary means of citizens and juridical persons and the placement of the said means in its name, on own conditions, and at own risk and the opening and conducting of bank accounts of citizens and juridical persons.

3. Banks shall be juridical persons. Banks may function as universal or as specialized – savings, investment, mortgage, settlement (or clearing).

4. The participation in management organs of banks, unless

provided otherwise by a law, of officials of agencies of State power and agencies of local self-government shall be prohibited.

5. Banks shall not be liable for obligations of the State, and the State shall not be liable for obligations of banks, except for instances provided for by a law and instances when the State in accordance with a law assumes such responsibility.

6. Banks shall be guided in their activity by the present Code, Law on Banks and Banking Activity, and other legislative acts.

7. A subject of economic management shall not have the right to use in its name the word "bank" without the registration of this subject as a bank in the National Bank of Ukraine, except for instances provided for by a law.

Article 335. National Bank of Ukraine. Council of National Bank of Ukraine

1. The National Bank of Ukraine shall be the central bank of the State whose basic function is ensuring the stability of the currency unit of Ukraine – the hrivna.

2. The legal status of the National Bank of Ukraine shall be determined by the Law on the National Bank of Ukraine.

3. The Council of the National Bank of Ukraine shall effectuate the working out of basic principles of monetary-credit policy and control over the fulfillment thereof. The legal status of the Council of the National Bank of Ukraine shall be determined by a law.

Article 336. Organizational-Legal Forms of Banks

1. Banks shall be created in the form of a joint-stock society, limited responsibility society, or cooperative bank.

2. Juridical persons and citizens, residents and nonresidents, and

also the State in the person of the Cabinet of Ministers of Ukraine or agencies empowered by it, may be participants of a bank. Juridical persons in which a bank has material participation, associations of citizens, religious and philanthropic organizations may not be participants of a bank.

3. It shall be prohibited to use for forming the charter fund of a bank budgetary means if such means have another special-purpose designation, means received on credit and under pledge, and also to increase the charter fund of a bank in order to cover losses.

4. Banks shall have the right to create banking association, the types of which shall be determined by a law, and also to be participants of industrial-financial groups. A bank may be a participant of only one banking association.

5. The conditions and procedure for the creation, State registration, licensing of the activity, and reorganization of banks, requirements for the charter, forming of the charter and other funds, and also the effectuation of the functions of baks, shall be established by the Law on Banks and Banking Activity. Legislation on economic societies and on cooperative societies shall extend to banks in the part not contrary to the present Code and said law.

Article 337. State Banks

1. A bank created by decision of the Cabinet of Ministers of Ukraine on the basis of State ownership shall be a State [bank].

2. The charter of a State bank shall be confirmed by decree of the Cabinet of Ministers of Ukraine.

3. The name of a State bank must contain the word "State".

4. The State shall effectuate the powers of possessor relative to stocks (or shares) belonging to it in the charter fund of a State bank through the management organs of the State bank.

5. In the event of the adoption of a decision concering the partial or full alienation by the State of share contributions of the State bank belonging to it, this bank shall lose the status of a State [bank].

Article 338. Cooperative Banks

1. A cooperative bank is a bank created by subjects of economic management, and also by other persons according to the principle of territoriality on the basis of voluntary membership and combining of share contributions for joint monetary-credit activity. Local and central cooperative banks may be created in accordance with a law.

2. The charter fund of a bank shall be divided into shares.

3. Each participant of a cooperative bank irrespective of his participation (or share) in the charter fund of the bank shall have one vote.

Article 339. Banking Operations

1. Financial intermediation shall be effectuated by banks in the form of banking operations. Deposit, settlement, credit, factoring, and finance lease operations shall be the principal types of banking operations.

2. A list of banking operations shall be determined by the Law on Banks and Banking Activity.

3. Banking operations shall be conducted in the procedure established by the National Bank of Ukraine.

Article 340. Deposit Operations of Banks

1. Deposit operations of banks shall consist of attracting means as contributions and the placement of savings (or deposit) certificates.

2. Deposits shall be formed at the expense of means in cash or noncash form, in hrivnas or in foreign currency placed by juridical

persons or citizens (clients) in their accounts in the bank on a contractual basis for a determined period of keeping or without an indication of such period and shall be subject to payment to the contributor in accordance with legislation and the conditions of the contract. A contract of bank contribution (or deposit) shall be concluded in written form.

Article 341. Settlement Operations of Banks

1. Settlement operations of banks shall be directed towards ensuring mutual settlements between participants of economic relations, and also other settlements in the financial sphere.

2. In order to effectuate settlements, subjects of economic management shall keep monetary means in branches of banks in respective accounts.

3. Noncash settlements may be effectuated in the form of payment commissions, payment demands, demands-commissions, bills of exchange, cheques, bank payment cards, and other debit and credit payment instruments which are applied in international banking practice.

4. In the event of noncash settlements all payments shall be conducted through branches of banks by means of transfer of the proper amounts from the account of the payer to the account of the recipient or by means of a set-off of mutual obligations and monetary claims. Payments shall be effectuated within the limits of available means in the account of the payer. When necessary, a bank may grant a credit to the payer for the effectuation of settlements.

5. Bank branches shall ensure settlements in accordance with legislation and the requirements of the client on conditions of a contract for settlement servicing. The contract must contain the requisites of the parties, conditions of opening and closing accounts, types of services which are rendered by the bank, duties of the parties, and responsibility for the failure to fulfill them, and also conditions for termination of the contract.

Article 342. Bank Accounts

1. Accounts of a juridical person who are a client of a bank shall be opened in branches of banks at the place of its registration or in any bank on the territory of Ukraine by consent of the parties. The procedure for opening accounts in branches of banks beyond the limits of Ukraine shall be established by a law.

2. Subjects of economic management having an autonomous balance sheet shall open accounts for settlements for products, the fulfillment of work, rendering of services, payment of earnings, payment of taxes and charges (or obligatory payments), and also other settlements connected with the financial provision of their activity.

3. A subject of entrepreneurship shall have the right to open accounts for keeping monetary means and the effectuation of all types of operations in any banks of Ukraine and other States at their choice and with the consent of these banks in the procedure established by the National Bank of Ukraine.

4. Juridical persons, branches thereof, divisions, and other solitary subdivisions not having the status of a juridical person and citizens-entrepreneurs shall open accounts to keep monetary means and effectuate all types of banking operations in any banks of Ukraine at their choice and with the consent of these banks in the procedure established by the National Bank of Ukraine.

5. Subjects of economic management who have been allotted means for special-purpose use from the State budget of Ukraine or local budgets shall apen accounts in accordance with a law.

6. The procedure for opening accounts in branches of banks, forms of settlement, and the procedure for the effectuation thereof shall be determined by the Law on Banks and Banking Activity, other laws, and also normative-legal acts of the National Bank of Ukraine.

Article 343. Responsibility for Violation of Periods of Settlements

1. Payers and recipients of means shall effectuate control over the timely conducting of settlements and consider claims which have arisen without the participation of branches of a bank.

2. The payer of monetary means shall pay to the benefit of the recipient of these means for delay of payment a forfeit in the amount which is established by agreement of the parties, but may not exceed twice the base rate of the National Bank of Ukraine which operated during the period for which the forfeit is paid.

3. In the event of delay in crediting monetary receipts to the account of the client, banks shall pay a forfeit to the benefit of the recipients of monetary means in the amount provided for by an agreement concerning the conducting of cashier-settlement operations, and in the absence of an agreement concerning the amount of forfeit – in the amount established by a law.

4. The payer shall be obliged autonomously to add the forfeit for the delayed amount of payment and give to the bank a commission concerning the transfer thereof from the means available in the account of the payer.

Article 344. International Settlement Operations

1. International settlement operations shall be conducted with regard to monetary demands and obligations arising when effectuating foreign economic activity between States, subjects of economic management, other juridical persons, and citizens situated on the territory of different countries.

2. Exports, importers, and banks acting in relations connected with the movement of goods-disposition documents and operational formalization of payments shall be subjects of international settlements.

3. International settlements shall be regulated by norms of international law, banking customs and rules, conditions of foreign economic contracts, and currency legislation of the countries-participants of the settlements.

4. General conditions of settlement operations with foreign States shall be determined by international treaties. The procedure for settlements and conducting of bank accounts shall be established by contracts which are concluded by empowered banks.

5. International settlements shall be effectuated through branches of banks, between which there are correspondent relations (or banks having an arrangement concerning the conducting of payments and settlements upon mutual commission).

6. In order to effectuate international settlements commercial documents shall be used: bill of lading, waybill, invoice, insurance documents (or insurance policy, certificate), document concerning right of ownership, and other commercial documents. The promissory note, bill of exchange, debt receipt, cheque, and other documents are which are used in order to receive payment shall be financial documents which are used to effectuate international settlements.

Article 345. Credit Operations of Banks

Credit operation shall consist of the placement by banks in their own names, on own conditions, and at own risk of attracted means of juridical persons (or borrowers) and citizens. Banking operations determined as such by the Law on Banks and Banking Activity shall be deemed to be credits.

Credit relations shall be effectuated on the basis of a credit contract, which shall be concluded between the creditor and the borrower in written form. The purpose, amount, and period of the credit, conditions and procedure for the issuance and repayment thereof, types of security of obligations of the borrower, interest rates, procedure of payment for the credit, duties, rights, and responsibility of the parties with regard to the issuance and repayment of the credit shall be provided for in a credit contract.

Article 346. Granting Credit to Subjects of Economic Management

1. In order to receive a bank credit the borrower shall provide the following documents to a bank:

petition (or application) in which the character of the credit transation is specified, purpose of use of the credit, amount of the loan, and period of use thereof;

feasibility study of the credit measure and calculation of economic effect of realization thereof;

other necessary documents.

2. In order to lower the degree of risk a bank shall grant a credit to the borrower when there are guarantees of solvency of the subject of economic management or suretyship of another bank, property belonging to the borrower under pledge and under other guarantees accepted in banking practice. For this purpose a bank shall have the right to study in advance the state of economic activity of the borrower, the solvency thereof, and to forecast the risk of nonpayment of the credit.

3. Credits shall be granted by a bank under interest, the rate of which, as a rule, may not be lower than the interest rate for credits which the bank itself assumes and interest rate which is paid by it for deposits. The granting of interest-free credits shall be prohibited, except for instances provided for by a law.

Article 347. Forms and Types of Bank Credit

1. In the sphere of economic management banking, commercial, finance lease, mortgage, and other forms of credit may be used.

2. Credits which are granted by banks shall be distinguished with regard to:

periods of use (short-term – up to one year; medium-term – up

to three years; long-term – in exceed of three years);
   means of security;
   degree of risk;
   methods of granting;
   periods of repayment;
   other conditions of granting, use, or repayment.

Article 348. Control of Bank Over Use of Credit

1. A bank shall effectuate control over the fulfillment of conditions of a credit contract, special-purpose use, timely and full repayment of the loan in the procedure established by legislation.

2. If the borrower does not fulfill its obligations provided for by the credit contract, the bank shall have the right to suspend the further issuance of the credit in accordance with the contract.

Article 349. Credit Resources

1. Banks shall effectuate credit operations within the limits of credit resources which they form in the process of their activity. They may borrow resources from one another on a contractual basis, attract and place means in the form of deposits and contributions, and effectuate mutual operations provided for by their charters.

2. In the event of the insufficiency of means for the effectuation of credit operations and fulfillment of obligations assumed, banks may receive loans from the National Bank of Ukraine. Credit resources of the National Bank of Ukraine shall comprise means of the charter and other funds and other means to be used as credit resources in accordance with a law.

3. General conditions of the use of credit resources shall be determined by the present Code and other laws.

Article 350. Factoring Services of Banks

1. The acquisition by a bank of the right of demand in monetary form with regard to the delivery of goods or rendering of services with acceptance of the risk of the fulfillment of such demand and acceptance of payments (factoring) shall be a banking operation which is effectuation on commission agency principles on a contractual basis.

2. Under a contract of factoring the bank assumes the obligation to transfer means for payment to the disposition of the client, and the client assumes the obligation to assign to the bank a monetary demand against a third person arising from relations of the client with this third person.

3. Factoring operations of banks may be accompanied by the rendering to clients of additional consultation and informational services.

4. A contract of factoring shall be valid irrespective of an agreement between the client and its debtor concerning a prohibition or limitation of transfer of the monetary demand.

5. General conditions and the procedure for the effectuation of factoring operations shall be determined by the Civil Code of Ukraine, the present Code, the Law on Banks and Banking Activity, other laws, and also normative-legal acts of the National Bank of Ukraine.

Article 351. Finance Lease Operations of Banks

1. Banks shall have the right to acquire for own monetary means for transfer thereof on finance lease means of production in compliance with requirements established in Article 292 of the present Code.

2. The general conditions and procedure for the effectuation of finance lease operations shall be determined by the Law on Banks and Banking Activity, other legislative acts, and also normative-legal acts of the National Bank of Ukraine.

§2. Insurance

Article 352. Insurance in Sphere of Economic Management

1. Insurance is an activity of specially empowered State organizations and subjects of economic management (insurers) connected with rendering insurance services to juridical persons or citizens (insureds) with regard to the defense of their property interests in the event of the ensuing of events (insured events) determined by a law or contract of insurance at the expense of monetary funds formed by means of payment by insurants of insurance payments.

2. Insurance may be effectuated on the basis of a contract between the insured and insurer (voluntary insurance) or on the basis of a law (obligatory insurance).

3. Subjects of economic management for the purpose of insurance protection of their property interests may create a mutual insurance society in the procedure and on the conditions determined by legislation.

Article 353. Subjects of Insurance Activity in Sphere of Economic Management

1. Subjects of economic management-insurers shall effectuate insurance activity on condition of receiving a license for the right to conduct a determined type of insurance. An insurer shall have the right to engage only in those types of insurance which have been determined in the license.

2. Only insurance, reinsurance, and financial activity connected with the forming and placement and management of insurance reserves may be the subject of direct activity of an insurer. The effectuation of the said types of activity in the form of rendering services for other insurers under a contract on joint activity shall be permitted.

3. Participants of economic relations which have concluded contracts of insurance with insurers or are insurants in accordance

with a law shall be defined as insurants in the present Code.

Article 354. Contract of Insurance

1. Under a contract of insurance the insurer shall be obliged when an insured event ensues to effectuate insurance payment to the insured or other person determined by the insured in a contract of insurance, and the insured shall be obliged to pay the insurance payments within the determined periods and fulfill other conditions of the contract.

2. The agency of State power empowered to effectuate supervision over insurance activity shall have the right in accordance with a law to establish additional requirements for contracts of insurance.

3. When concluding a contract of insurance, the insurer shall have the right to demand from the insured a reference concerning his financial state confirmed by an auditor (or audit organization).

4. The conclusion of a contract of insurance may be certified by an insurance certificate (or policy, certificate), which is a form of a contract of insurance.

Article 355. Legislation on Insurance in Sphere of Economic Management

Objects of insurance, types of obligatory insurance, and also general conditions for the effectuation of insurance, requirements for contracts of insurance and the procedure for the effectuation of State supervision over insurance activity, shall be determined by the Civil Code of Ukraine, the present Code, the Law on Insurance, and other legislative acts.

§3. Intermediation in Effectuation of Securities Operation. Stock Exchange

Article 356. Intermediation Connected With Issue and Circulation of Securities

1. Entrepreneurial activity of subjects of economic management (hereinafter – securities traders) for whom securities operations comprise the exclusive type of their activity or to whom such activity has been authorized by a law shall be intermediary activity in the sphere of the issue and circulation of securities.

2. Securities traders shall have the right to effectuate the following types of intermediary activity:
fulfillment on behalf of, in the name of, and at the expense of the emittent duties with regard to the organization of a subscription for securities or the realization thereof by other means;
purchase-sale of securities which is effectuated by a securities trader in his own name and on behalf of and at the expense of another person;
purchase-sale of securities which is effectuated by a securities trader in his own name and at his own expense.

3. Other types of intermediary activity with securities (or activity with regard to the management of securities, and so on) also may be provided for by a law.

Article 357. Licensing of Intermediary Activity in Sphere of Issue and Circulation of Securities

1. The effectuation of intermediary activity in the sphere of the issue and circulation of securities shall be permitted on the basis of a license issued in the procedure established by legislation.

2. Subjects of exclusive intermediary activity in the sphere of the issue and circulation of securities may effectuate individual types of activity connected with the circulation of securities (provision of

consultations to possessors of securities, and so on).

Article 358. Conditions Under Which Effectuation of Intermediary Activity Is Not Permitted in Sphere of Issue and Circulation of Securities

1. A securities trader who directly or indirectly possesses property of another securities trader whose value exceeds the amount established by a law may not receive a license for the effectuation of any kind of intermediary activity in the sphere of the issue and circulation of securities.

2. A securities trader having a license for the effectuation of any type of intermediary activity in the sphere of the issue and circulation of securities may not directly or indirectly possess property of another securities trader whose value exceeds the amount established by a law.

3. A securities trader may not effectuate trade in:
securities of own issue;
stocks of an emittent in which he directly or indirectly possesses property in an amount exceeding five percent of the charter fund.

Article 359. Conclusion of Securities Transactions

1. When accepting a commission for the purchase or sale of securities, the securities trader shall be obliged to provide to the person on whose behalf and account he is acting information concerning the quotation of the securities.

2. A securities trader shall be obliged to provide to the stock exchange information concerning all securities transactions concluded by him within the periods and in the procedure determined by the rules of the stock exchange.

3. Special requirements for the conclusion of securities transactions shall be established by a law.

4. The peculiarities of keeping bookkeeping records and securities operations shall be determined in accordance with a law.

Article 360. Stock Exchange

1. In order to ensure the organization of the functioning of the securities market a stock exchange-joint-stock society shall be formed which shall concentrate supply and demand of securities, promote the formation of the stock exchange quotation thereof, and effectuate its activity in accordance with the present Code, other laws, and also the charter and rules of the stock exchange.

2. A stock exchange shall be created by founders-traders in securities in the procedure established by a law.

3. The activity of a stock exchange shall be directed exclusively towards the organization of the conclusion of purchase-sale transactions of securities and derivatives thereof. A stock exchange may not perform securities operations in its own name and on behalf of clients, and also fulfill the functions of depositary.

4. A stock exchange shall acquire the status of a juridical person from the day of State registration thereof in accordance with a law.

Article 361. Special Conditions of Termination of Activity of Stock Exchange

1. The activity of a stock exchange shall terminate on condition that the number of its members during a period established by a law remains lower than the minimum number determined by a law.

2. The activity of a stock exchange shall terminate in the procedure established for the termination of activity of economic societies, unless provided otherwise by a law.

§4. Audit

Article 362. Auditor Activity

1. The activity of citizens and organizations, the subject of which is the effectuation of an audit, organizational and methods provision of the audit, and rendering of other auditor services shall be deemed auditor activity.

2. Auditor activity shall be regulated by the present Code, the Law on Auditor Activity, and other normative-legal acts adopted in accordance therewith.

Article 363. Audit

1. An audit is a verification of bookkeeping reporting, records, primary documents, and other information concerning the financial-economic activity of subjects of economic management for the purpose of determining the reliability of their reporting and records, the completeness thereof in accordance with legislation and established normative standards.

2. An audit shall be effectuated by independent persons (or auditors) or auditor organizations which have been empowered by the subjects of economic management to conduct it.

3. An audit may be conducted at the initiative of subjects of economic management, and also in the instances provided for by a law (obligatory audit).

Article 364. Auditor and Auditor Organization

1. A citizen of Ukraine having a qualifications certificate concerning the right to engage in auditor activity on the territory of Ukraine may be an auditor.

2. An auditor shall have the right to combine with other auditors

in a union in compliance with the requirements of legislation.

3. An auditor organization shall be an economic organization created in accordance with the requirements of a law.

4. The conditions and procedure for the effectuation of auditor activity and the rights and duties of auditors and auditor organizations shall be determined by a law and other normative-legal acts.

Article 365. Auditor Chamber of Ukraine

1. The Auditor Chamber of Ukraine is a self-governing agency which effectuates the certification of subjects intending to engage in audit activity, confirms programs for the training of auditors, norms and standards of an audit, and records audit organizations and auditors.

2. The legal status and procedure for the activity of the Auditor Chamber of Ukraine shall be determined by the Law on Auditor Activity and other normative-legal acts adopted in accordance with it.

Chapter 36
Use in Entrepreneurial Activity of Rights of Other Subjects of Economic Management (Commercial Concession)

Article 366. Contract of Commercial Concession

1. Under a contract of commercial concession, one party (right-possessor) shall be obliged to grant to the other party (user) for a period or without determination of a period the right of use in entrepreneurial activity of the user the complex of rights belonging to the right-possessor, and the user shall be obliged to comply with the conditions of use of the rights granted to him and to pay the right-possessor the remuneration stipulated by the contract.

2. A contract of commercial concession shall provide for the use of a complex of rights granted to the user, business reputation and

commercial experience of the right-possessor in a determined amount, with or without an indication of the territory of use relating to the determined sphere of entrepreneurial activity.

Article 367. Form and Registration of Contract of Commercial Concession

1. A contract of commercial concession must be concluded in written form in the form of a single document. The failure to comply with this requirement shall entail the invalidity of the contract.

2. A contract of commercial concession shall be subject to State registration by the agency effectuating registration of the subject of economic management acting under the contract as the right-possessor. If the right-possessor has been registered as a subject of economic management not in Ukraine, the registration of the contract of commercial concession shall be effectuated by the agency which registered the subject of economic management which is the user.

3. In relations with third persons the parties to a contract of commercial concession shall have the right to refer to the contract only from the day of the State registration thereof. The absence of registration of a contract shall deprive the parties of the right in the event of a dispute to refer to the present contract.

4. Other requirements for the conclusion of a contract of commercial concession shall be established by a law.

Article 368. Commercial Subconcession

1. The right of the user to authorize the use to other persons of the complex of rights or part of this complex granted to him on conditions of a commercial subconcession agreed by him with the right-possessor or determined in the contract of commercial subconcession may be provided for by a contract of commercial concession.

2. If a contract of commercial concession is deemed invalid, the

contracts of commercial subconcession concluded on the basis thereof also shall be invalid.

Article 369. Remuneration Under Contract of Commercial Concession

Remuneration under a contract of commercial concession may be paid by the user to the right-possessor in the form of one-off or periodic payments or in another form provided for by the contract.

Article 370. Duties of Right-Possessor

1. A right-possessor shall be obliged to:
transfer to the user the technical and commercial documentation and provide other information necessary for the user for the effectuation of the rights granted to him under the contract of commercial concession, and also train the user and his workers with regard to questions connected with the effectuation of these rights;
issue to the user a license (or authorization) provided for by the contract, having ensure the formalization thereof in the procedure established by legislation.
2. Unless provided otherwise by the contract of commercial concession, the right-possessor shall be obliged to:
ensure the registration of the contract of commercial concession;
render constant instruction and consultative assistance to the user, including assistance in training and raising the qualifications of workers;
control the quality of goods (or work, services) which are produced (or fulfilled or rendered) by the user on the basis of the contract of commercial concession.

Article 371. Duties of User

Taking into account the character and peculiarities of activity being effectuated by a user under a contract of commercial concession, a user shall be obliged to:
use the trademark and other designations of the right-possessor

determined by a means in the contract when effectuating the activity provided for by the contract;

ensure the conformity of quality of the goods produced, work fulfilled, or services rendered by him on the basis of the contract to the quality of such goods (or work, services) which are produced (or fulfilled or rendered) directly by the right-possessor;

comply with instructions and directions of the right-possessor directed towards ensuring the conformity of the character, means, and conditions of use of the complex of rights granted to the use of these rights by the right-possessor;

render to the purchasers (or customsers) additional services on which they may count upon in purchasing (or ordering) the good (or work, service) directly from the right-possessor;

inform the purchasers (or customers) of the most obvious means for them concerning the use by him of the trademark and other designations of the right-possessor under the contract of commercial concession;

not divulge production secrets of the right-possessor and other confidential information received from him;

pay the right-possessor the remuneration stipulated by the contract.

Article 372. Limitations of Rights of Parties Under Contract of Commercial Concession

Limitations of rights of the parties under this contract may be provided for by a contract of commercial concession, in particular:

the duty of the right-possessor to provide to other persons analogous complexes of rights for the use thereof on a territory consolidated to the user or refrain from own analogous activity on this territory;

the duty of the user not to permit his competition with the right-possessor on the territory to which the operation of the contract of commercial concession extends with respect to the entrepreneurial activity being effectuated by the user with the use of the rights which belong to the right-possessor;

the renunciation of the user to receive under the contract of commercial concession analogous rights from competitors (or potential competitors) of the right-possessor;

the duty of the user to agree with the right-possessor the location of production premises which must be used when effectuating the rights granted under the contract, and also the internal and external design thereof.

2. Conditions of limitation may be deemed invalid if these conditions are contrary to legislation.

Article 373. Responsibility of Right-Possessor With Regard to Demands Presented to User

1. The right-possessor shall bear subsidiary responsibility with regard to demands presented against the user of a commercial concession in the event the quality of the goods (or work, services) which are sold (or fulfilled, rendered) by the user fails to conform.

2. With regard to demands which are presented against the user as the producer of products (or goods) of the right-possessor, the last shall be liable jointly and severally with the user.

Article 374. Change and Dissolution of Contract of Commercial Concession

1. A contract of commercial concession may be changed in accordance with the provisions established by Article 188 of the present Code.

2. In relations with third persons the parties to a contract of commercial concession shall have the right to refer to a change of the contract only from the day of State registration of this change in accordance with Article 367 of the present Code unless it is proved that the third person knew or should have known about the change of the contract earlier.

3. Each of the parties to a contract of commercial concession concluded without a specified period shall have the right at any time to

renounce the contract, having informed the other party six months in advance unless a longer period has been provided by the contract.

4. Dissolution before time of a contract of commercial concession concluded for a determined period, and also dissolution of the contract concluded without determination of a period, shall be subject to State registration in accordance with Article 367 of the present Code.

5. In the event of the right-possessor or user declaring insolvency (or bankruptcy), the contract of commercial concession shall terminate.

Article 375. Consequences of Change of Trademark or Other Designation of Right-Possessor

1. In the event of a change of a trademark or other designation of a right-possessor, the rights to the use of which are within a complex of rights under a contract of commercial concession, this contract shall retain operation with respect to the new designations of the right-possessor unless the user requires dissolution of the contract.

2. In the event of the continuation of the operation of the contract of commercial concession the user shall have the right to demand a respective reduction of the remuneration due to the right-possessor.

3. If within the period of operation of a contract of commercial concession the right has terminated, the use to which was granted under this contract, the contract shall continue its operation except for provisions affecting the right being terminated, and the user, unless provided otherwise by the contract, shall have the right to demand the respective reduction of remuneration due to the right-possessor.

Article 376. Legal Regulation of Commercial Concession

1. Relations connected with the use in entrepreneurial activity or the rights of other subjects of economic management shall be regulated by the present Code and by other laws.

Section VII
Foreign Economic Activity

Chapter 37
General Provisions

Article 377. Concept of Foreign Economic Activity

1. Economic activity which in the process of the effectuation thereof requires crossing the customs boundary of Ukraine by property specified in Article 139, paragraph one, of the present Code, and/or work force, shall be foreign economic activity of subjects of economic management.

2. Foreign economic activity shall be effectuated on the principles of the freedom of the subjects thereof to enter into foreign economic relations, effectuate them in any forms not prohibited by a law, and equality before the law of subjects of foreign economic activity.

3. General conditions and the procedure for the effectuation of foreign economic activity by subjects of economic management shall be determined by the present Code, the Law on Foreign Economic Activity, and other normative-legal acts.

Article 378. Subjects of Foreign Economic Activity

1. There shall be subjects of foreign economic activity:
subjects of economic management specified in Article 55, paragraph two, points (1) and (2) of the present Code;
subdivisions (or structural entitles) of foreign subjects of economic management which are not juridical persons according to legislation of Ukraine (branches, divisions, and so on) but have a permanent location on the territory of Ukraine and have been registered in the procedure established by a law.

2. Foreign economic organizations having the status of a juridical person formed in Ukraine in accordance with a law by agencies of

State power or agencies of local self-government also may take part in foreign economic activity.

3. The State shall guarantee identical defense for all subjects of foreign economic activity.

Article 379. Types of Foreign Economic Activity and Foreign Economic Operations

1. All subjects of foreign economic activity shall have the right to the effectuation of any types of foreign economic activity and foreign economic operations unless established otherwise by a law.

2. Types of foreign economic activity, a list of foreign economic operations effectuated on the territory of Ukraine, the conditions and procedure of the effectuation thereof by subjects of foreign economic activity, and also a list of goods (or work, services) prohibited for export and import, shall be determined by a law.

Article 380. State Regulation of Foreign Economic Activity

1. State regulation of foreign economic activity shall be directed towards the defense of the economic interests of Ukraine, rights and legal interests of subjects of foreign economic activity, creation of equal conditions for the development of all types of entrepreneurship in the sphere of foreign economic relations and use by subjects of foreign economic activity of revenues and investments, encouragement of competition, and limitation of monopolism of subjects of economic management in the sphere of foreign economic activity.

2. Agencies of State power and agencies of local self-government shall not have the right to interfere in the operational activity of subjects of foreign economic activity except for instances provided for by a law.

3. A list and the powers of agencies of state power effectuating the regulation of foreign economic activity, and also the forms of State

regulation and control thereof, shall be determined by the present Code, the Law on Foreign Economic Activity, and other laws.

Article 381. Licensing and Quotaing of Foreign Economic Operations

1. The Cabinet of Ministers of Ukraine may establish a list of goods (or work, services) whose export and import shall be effectuated by subjects of foreign economic activity only when there is a license.

2. The procedure for licensing of export-import operations and types of licenses shall be determined by a law.

3. The regime of quotaing foreign economic operations shall be introduced in instances provided for by a law and international treaties of Ukraine in force, and shall be effectuated by means of a limitation of the total quantity and/or total customs value of goods which may be brought in (or carried out) for a determined period. The procedure for quotaing the said operations and types of quotas shall be determined by a law.

4. Information concerning the introduction of the regime of licensing or quotaing shall be published in official publications in the procedure established by a law.

Article 382. Foreign Economic Contracts

1. Subjects of foreign economic activity shall have the right to conclude any foreign economic contracts, except those whose conclusion is prohibited by legislation of Ukraine.

2. A foreign economic contract shall be concluded in written form unless established otherwise by a law or international treaty in force, consent to the bindingness of which has been given by the Supreme Rada of Ukraine.

3. The form of a foreign economic contract shall be determined

by the law of the place of conclusion thereof. The place of conclusion of a contract shall be determined in accordance with laws of Ukraine.

4. The form of foreign economic contracts concerning land plots, buildings, and other immoveable property located on the territory of Ukraine shall be determined by laws of Ukraine.

5. The rights and duties of parties to a foreign economic contract shall be determined by the law of the place of conclusion thereof unless the parties have agreed otherwise. The procedure for the determination of the law which should be applied to a contract in the event of the failure to reach agreement of the parties relative to the said procedure shall be established by the Law on Foreign Economic Activity.

6. A foreign economic contract may be deemed invalid in a judicial proceeding if it does not correspond to the requirements of laws of Ukraine or international treaties in force, consent to the bindingness of which has been given by the Supreme Rada of Ukraine.

7. A special procedure for the conclusion, fulfillment, and dissolution of individual types of foreign economic contracts may be established by a law.

Article 383. State Registration of Foreign Economic Contracts

1. The Cabinet of Ministers of Ukraine may for the purpose of ensuring the conformity of foreign economic contracts to legislation of Ukraine introduce the State registration thereof.

2. Types of foreign economic contracts subject to State registration, and also the procedure for the effectuation thereof, shall be determined by the Law on Foreign Economic Activity and other normative-legal acts adopted in accordance with it.

3. The fulfillment of obligations arising from foreign economic contracts not registered in the procedure established by a law shall

entail the application to subjects of economic management which have violated this requirement administrative-economic sanctions provided for by a law.

Article 384. Customs Regulation in When Effectuating Foreign Economic Activity

1. The State shall effectuate customs regulation of foreign economic activity.

2. Customs regulation of foreign economic activity shall be effectuated in accordance with the Customs Code of Ukraine, the Law on Foreign Economic Activity, other laws, the Unified Customs Tariff, and international treaties in force, consent to the bindingness of which has been given by the Supreme Rada of Ukraine.

3. Customs control on the territory of special (free) economic zones shall be regulated by individual laws and international treaties inforce, consent to the bindingness of which was given by the Supreme Rada of Ukraine, which shall establish the special legal regime of the said zones in accordance with Section VIII of the present Code.

Article 385. Principles of Taxation When Effectuating Foreign Economic Activity

1. Taxation of subjects of foreign economic activity must be effectuated according to the following principles:
establishment of the level of taxation by proceeding from the need to achieve and maintain the nonsubsidy of subjects of foreign economic activity and ensure a nondeficit balance of payments of Ukraine;
guarantee of the stability of types and amounts of taxes, establishment of taxes and charges (or obligatory payments), and also the status of foreign currencies on the territory of Ukraine, exclusively by a law;
equality of subjects of foreign economic activity when establishing tax rates;

encouragement of the export of products of fatherland production.

2. Tax privileges shall be granted exclusively in accordance with a law, as a rule, to subjects of foreign economic activity which stably export scientific, scientifically-intensive products, those export exceeds import for the financial year and the amount of export of which comprises not less than five percent of the volume of goods realized for the financial year.

3. Tax rates shall be established and repealed in accordance with laws on taxation.

Article 386. Hard Currency Accounts of Subjects of Foreign Economic Activity

1. Subjects of foreign economic activity shall have the right to open any hard currency accounts not prohibited by a law in bank branches located on the territory of other States.

2. The procedure for opening hard currency accounts in bank branches on the territory of other States shall be regulated by the legislation of the respective State. When opening a hard currency account in a bank branch beyond the limits of Ukraine, a subject of foreign economic activity shall be obliged to inform the National Bank of Ukraine thereof not later than within a three-day period. A violation of this requirement shall entail administrative-economic responsibility in the procedure established by a law.

3. The opening of a hard currency account in the branch of a bank beyond the limits of Ukraine by a subject of foreign economic activity in whose charter fund there is a participatory share of State property shall be effectuated by agreement with the State Property Fund of Ukraine.

4. Subjects of foreign economic activity shall be obliged to provide information concerning the use of their hard currency accounts

to tax agencies in the procedure established by legislation.

5. The procedure for the effectuation of the settlement of accounts in foreign hard currency by subjects of foreign activity shall be established by a law.

Article 387. Hard Currency Receipts from Foreign Economic Activity

1. Subjects of foreign economic activity after the payment of taxes and charges (or obligatory payments) provided for by a law shall autonomously dispose of hard currency receipts from operations conducted by them, except for instances determined by a law in accordance with the present Code.

2. A regime of obligatory distribution of receipts from foreign economic operations in foreign hard currency between subjects of foreign activity and empowered State hard currency funds, and also the procedure and amounts of deductions of foreign hard currency, may be introduced by a law. Information concerning the introduction of the said regime must be published in an official printed organ of the Cabinet of Ministers of Ukraine not later than two months before the introduction of this regime.

Article 388. Receipt by Subjects of Foreign Economic Activity of Credits in Foreign Financial Institutions

1. Subjects of foreign economic activity may receive hard currency credits on a contractual basis in foreign financial institutions. In so doing the conditions of the credit contract may not be contrary to legislation of Ukraine.

2. Subjects of foreign economic activity in whose charter fund there is a participatory share of State property may conclude credit contracts with foreign financial institutions only with the consent of the State Property Fund of Ukraine.

3. The types of property which may not be the subject of pledge when receiving a hard currency credit in a foreign financial institution shall be determined by a law.

Article 389. Defense by State of Rights and Legal Interests of Subjects of Foreign Economic Activity

1. The State shall effectuate the defense of the rights and legal interests of subjects of foreign economic activity beyond the limits of Ukraine according to norms of international law. Such defense shall be effectuated through diplomatic and consular institutions, State trade representations representing the interests of Ukraine, and also other means determined by a law.

2. The State shall take necessary measures in response to discriminatory and/or unfriendly actions on the part of other States, customs unions, or economic groupings limiting the rights and legal interests of subjects of foreign activity of Ukraine.

3. Special measures with regard to the defense of a national goods-producer against dumping imports and special measures with regard to import which cause or may cause material harm to national goods-producers may be provided for by a law, and also a list determined of types of goods and services whose export, import, and transit across the territory of Ukraine is prohibited.

4. In instances of unfair competition against subjects of foreign economic activity or their foreign contracting parties sanctions shall be applied inaccordance with the Law on Foreign Economic Activity and other laws.

Chapter 38
Foreign Investments

Article 390. Foreign Investors

The following subjects effectuating investment activity on the territory of Ukraine shall be deemed to be foreign investors:

juridical persons formed according to the legislation other than the legislation of Ukraine;

foreigners and stateless persons not having a permanent place of residence on the territory of Ukraine;

international intergovernmental and nongovernmental organizations;

other States;

other foreign subjects of investment activity determined by legislation.

Article 391. Types of Foreign Investments

1. Foreign investors shall have the right to effectuate investments on the territory of Ukraine in the form of foreign currency which is deemed to be convertible by the National Bank of Ukraine, any moveable and immoveable property and property rights connected therewith; other valuables (or property) which in accordance with a law are deemed to be foreign investments.

2. A prohibition or limitation of any types whatsoever of foreign investments may be effectuated exclusively by a law.

Article 392. Forms of Effectuating Foreign Investments

1. Foreign investors shall have the right to effectuate all types of investments specified in Article 391 of the present Code in the following forms:

participation in economic organizations which are created jointly with fatherland juridical persons or citizens, or the acquisition of a participatory share in operating economic organizations;

creation of foreign enterprises on the territory of Ukraine, branches or other structural subdivisions of foreign juridical persons or acquisition in ownership of operating enterprises;

acquisition directly of immoveable or moveable property not prohibited by laws of Ukraine, or acquisition of stocks or other securities;

acquisition autonomously or with the participation of citizens or fatherland juridical persons of the rights of use of land and use of natural resources on the territory of Ukraine;

economic activity on the basis of production sharing agreements;

acquisition of other property rights;

in other forms not prohibited by a law.

2. The prohibition or limitation of any forms whatsoever of the effectuation of foreign investments may be only by a law.

3. Relations arising in connection with the acquisition by a foreign investor of property rights to land and other natural resources in Ukraine shall be regulated respectively by land and other legislation of Ukraine.

Article 393. Valuation of Foreign Investments

The valuation of foreign investments, including contributions to the charter fund of an enterprise with foreign investments, shall be effectuated in foreign convertible currency and in hrivnas by agreement of the parties on the basis of international market prices or the market of Ukraine. In so doing the conversion of the amounts in foreign currency into hrivnas shall be at the exchange rate established by the National Bank of Ukraine.

Article 394. Legal Regime of Foreign Investments

1. The national regime of investment activity shall be established on the territory of Ukraine with respect to foreign investments, with the exceptions provided for by the present Code, other laws, and international treaties in force, consent to the bindingness of which was given by the Supreme Rada of Ukraine.

2. Relations with regard to the taxation of foreign investors and enterprises with foreign investments shall be regulated by tax legislation of Ukraine.

3. The establishment of additional privileges for subjects of economic management effectuating activity in these spheres may be provided for by State programs for the attraction of foreign investments in priority branches of the economy and social sphere.

4. The activity of foreign investors and enterprises with foreign investments in individual branches of the national economy or within the limits of individual territories of Ukraine, proceeding from the interests of the national security of Ukraine, may be limited or prohibited by a law.

Article 395. State Registration of Foreign Investments

1. State registration of foreign investments shall be effectuated by the Council of Ministers of the Autonomous Republic Crimea, regional, Kiev, and Sevastopol city State administrations within three work days after the actual submission thereof in the procedure established by the Cabinet of Ministers of Ukraine.

2. A refusal of State registration of foreign investments shall be possible only in the event of a violation of legislation of Ukraine on foreign investing. A refusal of State registration of foreign investments may be appealed in a judicial proceeding.

3. Unregistered foreign investments do not give the right to receive privileges and guarantees provided for by the present Code and other laws for foreign investors and enterprises with foreign investments.

Article 396. Activity of Subjects of Economic Management with Foreign Investments in Ukraine

1. Subjects of economic management with foreign investments effectuating their activity in the forms of an enterprise with foreign

investments (Article 116 of the present Code), foreign enterprise (Article 117 of the present Code), branch, or representation of a foreign juridical person, and other forms not prohibited by a law may be created and operate on the territory of Ukraine.

2. The procedure for the formation of enterprises with foreign investments and foreign enterprises shall be regulated by the present Code and other laws adopted in accordance therewith. The peculiarities of the creation of banking, insurance, and other financial institutions with the participation of a foreign investor shall be determined by the respective laws.

Article 397. Guarantees of Effectuation of Foreign Investments

1. For the purposes of ensuring the stability of the legal regime of foreign investing the following guarantees shall be established for foreign investors:

application of State guarantees of the defense of foreign investments in the event of a change of legislation on foreign investments;

guarantees relative to compulsory seizure, and also against illegal actions of agencies of power and officials thereof;

contributory compensation and compensation of losses to foreign investors;

guarantees in the event of the termination of investment activity;

guarantees of the transfer of profits and use of revenues from foreign investments;

other guarantees for the effectuation of investment activity.

2. In the event of a change of legislation on the regime of foreign investing with regard to a demand of a foreign investor in the instances and in the procedure determined by a law, State guarantees shall apply which are determined by legislation in force at the moment of making the investments.

3. Foreign investments in Ukraine shall not be subject to nationalization.

4. Agencies of State power and officials thereof shall not have the right to requisition foreign investments except for instances of the effectuation of rescue measures in the event of a natural disaster, accidents, epidemics, and epizootics. The said requisition may be effectuated only on the basis of the decision of agencies empowered by the Cabinet of Ministers of Ukraine and in the procedure established by a law.

5. Foreign investors shall have the right to demand compensation of losses caused to them by illegal actions or failure to act of agencies of State power or agencies of local self-government and officials thereof. Losses of foreign investors must be compensated according to current market prices or on the basis of substantiated valuations confirmed by an independent auditor (or audit organization).

6. Contributory compensation to be paid to a foreign investor by way of compensation of losses must be adequate, effective, and determined at the moment of fulfillment of the decision concerning compensation of losses. The amount of contributory compensation under this decision must be immediately paid in the currency in which the investments were effectuated, or in another currency acceptable for the foreign investor in accordance with currency legislation. The calculation of interest on the amount of contributory compensation may be provided for by a law.

7. Contributory compensation of losses to foreign investors shall be effectuated in the procedure established by a law.

Article 398. Guarantees of Transfer and Use of Revenues from Foreign Investments

1. To foreign investors shall be guaranteed after the payment of taxes and charges (or obligatory payments) by them the unobstructed immediate transfer abroad of their revenues, profits, and other means in foreign currency received on legal grounds from the effectuation of investments.

2. The procedure for the transfer abroad of the said means shall be established by the National Bank of Ukraine. Revenue of a foreign investor or other means received in Ukraine in hrivnas or foreign currency from the effectuation of investments may be reinvested in Ukraine in the procedure established by legislation.

Article 399. Guarantees to Foreign Investors in Event of Termination of Investment Activity

In the event of the termination of investment activity on the territory of Ukraine a foreign investor shall have the right to return of his investments not later than six months after the termination of this activity, and also revenues with regard to these investments in monetary or goods form, unless established otherwise by a law or by agreement of the parties.

Article 400. Legislation on Foreign Investments

Relations connected with foreign investments in Ukraine shall be regulated by the present Code, Law on the Regime of Foreign Investing, other legislative acts, and international treaties in force, consent to the bindingness of which has been given by the Supreme Rada of Ukraine. If other rules have been established by an international treaty than those which have been provided for by legislation of Ukraine on foreign investments, the rules of the international treaty shall apply.

Section VIII
Special Regimes of Economic Management

Chapter 39
Special (Free) Economic Zones

Article 401. Definition of Special (Free) Economic Zone

1. A part of the territory of Ukraine on which a special legal

regime of economic activity is established and a special procedure for the application and operation of legislation of Ukraine shall be considered to be a special (free) economic zone.

2. Special (or free) economic zones shall be created for the purposes of attracting investments and the effective use thereof, activization with foreign investors of entrepreneurial activity for the purpose of increasing the export of goods and deliveries to the internal market of high-quality products and services, introduction of new technologies, development of market infrastructure, improvement of the use of natural, material, and labor resources, and acceleration of the socio-economic development of Ukraine.

Article 402. Territory and Status of Special (Free) Economic Zone

The territory and status of a special (free) economic zone, including the period for which it is created, shall be determined by an individual law for each special (free) economic zone.

Article 403. Types of Special (Free) Economic Zones

Special (free) economic zones of various functional types may be created on the territory of Ukraine: free customs zones and ports, export, transit zones, customs warehouses, technology parks, technology belts, integrated production zones, tourist-recreational, insurance, banking zones, and so on. Individual economic zones may combine functions inherent to various types of special (free) economic zones specified in the present Article.

Article 404. State Guarantees of Investments in Special (Free) Economic Zone

A system of State guarantees of defense of investments provided for by legislation on investment activity and on foreign investments shall extend to all subjects of economic management effectuating investments in a special (free) economic zone. The State shall guarantee to subjects of economic management of a special (free) economic zone the right to take out profit and investments beyond the limits of the particular zone and the limits of Ukraine in accordance with a law.

Article 405. Legislation Operating on Territory of Special (Free) Economic Zone

Legislation of Ukraine, taking into account peculiarities provided for by the present Code, the Law on General Principles of the Creation and Functioning of Special (Free) Economic Zones, and also the law on the creation of a specific special (free) economic zone adopted in accordance with the present Code, shall operate on the territory of a special (free) economic zone.

Chapter 40
Concessions

Article 406. Concession Activity in Ukraine

1. A concession is the granting for the purpose of satisfaction of social requirements by an empowered agency of State power or agency of local self-government on the basis of a concession contract ona paid and fixed-term basis to fatherland or foreign subjects of economic management (concessionaires) rights to the creation (or construction) and/or management (or exploitation) of the object of the concession on condition of the assumption by the concessionaire of respective obligations, property responsibility, and entrepreneurial risk.

2. Spheres of economic management in which concession activity is authorized, objects of the right of State or municipal ownership which may be granted on concession, and also types of entrepreneurial activity which are not authorized to be effectuated on a concession basis, shall be determined by a law.

Article 407. Principles of Concession Activity

Concession activity in Ukraine shall be based on the following principles:

combining of State regulation of concession activity and effectuation thereof on basis of concession contract;

selection of concessionaires primarily on competition basis;

integrated and paid use of object of concession, participation of State, agencies of local self-government, and private financing of objects of concession of social designation;

mutual advantage of parties to concession contract, distribution of risks among parties to concession contract;

State guaranteeing of investments of concessionaires;

stability of conditions of concession contracts;

ensuring rights and legal interests of consumers of products (or services) provided by concessionaires.

Article 408. Concession Contract

1. Concession activity shall be effectuated on the basis of concession contracts which shall be concluded in accordance with legislation of Ukraine with concessionaires, including foreign investors, by the Cabinet of Ministers of Ukraine or agency of State power empowered by it, or by agencies of local self-government determined by a law.

2. The period of operation of a concession contract shall be established by the parties to the contract depending upon the character and conditions of the concession. This period may not be less than ten years nor more than fifty years.

3. The Cabinet of Ministers of Ukraine may confirm standard concession contracts for the effectuation of determined types of concession activity.

4. Requirements for concession contracts, the procedure for concluding them, and also other questions of legal regulation of concession activity, shall be determined by the Law on Concessions and by other laws.

Article 409. Termination of Activity of Enterprise Whose Property Is Transferred to Concession

1. The termination of the activity of a State or municipal enterprise whose property is transferred to a concession shall be effectuated by means of the liquidation of the particular enterprise, with the termination of the right of economic jurisdiction over property consolidated to this State or municipal enterprise.

2. Maximum use in concession activity of the labor of citizens of Ukraine, including those dismissed in connection with the liquidation of a State or municipal enterprise whose property was transferred to a concession, must be provided for by the conditions of a concession contract.

Article 410. Legislation on Concessions

1. Relations connected with concession activity shall be regulated by the present Code the Law on Concessions, and other normative-legal acts adopted in accordance therewith.

2. The peculiarities of the effectuation of concession activity in individual spheres of economic management may be determined by special laws.

Chapter 41
Other Types of Special Regimes of Economic Activity

Article 411. Exclusive (Maritime) Economic Zone of Ukraine

1. Maritime areas externally adjacent to the territorial sea of Ukraine, including areas around islands belonging thereto, shall comprise the exclusive (maritime) economic zone of Ukraine.

2. The breadth of the exclusive (maritime) economic zone shall comprise up to two hundred nautical miles calculated from those same

baselines as the territorial sea of Ukraine.

3. For the purpose of ensuring the sovereign rights of Ukraine to the exploration, exploitation, and preservation of living resources and the management thereof in the exclusive (maritime) economic zone the State shall take measures (including surveillance, inspection, arrest, and judicial consideration) with regard to ensuring compliance by subjects of economic management of legislation of Ukraine.

4. The State shall in the exclusive (maritime) economic zone of Ukraine have the exclusive right to create, and also to authorize and regulate, the erection, exploitation, and use of artificial islands, devices, and installations for marine scientific research, the exploration and development of natural resources, and other economic purposes in accordance with legislation of Ukraine.

5. The regime for the effectuation of economic activity in the exclusive (maritime) economic zone shall be established in accordance with the present Code by the Law on the Exclusive (Maritime) Economic Zone of Ukraine and other legislative acts regulating questions connected with the legal regime of the exclusive (maritime) economic zone of Ukraine.

Article 412. Peculiarities of Effectuation of Economic Activity on State Boundary of Ukraine

1. Economic activity on the State boundary of Ukraine (navigation, use of water objects for needs of timber rafting, and other types of water use, creation of hydroinstallations, conducting of other work in internal waters of Ukraine, use of land, forests, objects of fauna, conducting of geological prospecting, and other economic activity) shall be effectuated by taking into account the peculiarities of the regime of the State boundary of Ukraine in accordance with legislation of Ukraine and international treaties in force, consent to the bindingness of which was given by the Supreme Rada of Ukraine.

2. The conditions for the effectuation on the State boundary of

Ukraine of economic activity shall be determined by the respective agencies of State power of Ukraine, taking into account local conditions according to the requirements of a law.

3. In the instances and procedure provided for by a law communication across the State boundary of Ukraine at individual sectors may by decision of the Cabinet of Ministers of Ukraine be temporarily limited or terminated or measures of quarantine established for people, livestock, cargoes, seed and garden material, and other products of fauna and flora origin which cross the State boundary of Ukraine.

Article 413. Peculiarities of Effectuation of Economic Activity in Sanitary-Protective and Other Protection Zones and at Specially-Protected Territories and Objects

1. Economic activity in sanitary-protective, water protection zones, sanitary protection zones, and other protection zones shall be effectuated by taking into account the legal regime of such zones established by a law.

2. Economic activity on territories and at objects of the nature-preserve fund of Ukraine, resort, treatment-therapeutic, recreational, and other territories and objects relegated by legislation to specially-protected shall be effectuated in accordance with the requirements of the legal regime of these territories and objects established by a law and other legislative acts.

3. Additional requirements with regard to the effectuation of economic activity and social guarantees of persons working on territories radioactively polluted as a result of the Chernobyl catastrophe shall be established by a law.

Article 414. Special Regime of Economic Management in Individual Branches of National Economy

1. In the event of the necessity of stabilization or acceleration of the development of individual branches of the national economy, a special

regime of economic management in those branches may be established by a law upon the recommendation of the Cabinet of Ministers of Ukraine.

2. Only noncommercial (or nonprofit) economic activity may be effectuated in the Armed Forces of Ukraine.

3. Economic activity in the Armed Forces of Ukraine is a specific activity of military units, establishments, institutions, and organizations of the Armed Forces of Ukraine connected with ensuring their day-to-day vital activity which provides for the conducting of subsidiary husbandry, production of products, fulfillment of work, and rendering of services, transfer on lease of moveable and immoveable military property (except for armaments, ammunition, combat and special technology) within the limits and in the procedure determined by a law.

4. Relations connected with the effectuation of economic activity in the Armed Forces of Ukraine shall be regulated by the present Code and other laws.

Article 415. Peculiarities of Effectuation of Economic Activity on Territory of Priority Development

1. By a law may be determined upon the recommendation of the respective agency of local self-government within the limits of a city or district of a territory on which unfavorable socio-economic conditions have formed and on which, on the grounds and in the procedure provided for by a law a special regime for investment activity for the purpose of creating new jobs (territory of priority development) is introduced.

2. The procedure for the effectuation of economic activity on a territory of priority development shall be established by a law.

Article 416. Procedure for Effectuation of Economic Activity Under Conditions of Extraordinary Situation and Extraordinary Ecological Situation

1. Economic activity under conditions of an extraordinary situation – a special legal regime of activity of agencies of State power and agencies of local self-government, enterprises, institutions, and organizations provided for by the Constitution of Ukraine, which temporarily permits limitations in the effectuation of constitutional rights and freedoms of citizens, and also rights of juridical persons and placed on them additional duties – may be effectuated by taking into account the limitations and obligations established by an edict of the President of Ukraine issued in accordance with the Constitution of Ukraine on the introduction of an extraordinary situation in Ukraine and individual localities thereof.

2. Powers of agencies of State power and agencies of local self-government with respect to participants of economic relations, measures adopted under conditions of an extraordinary situation, and also responsibility for a violation of the regime of an extraordinary situation, shall be determined by the Law on an Extraordinary Situation.

3. The rules of the present Article concerning the effectuation of economic activity shall also apply when declaring individual localities to be zones of an extraordinary ecological situation.

Article 417. Procedure for Effectuation of Economic Activity Under Conditions of Military Situation

During the period of operation of a military situation introduced on the territory of Ukraine or individual localities, the legal regime of economic activity shall be determined on the basis of the Law on Defense of Ukraine, other legislative acts with regard to ensuring the defense capability of the State, and legislation of the regime of a military situation.

Article 418. Guarantees of Rights of Participants of Economic Relations Under Conditions of Special Regime of Economic Management

1. The introduction of special regimes of economic management not provided for by the present Code by which limitations of the rights of subjects of economic management are established shall not be permitted.

2. The State shall guarantee to subjects of economic management and other participants of economic relations the right of recourse to a court for defense of their property and other rights against illegal limitation under conditions of any special regime whatsoever of economic management provided for by the present Code.

Section IX
Concluding Provisions

1. The present Code shall enter into force from 1 January 2002.

2. To deem to have lost force form 1 January 2004:
Law of Ukraine "On Entrepreneurship" (Ведомости Верховного Совета УССР (1991), no. 14, item 168), with subsequent changes, except Article 4 of the Law;
Law of Ukraine "On Enterprises in Ukraine" (Ведомости Верховного Совета УССР (1991), no. 24, item 272), with subsequent changes.

3. The Cabinet of Ministers of Ukraine shall:
(1) submit to the Supreme Rada of Ukraine within a three-month period from the day of publication of the Economic Code of Ukraine:
a list of legislative acts (or individual provisions thereof) which must be deemed to have lost force and a list of legislative acts in which changes should be made in connection with the entry of the present Code into force;
proposals concerning the clarification, when necessary, of the

procedure for the entry into force of individual provisions of the present Code;

(2) confirm normative-legal acts provided for by the present Code;

(3) ensure the revision, bringing into conformity with the present Code, or deeming to have lost force of normative-legal acts of the Cabinet of Ministers of Ukraine and normative-legal acts of ministries and other central agencies of executive power;

(4) determine the subjects of economic management relating to the State sector of the economy in accordance with the requirements of the present Code;

(5) submit for consideration of the Supreme Rada of Ukraine a draft law on the list of types of activity in which entrepreneurship is prohibited and the types of economic activity which State enterprise, institutions, and organizations shall be authorized to effectuate exclusively;

(6) ensure the forming and keeping of the Register of State corporative rights in accordance with the requirements of the present Code.

4. To establish that the Economic Code of Ukraine shall apply to economic relations which arose after the entry into force of its provisions in accordance with the present Section.

To economic relations which arose before the entry into force of the respective provisions of the Economic Code of Ukraine the said provisions shall apply relative to those rights and duties which continue to exist or arose after the entry into force of these provisions.

5. The provisions of the Economic Code of Ukraine concerning responsibility for a violation of rules for the effectuation of economic activity, and also for a violation of economic obligations, shall apply if these violations were committed after the entry into force of the said provisions, except for instances when for a violation of economic obligations other responsibility has been established by a contract concluded before the period specified in point 1 of the present Section.

The provisions of the Economic Code of Ukraine concerning responsibility for violations specified in paragraph one of the present point committed before the entry into force of respective provisions of the present Code concerning responsibility of participants of economic relations shall apply if they mitigate responsibility for the said violations.

6. To establish that to the economic relations specified in paragraph two of point 4 of the present Section shall apply the period of limtation provided for by the Economic Code of Ukraine in the following sequence:

special periods of limitation established by legislation operating before the entry into force of the present Code if the said periods exceed the period established by the present Code;

increased special periods of limitation in accordance with periods established by the present Code if the duration of the periods previously operative is less in comparison with the periods of limitation established by the present Code.